SURVIVAL GUIDE FOR CHESS PARENTS

TANYA JONES

EVERYMAN CHESS

Gloucester Publishers plc   www.everymanchess.com

First published in 2003 by Gloucester Publishers plc (formerly Everyman Publishers plc), Gloucester Mansions, 140A Shaftesbury Avenue, London WC2H 8HD

British Library Cataloguing-in-Publication Data
A catalogue record for this book is available from the British Library.

ISBN 1 85744 340 3

Distributed in North America by The Globe Pequot Press, P.O Box 480, 246 Goose Lane, Guilford, CT 06437-0480.

All other sales enquiries should be directed to Everyman Chess, Gloucester Publishers plc, Gloucester Mansions, 140A Shaftesbury Avenue, London WC2H 8HD
tel: 020 7539 7600 fax: 020 7379 4060
email: info@everymanchess.com
website: www.everymanchess.com

Everyman is the registered trade mark of Random House Inc. and is used in this work under license from Random House Inc.

EVERYMAN CHESS SERIES (formerly Cadogan Chess)
Chief advisor: Garry Kasparov
Commissioning editor: Byron Jacobs

Typeset and edited by First Rank Publishing, Brighton.
Cover design by Horatio Monteverde.
Production by Navigator Guides.
Printed and bound in the United States by Versa Press.

Contents

Bibliography

Attacking with 1 d4, Dunnington, Angus (Everyman 2001)

Attacking with 1 e4, Emms, John (Everyman 2001)

Checkmate at Chess City, Harper, Piers (Walker Books, 2000)

Development of a Grandmaster, Adams, Bill & Michael (Pergamon 1991)

Encylopaedia of Chess Openings, Krnic, J et al, (Sahovski Informator 2000)

How to Cheat at Chess, Soft Pawn, Hartson, William (Cadogan 1995)

My System, Nimzowitsch, Aron (trans. Philip Hereford), (Batsford 1987)

Nunn's Chess Openings, Nunn, John et al, (Everyman/Gambit 1999)

Rate Your Endgame, Mednis, Edmar & Crouch, Colin, (Cadogan 1992)

Searching for Bobby Fischer, Waitzkin, Fred (Random House 1988)

Starting Out in Chess, Jacobs, Byron (Everyman 2001)

Steve Davies Plays Chess, Davis, Steve & Norwood, David (Batsford 1995)

Test Your Positional Play, Bellin, Robert & Ponzetto, Pietro (Batsford 1985)

The Chess Mysteries of the Arabian Knights, Smullyan, Raymond, (Oxford 1992)

The Chess Organiser's Handbook, Reuben, Stewart (Cadogan 1997)

The Even More Complete Chess Addict, Fox, Mike & James, Richard (Faber 1993)

The Flanders Panel, Perez-Reverte, (trans. M. J. Costa) (Hamill 1994)

The Inner Game, Lawson, Dominic (Macmillan 1993)

The Lewis Chessmen and what happened to them, Finkel, Irving, (British Museum Press 1995)

The Luneburg Variation, Maurensig, Paolo (Weidenfield & Nicholson 1998)

The Oxford Companion to Chess, Hooper David and Whyld, Kenneth (Oxford 1992)

Trotter's Bottom, Jones, Tanya (Headline 1997)

USCF Official Rules of Chess, Goichberg, Bill et al, (USCF 1993)

Notation and Symbols

The games in this book are written in algebraic notation, using an initial letter for each piece, followed by the co-ordinates of the square to which it moves.

e.g. Bb2 – bishop moves to the b2-square.

The squares are indicated horizontally by letters a to h, beginning on White's left hand side (the files), and vertically by numbers 1 to 8, beginning on White's side of the board (the ranks).

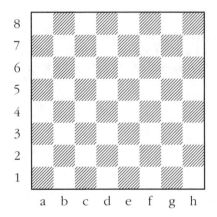

The pieces are designated as follows:

K – king, Q – queen, R – rook, N – knight, B – bishop

If no initial letter is given then the move is made by a pawn.

e.g. e4 – pawn moves to e4

Survival Guide for Chess Parents

Sometimes further information is given, e.g. when one of two pawns could capture the same piece or one of two rooks could move to the same square.

e.g. R8h4 – rook on the eighth rank moves to h4

Other symbols are used as follows:

x – captures	!! – outstanding move
+ – check	? – weak move
0-0 – castles kingside	?? – very weak move: a 'blunder'
0-0-0 – castles queenside	!? – interesting move
! – good move	?! – doubtful move

The moves are numbered, with White's move given first, as it is played. If there is a break for analysis after a White move, then the following Black move is indicated with three dots.

e.g. 1 e4. The most popular opening move. 1...c5

The moves actually played in the game are indicated in bold, while the moves in ordinary type are variations which might have occurred. Where necessary, brackets are used within the variations to make them easier to follow.

Introduction

Chess, like the past, is another country, and they do things differently there. It is a beautiful land, steeped in history and legend, logical yet intuitive, a source of infinite challenge, fascination and friendship to those who find their way inside. Playing chess, for both adults and children, can be a way to extend their horizons in all directions: mental, social, geographical and imaginative. But, like any other country, chess takes time and energy to discover. Its language, its institutions and its etiquette are unique, complex and, to the newcomer, often incomprehensible.

I have aimed firstly, therefore, to make this book a kind of travellers' guide. It gives the reader, whether parent, junior or adult novice, an introductory map of the terrain, of clubs, tournaments and championships, ratings, resources and the esoteric mysteries of blitz, bughouse and the blindfold simul. Practical advice is given upon joining a chess club, playing in tournaments, finding professional help and using the Internet.

Secondly, and perhaps more importantly, I have tried to give an idea of what it actually means to play chess, of the particular psychological pressures and stimuli experienced by the chess player and the effect of these upon relationships, at school, at home and with other players. From our own experience and that of other families, I look at how we can best help our chess-playing children and teenagers, both practically and emotionally, and how we can balance their needs with those of the rest of the family. The book covers the full range of age and ability, from the pre-school child learning the first moves to the young adult contemplating a professional chess career. Chess is, of course, played by both men and women, boys and girls, and in order to reflect this[1], I have used the fictional players 'Charlie' and 'Alice' in alternate chapters.

---

[1] and in homage to Charles Dodgson, better known as Lewis Carroll, from whose *Through the Looking Glass and what Alice found there* the quotations at the beginning of each chapter are taken.

Our son Gawain has been playing competitive chess for nearly ten years, since he was six, and the book is illustrated by his own games, covering the spectrum of his experience, from his first friendly club matches to international tournaments and championships. The moves are explained and discussed in his own notes, designed to be interesting and comprehensible to novice parents as well as to their expert offspring.

An experienced chess-player, with the ability, peculiar to the species, of mentally visualizing the board, will be able to appreciate these games and their analysis simply by reading them. For the beginner, however, and for those, including most parents, whose brains are constructed in the conventional manner, a board or at least a computer screen will be essential. In the first instance you may prefer to look only at the actual moves of the game, those printed in bold type, without wandering down the byways of the suggested variations. Playing the moves on an actual physical chess board[2] will probably be the easiest way to follow them and to understand the comments which Gawain makes. If you are looking at the games with your child (as I did with Gawain's five year old brother), then he or she can of course take a colour (maybe the winning one!) and perhaps try to predict the moves before they are played.

Later, if your spatial awareness is up to it[3], you can investigate the suggested variations, alternative moves which, if played, might have changed the whole course of the game. These will perhaps be of especial interest to the older or more experienced junior who will be able to follow the analysis by him – or herself[4] and will, we hope, find ideas and inspiration for his or her own future games.

Finally, we would like to thank you for buying this book (or for being about to buy it, if you are still hovering at the bookstall). Writing it has been an enjoyable and sometimes illuminating experience for us (with a strict minimum of gratuitous bishop-hurling) and we hope that reading it will be equally entertaining and informative. Chess is a fascinating game, ancient and yet still evolving, with rich opportunities for development, travel and friendship. We hope that this book will help you to take advantage of these, and, most of all, to enjoy yourselves while doing so. Good luck in all your games, tournaments, championships, attempts to read the map and choices of three-volume novels to while away the waiting hours. And yes, it is worth the wait...

Tanya Jones
Lucca, Italy,
November 2003

---

[2] On the other hand a computer chess program, while less tactile, will allow you to check that you have moved the pieces correctly and can be especially useful if and when you move on to complex variations.

[3] I have never been able to get to the end of even a four-move variation without getting confused, but then neither have I been able to follow the simplest sketch map to a new tournament venue without at least one or two unscheduled three-point turns.

[4] no doubt closeted in the bedroom, on the floor of which, under last week's socks and last month's homework, you will eventually find this book again.

Chapter One

The Noah's Ark Trap[5]:
Beginnings and the Very Young

Kitty, can you play chess? Now, don't smile, my dear, I'm asking it seriously. Because, when we were playing just now, you watched just as if you understood it: and when I said 'Check!' you purred![6]

There is something inevitable and oddly comforting about teaching your child to play chess. Like cleaning his teeth alone, riding a bike without stabilisers or his first unsigned Valentine, it is part of the continuum of childhood, an assurance of the stability of the generations. In a world of Playstations and mobile phones, the game of chess reassures us that our children are not so very different from us, just as we, despite our Choppers and inexplicable passion for the Bay City Rollers, were basically the same species as our own parents.

And, for most families, this is as far as the thing will go, a few desultory games with one of the pawns missing and replaced by a bottle top, some confusion over the relative status of the knight and rook, one or two half-hearted accusations of cheating, or at least, a selective interpretation of the rules, and the final consignment of the set back up to the attic until the grandchildren come along. But for a few children, often quite unexpectedly and without rational explanation, the game takes a mysterious hold and becomes, not just an isolated rite of passage, but the onset of a lifetime's passion. It is for the parents of these odd aficionados that this book has been written.

You may already have received hints that Charlie might turn into one of these weird creatures, although you probably only recognize them with hindsight. There seem to be two principal methods by which chess fastens itself upon the child's imagination; either as a puzzle or as a war. If Charlie is one of the peaceful puzzlers, then he may have shown an early fascination with jigsaws, Rubik's cubes or those mysterious pieces of twisted metal without which no box of Christmas crackers could possibly be complete.

---

[5] Literally, a variation in which a white bishop is trapped by black pawns, rather the way you feel when cajoled into your first game of chess for the past fifteen years.
[6] Lewis Carroll, *Through the Looking Glass and what Alice found there* (1887)

If, on the other hand, he comes to chess by the martial route, you may already bear the scars of green plastic soldiers, miniature cannon and medieval knights with perilously authentic spurs and lances. Perhaps these early preferences are later translated into playing styles, so that the jigsaw solving infant becomes the sort of vegetarian individual who sets and solves ingenious help-mates[7], while the more bloodthirsty youngster will specialize in violent and probably unsound sacrificial attacks, counting the game contemptible until the table before him is littered with butchered pawns, slaughtered pieces and small parts of his opponent's anatomy. Or perhaps not.

Whichever the route, the end is the same; a child, anywhere between three and seventeen, who cannot pass a chess board without stopping to look at the game with swift recognition or a long patient gaze, as though he is listening to its secrets on a wavelength that no one else can hear. Probably, you are quite pleased. There is, after all, something reassuringly wholesome about the game, like honey sandwiches or camping in the rain. Chess, you reflect smugly, needs little specialist equipment and no designer sportswear, does not require long parental hours on a damp touchline and bears a relatively low risk of grievous bodily harm. What is more, there are popularly believed to be statistical links between ability at chess, general intelligence and a slightly nerdy type of good behaviour. There appears therefore to be nothing about Charlie's new interest to alarm elderly relatives and much reflected glory in which to bask, whether you incline to the genetic or environmental theories of development.

Faced with these shining advantages, and the prospect of a happy and fulfilled future for Charlie as the next Garry Kasparov, it is worth making a modest investment in a proper chess set. Great Uncle Harold's boyhood pieces, with all the knights decapitated, the kings and queens indistinguishable and half the pawns missing may be enough for the Boxing Day grudge match, but will be highly frustrating for everyday use. Similarly, to rely upon novelty sets, whether the pieces are in the shape of The Simpsons or of eminent Victorian statesmen, is to invite inevitable confusion, dispute and probable bloodshed, when, in the closing stages of a crucial game, no one can quite remember whether Gladstone is a queen or a mere bishop. A standard, boring Staunton style set, large enough for the pieces to be clearly distinguishable but not too big to fit on a coffee table, is probably your safest choice.

The other early essential is to make sure that you know the rules. Like Monopoly and Scrabble, chess tends to collect private family variations, which, while entertaining, are liable to cause embarrassment in the outside world. The harassed controller of a prestigious junior tournament will not be impressed by Charlie's impassioned insistence that, according to his Dad, pawns can always capture backwards, or that, on his birthday, he is to be allowed a third bishop. Get yourself a copy of the rules from a reputable source, preferably not translated verbatim from the Korean as part of your Giant Compendium of Games, and make sure you know them yourself before teaching anyone else. Castling, pawn promotion (to a queen, rook, bishop or knight, *not* a second king) and the circumstances

---

[7] A type of chess problem which requires the losing player to acquiesce in his own vanquishment by deliberately playing the moves most beneficial to his opponent.

in which a draw can be claimed are particularly dodgy areas. By the way, if you want Charlie to retain any street cred (if there is such a thing in chess), please remember not to refer to a rook as a castle and certainly not to a knight as a 'horsey'. Talking about prawns instead of pawns is amusing for about thirteen seconds.

Neither is it generally advisable, unless you are prepared to risk a seriously overheated brain, to attempt to make any kind of logical sense out of the rules of chess. No doubt there is some intricate military reason for the fact that pawns capture diagonally but cannot retreat, or that knights perform such an odd L-shaped manoeuvre, but, unless you are a specialist in ancient Babylonian armoury, it is probably wisest not to enquire. 'Because it *does*,' should be sufficient explanation for all but the most irritatingly inquisitive child, and if they are that anxious to find out then they can jolly well get the bus down to the library and consult the *Encyclopaedia Britannica* (or more likely download the answer from the Net before you have managed to explain what a bus used to be).

If you cannot face the task yourself, then there are plenty of books, videos, computer programmes and special sets designed to teach the essentials of chess. Tedious as it may be, if you decide to use one of these then it might be wise to work through it yourself first, just to make sure that it really does as it promises.

Some of these teaching aids, especially those aimed at the very young, introduce each piece individually and devise a kind of simplified chess for each stage, so that the first level uses pawns only, the next bishops and so on, gradually building up to the complete game. This may be helpful to some, perhaps to the under eights (or feeble-minded parents) but most children with any aptitude for chess, once they are old enough to appreciate the game at all, are capable of comprehending all the piece moves more or less at once. There is inevitably something artificial about, for example, a pawns-only game, and so it may be more satisfying for you both to introduce Charlie as quickly as possible to the interrelation of all the pieces on the board. All that matters, at this stage, is that you have a clear and accurate understanding of the rules, and, most importantly of all, that both you and Charlie are having fun. There is no necessity for any child to learn chess and, especially for an absolute beginner, if the experience is not enjoyable then there is no point in it whatsoever. However convinced you may be that Charlie could be a brilliant player, however many times he himself has gazed upon the board with fascination and longing, frustration and tears are a price too high to pay. Much better to put the set away for a while and go back to the jigsaws or toy soldiers. Chess has been around for the last few thousand years; it will wait another six months for Charlie.

But however long you manage to fob him off with Snakes and Ladders or Sesame Street dominoes, the time will eventually come when, having ploughed through the rules from a-pawns to zugzwang[8], you are obliged to put them into practice.

---

[8] Not strictly part of the rules of chess at all, but one of those usefully arcane chess words which are both relatively easy to understand and remember and also mysteriously impressive to non-chess players. It means, roughly speaking, a situation in which every possible move weakens the player's position. As this is a very common predicament for the weak or inexperienced player, a great psychological benefit can

At this point, remembering, perhaps, that chess is, after all, a game and thus theoretically a pleasurable experience, should you use a little judicious deception to even out the stakes? There can be little more dispiriting to a child, his head reeling with knights, castles and sacrifices, than to find himself lost every time within the first ten moves. Often you need only to overlook the fact that your queen is *en prise*[9] but occasionally you may have to try more drastic measures, subtly whisking one of your rooks off the board or, when returning to a game after supper, forgetting that you were originally White and taking up Black's completely lost position. These tactics should be temporary, and used with care, for if Charlie is to play chess at all outside the smallest family circle, he will soon have to learn, and relearn, the raw and bloody pain of losing, losing badly and losing repeatedly. Similarly, if he is ever to play in a tournament or any kind of official game, it must be instilled immutably into his brain that cheating of any kind is always and invariably absolute anathema. So, fix the game if you have to, but only for the youngest children or in the first few weeks, and don't let them notice what you are doing. Cheating on your own behalf, in a feeble attempt to scrape a draw from your superior teenage children, I leave to your own conscience.

For a few children, the question of how much help to give hardly arises at all, or, if it does, it is more a matter of how much help they ought to give to you. These are the scary ones, the ones who, while still at infant school or kindergarten show a reckless disregard for the proprieties of family life by not only beating their elder brothers and sisters but also their parents, grandparents and even Uncle Eric, who once played for his house at school and was always previously acknowledged as the family champion.

It is difficult to know quite what to do with one of these, short of locking him in a cupboard for the next ten years with a copy of the *Encyclopaedia of Chess Openings* (and with or without Uncle Eric). Almost inevitably, there will be a degree of potential conflict between your wish to nurture his talent, allowing him to explore and enjoy it to the full, and your paramount concern that, as a young child, he needs, above all else, a safe, happy and tranquil environment in which to grow.

Exactly how you resolve this dilemma will depend upon your particular circumstances, Charlie's age and character and your access to expert help and facilities. For each family the balance will be slightly different, but you are unlikely to go far wrong so long as you remember that, however good a chess player Charlie may eventually become, he is first and foremost a child, with the same basic needs as any other. Although others may in time assume the responsibility of directing his chess development (and should generally be left to do so without your interference), you are still his parents, with a constant duty to watch over his general welfare. You may not know a forced mate from a fianchetto but you know your own child and can recognize the signs of tiredness, frustration, bump-

---

be obtained by muttering sagely, 'I appear to be somewhat zugswanged', in place of the verb that you would otherwise, were it not for the children's delicate ears, be tempted to employ.

[9] In a position where it can be captured immediately, with no, or insufficient compensation.

tiousness or simple boredom. Upon any point that touches his health, happiness, safety or behaviour, you are always entitled to intervene, no matter how exalted a chess personage you may have to defy. Most organizers, coaches and officials, particularly in junior chess, are themselves parents or teachers, or at the least can recall a little of their own childhood, and see junior players as children first, and as chess players second. In a few cases, however, the perception seems to become reversed, so that they see the child almost as a little bundle of grades, ratings and tournament performances, with a human body and soul tacked on as an afterthought.

It is up to you to watch out for this tendency, to counterbalance it wherever you can and generally to help Charlie to grow into a happy and fulfilled adult, at peace with himself and his neighbours. A brief skim through a few biographies will show that these are not always the defining characteristics of a great player. Overbearing or morbidly timid, paranoid, neurotic or just plain dotty, the story of the historic masters can sometimes seem like a parade of isolation, eccentricity and mania. However, before you lock up the pawns and throw away the key, take a look at the present generation of professional players, who are, in the vast majority, pleasant, civilised and stable, quite capable of tying their shoelaces, holding a knife and fork and conducting happy and fruitful family lives as well as writing abstruse volumes delineating the latest tendrils of theory.

For the first few months, and longer for a very young child, most of his chess playing will take place at home, under your own supervision. Usually there will be little beyond the basics that you yourself can teach, other than a few simple principles (not moving a piece twice in the opening, developing pieces quickly, controlling the centre etc.) that most children with a talent for the game seem to know instinctively in any case. But it is here that the plethora of chess computer games, videos, and books (discussed in more detail in Chapter Nine) really come into their own. If you have a PC available for Charlie's use (i.e. one which can safely be doused in Coke and have its hard disk battered into oblivion, then a sensible[10] chess program may be the simplest option. Otherwise it may be better to buy a stand-alone computer chess game, with a touch sensitive board. You may be reluctant to see Charlie playing on a computer for hours on end, but it is probably better than your trying to obtain a comprehensive mastery of the Najdorf Variation between the breakfast washing-up and the morning school run. If you are concerned about fresh air, exercise, social interaction and all the other things that a responsible parent ought to be concerned about, you can always reserve to yourself the right of absolute veto and impose an occasional game of soccer. In any case, at best you are only anticipating the inevitable computer domination by a few months, unless you live in some undiscovered warp of space and time as yet unvisited by Nintendo, Playstation or the X-Box.

Of course, constant cyber-opposition needs leavening with the human variety and so you, your spouse, father-in-law, cat and hamster should also play as often as you can stand it, even if the outcome is a completely predictable pasting. Your chess-playing child will never tire of beating you and, provided that he himself is

---

[10] i.e. not one which requires ten minutes of blood-splattered animation to indicate that a piece has been captured

defeated often enough (remember to set the computer rating progressively higher to reflect his own improvement), it will not do him any lasting psychological damage. Be careful, however, with your other children. If you have a much older child who is himself good at chess (i.e. significantly better than the younger) then it does no harm to cajole, threaten or bribe him into playing a game or two (and even into losing once in a while). In general, however, unless your other children particularly want to play (and they will let you know if they do), they should not be pressured to do so. Chess is a source of endless fascination to those who enjoy it, but of equally boundless irritation and boredom to those who don't. If Charlie fulfils his early promise then his brothers and sisters will inevitably be dogged by the game for many years to come. It seems rather unfair to inflict it on them so early, in the peace of their own home. Meanwhile, the talent of one child need not necessarily be a source of injustice or resentment to the others, but an inspiration to discover and develop their own particular skills. So, rather than nagging at them to give Charlie yet another a game, leave Charlie to his computer, and concentrate on giving the others the time and facilities to enjoy their own peculiar talents. That way, if and when the occasion arises, they are far more likely to enjoy basking in the reflected glory of their brother's success instead of stomping about the house like the *Dreamcoat* fraternity, making unguarded remarks to hovering reporters.

Visitors, friends and relatives can present a dilemma. Perhaps Charlie is a bumptious and confident child, desperate for opponents, who would dragoon the man who comes to read the electricity meter, several election canvassers and a brace of Jehovah's Witnesses into an impromptu simul[11] sooner than you can say 'Bedtime'. On the other hand, he may be excruciatingly shy, collapsing into something resembling a grilled tomato if the subject of chess is so much as mentioned, despite secretly longing for a real game against a worthy opponent. You therefore have the delightful choice of appearing either as an unbearably pushy parent or as a pathetic wimp who cannot even control her big-headed and brash eight year old. The answer may be to have a quiet chat with Charlie, both generally and before an expected visit, explaining that it is polite to play a game if, and only if, an adult asks him first. Then a chess set can be visibly but unobtrusively left on a table in the sitting room and developments awaited. You may be surprised at how many of your old friends have a secret chess-playing past, sometimes to quite a high level, about which they have been suspiciously quiet for all the years that you have known them.

So when is the best age to start playing chess? Biographies of successful players often tell how the future grandmaster eavesdropped upon his elder brother's first chess lesson, grasping the basics of the game within minutes and proceeding to beat his hapless sibling hollow. Oddly, no instances of subsequent fratricide are recorded. Meanwhile, a media silly season standby is the breathtaking account of some photogenic three year old's tournament debut, complete with lisp and sandaled feet swinging a good yard above the floor. At the other extreme, many

---

[11] short for 'simultaneous display', a 'match' where one strong player plays simultaneously against a number of opponents (typically 20-30), moving from board to board with each move.

players who come to the game in their teens or even as adults, regret not having learned it earlier, before their free time was circumscribed by the demands of exams, employment and the emotional entanglements of the Great Wide World.

There is no doubt that many two year olds, given sufficient time to watch and copy, are able to set up the pieces on the board accurately and that, by the time they are four, some have grasped the rudiments of the game. But, like Doctor Johnson's upright dog, 'it is not done well, but you are surprised to find it done at all'[12]. Very few children, under the age of five or six, are able to develop any real sense of strategy, or to think ahead beyond the next move. Most pre-school children will regularly need to be reminded of how a knight moves, how many squares each of their own pawns can advance, how to castle and not to cheat by removing their opponent's queen when she goes out to switch the oven on. It will be rare for a game to be finished, especially one where the child is not certain to win, and defeat will seldom be welcomed with good grace. There is little point, unless you particularly enjoy seeing the board awash with tears (both Charlie's and your own) in trying to persuade him to take the game at all seriously unless and until he is clearly ready, probably well after he has started full-time school.

Generally speaking, of course, there is no reason why Charlie should, at this age, be interested in chess at all, or even know of the game's existence, unless he has an older relative who plays regularly. In this case, if he really clamours to know, there is no harm in showing him the moves, provided that he is not expected to remember or apply them consistently. Meanwhile the world, your High Street toyshop and Granny's cupboard are crammed with toys and games that are easier, more brightly coloured and more fun to explore during the Play-Doh years. It would be a shame for Charlie to miss his brief months of enjoying these in favour of the cheap prestige of the ghastly word 'prodigy'. And even if he is to be a great player by the hoary old age of seven or eight, his mental faculties are unlikely to be severely blunted by Animal Lotto and a jigsaw or two.

But, when chess and only chess will do, should you send your pre-school player out into the great wide world of clubs, tournaments and ratings? In Chapter Two we will look at junior clubs, and it may be that an unusually precocious four year old (in terms of confidence and behaviour as well as chess ability) could survive in an unusually tranquil junior club with a particularly understanding organizer. You could certainly, in such a position, contact the organizer and ask his advice. I would not normally suggest that you contact an adult club at this stage. As we will see in Chapter Three, many are unsympathetic to the membership of junior players at all, and most would seriously blanch at the thought of an under-five. An unhelpful response at this stage would only make it awkward for all concerned when, in a few years' time, Charlie really is ready to join a club.

Another possibility is to enter Charlie directly into a tournament. This is sometimes done, but it is difficult to see what good it really serves. Chess tournaments are, on the whole, silent and intense affairs, often held in uncomfortable halls, either too hot or too cold, full of silent and intense men hunched over their boards. Few infractions of either the rules or conventions will be tolerated by

---

[12] James Boswell, *The Life of Samuel Johnson* (1791)

these players and they expect the same standards of behaviour from children as from their contemporaries. The games are either long and drawn-out, or painfully brief and disaster is horribly public. Little is worse for a chess player than being beaten by an infant, and so Charlie's opponent will not hesitate to use all the tricks and stratagems at his disposal. If, despite this, Charlie wins the game, his antagonist will probably be graceful and generous in defeat but sometimes may not. I have known adult men to swear at children at the conclusion of a game. Junior tournaments may not be much better, especially important championships, where parents loom as close to the boards as they are allowed, huge, prepossessing and eagle-eyed for any excuse for interference. What is more, in almost all tournaments, players are required to write down their moves and those of their opponent as soon as they have been played. While for most adult players this is the easiest part of the whole process, for a small child it will be daunting and perhaps impossible. Finally, you should consider the attention, not all of it positive, which will be directed towards a very young child at a chess tournament. It may be exciting for Charlie to see his picture in the local, or even national paper, but the story alongside the photograph will not always be sympathetic or measured. It can leave a nasty taste in the mouth to see one's child described, even if in not so many words, as a freak.

Unless, therefore, you discover a really positive, child-friendly junior tournament (and such do exist), where the venue, time controls and rules about recording games are all appropriate to Charlie's development, it is probably best to wait a year or two. When Charlie has been at school for some time, long enough to be confident in writing letters and numbers, to be accustomed to sitting still and quietly, and to be able to deal with public disappointment, he will be able to enjoy a tournament properly, and to make full use of his talents. Until then, you may as well make the most of his infancy, his presence at home and the moments of peace afforded to you by the distant hum of his chess computer.

Chapter Two

Skittles[13] and Scholar's Mate[14]:
Schools and Junior Clubs

'It's something very like learning geography', thought Alice, as she stood on tiptoe in hopes of being able to see a little further.

By the time Alice begins to play serious chess, she will usually already be at school and is likely to remain in the educational system for the next ten to fifteen years. Although the correlation between chess and general intelligence is not as straightforward as fond parents might believe, it is nonetheless still the fact that an aptitude for the game tends to be accompanied, in the long run, by high academic achievement.

I say 'in the long run' because the intellectual development of young chess players, especially those gifted at mathematics, is often rather different from the average. Many begin to read comparatively late, sometimes not until they are nine or ten, although thereafter they swiftly catch up and usually overtake their peers. In the meantime, however, they may have been labelled as having special educational needs (or with whatever is the current euphemistic formula) by bureaucracies that find it difficult to integrate deviations from the developmental norm. It may be partly as a result of this type of rigid thinking that a comparatively high proportion of young chess players seem to be taught at home, in both Britain and the United States, at least for the primary or elementary years.

While the majority of children who play chess experience no such extreme conflict with the educational establishment, the relationship between school and chess is often complex. When Alice begins to play chess, especially if she enjoys some early success, she may be met by a range of various and unpredictable responses from the adults around her, as well as from her contemporaries at school. Individual teachers' attitudes vary from a kind of reverent awe, rather as if Alice had been anointed as the next Dalai Lama, to a suspicious contempt, conveying the strong impression that the whole thing is simply an elaborate ruse to

---

[13] A quick, friendly game.

[14] An early (sometimes fourth move) mate by the queen, capturing the opponent's f-pawn.

evade hockey practice. Both of these extremes tend to be found in teachers who have never, either through inability or disinclination, learned to play chess themselves. In between is the comparatively level-headed majority whose general view is one of benevolent boredom, shading into mild enthusiasm at one end and incredulity at the other. Chess fervour is occasionally found in the staff room but generally only in combination with a shyness so paralysing as to prevent the teacher so afflicted from ever communicating either with you or with Alice beyond an annual embarrassed nod.

These various viewpoints are frequently mirrored by the attitudes of head teachers and of schools in general. There are two potential and opposing pitfalls: an ethos that pays too much attention to chess and one that pays too little. The first, commoner among high-flying academic schools, in the private or state sector, conscious of publicity and league table positions, can lead to Alice's talent being effectively hijacked by the school so that her every game becomes a test of corporate honour. Though the attention can be gratifying so long as Alice is successful, it puts enormous extra pressure on what is already a stressful activity, and can lead to her feeling that she is only valued by the school in terms of her chess achievements. The opposite extreme, sometimes found in schools which like to boast of their anti-elitism and inclusiveness, is a virtually open hostility to the game, which is seen as somehow regressive, elitist and probably imperialistic. No doubt such schools have no intention of transferring their dislike of the game to Alice herself, but it is difficult, in practice, to separate the two, and she may well be left feeling uncomfortable and isolated.

There are schools, of course, and many of them, which successfully steer their path between this Scylla and Charybdis, recognizing and rejoicing in their students' talents without exploiting them for their own ends. Such schools will expect, naturally, that a strong player will support the school team, if any, but equally will allow suitable time and support for chess-playing activities further afield. Children are naturally generous towards another's success and a good teacher will enjoy encouraging Alice to share her interests and good news, provided that she herself keeps a sense of proportion.

Playing for a school team can be particularly enjoyable for a strong player, with its combination of camaraderie and relatively undemanding chess. In this game, played when Gawain was nine, he made one or two misjudgements but managed to impress his opponent sufficiently to come away with an early victory.

□ **Robert Price** ■ **Gawain Jones**
Northern Preparatory Schools Semi-Final 1997
Benko Gambit

---

1 d4 Nf6 2 c4 c5 3 d5 b5

This is the Benko Gambit, in which Black sacrifices a pawn to get quick development and opportunities for active play. It is a good line to play as you don't need to learn reams of theory but only to be familiar with the plans of the position.

4 Nc3 b4

Taking the pawn on c4 is possible but it gives White an easy position to play. Not in the spirit of the Benko!

5 Na4 Qa5

Simply defending the pawn with 5...d6 would be better. Remember the motto, 'Don't move your queen early in the opening!'

6 b3 g6 7 Bg5 d6?! Bg7

An easy developing move would be better or alternatively 6...Ne4 attacking the bishop. Another familiar motto is 'Don't move the same piece twice in the opening.' However, this time it would be justified, as White has already moved his own knight twice without achieving very much.

8 Nf3?!

Here White should have taken on f6 doubling Black's pawns and taking Black's dangerous knight. 'Doubled' pawns are two on the same file and can be a serious weakness, as they are no longer able to defend one another.

8...Bg7 9 e3 Bd7 10 Rc1

Moving the rook off the dangerous diagonal away from the attack of Black's dark-squared bishop.

10...Ne4?!

Here it would be better to keep with my original plan and take the knight on a4 thus doubling White's pawns.

11 Bd3 Nxg5 12 Nxg5 Bxa4!

Taking off the knight, doubling White's a-pawns and threatening a nasty discovered check. (A discovered check is one in which a piece moves out of the way, revealing a check given by another piece of the same colour.)

13 bxa4 b3+ 14 Kf1 bxa2 (diagram 1) 15 Ra1!

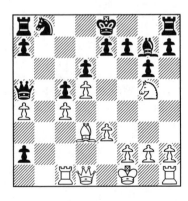
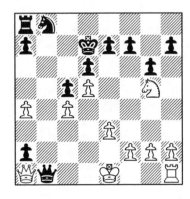

Diagram 1   **Diagram 2**

A good move giving up material but creating counterplay.

15...Bxa1 16 Qxa1 Qd2

Castling would perhaps be a better move but this at least keeps Black with the attack.

17 Qxh8+ Kd7 18 Qa1

18 g3, which lets White's rook into the game after the king moves, would be better.

18...Qxd3+ 19 Ke1 Qb1+? (diagram 2) 0-1

Letting White's king out of the net. Instead 19...Na6! followed by either ...Rb8-b1 or ...Na6-b4-c2 would be winning easily. You have to remember to attack with more than just your queen! Strangely enough just after I let out his king, giving White chances, he resigned! Remember 'No one ever won by resigning'! 20 Kd2 attacking black's queen with the h1-rook would have kept White in the game!

A few schools go further than this, including chess in their curriculum, generally for all children and not only the especially talented. Such initiatives may arise out of a perception of chess as valuable for its own sake but more often as a kind of intellectual warm-up, preparing the mental muscles for the serious matters of trigonometry or business studies. Whatever the motives, a growing number of schools, mainly in the private secondary sector, employ specialist chess teachers, often titled players, to give specific lessons within the school timetable.

Many more schools have chess clubs, even now, when the opportunities for extra-curricular activities are often much more limited than they were for our generation. These clubs normally meet after school or at lunchtime, and may often be found in primary as well as secondary schools. Many are excellent, full of enthusiastic students and run efficiently and well, producing school teams who compete in regional and national competitions. Unfortunately, a talent for chess is not always accompanied by one for discipline and, without this, some school clubs descend into chaos, transformed into a teacher-baiting arena where the children who actually want to play chess cower in corners, their interest in the game waning with every week. Bear in mind also that, even if undisturbed chess is played at the club, it will not necessarily be at an appropriate level for Alice. It is difficult for an eleven-year old novice to hold her own among a group of confident sixth-formers, expertly debating the latest variations in the Marshall Attack, and equally difficult for an outstanding player to cope with the social dilemmas of perpetual victory. It can be a lonely place at the top of the chess ladder, where her wins are taken for granted, as further evidence of her weirdness, while any losses are headline news for weeks. It takes a confident and popular child, with generous and supportive friends, to deal positively with that kind of attention. Even with these advantages, life for a chess-playing child within a hostile or derisive school atmosphere may be very difficult. It is not surprising that many strong junior players choose to keep their school and chess lives separate. By all means, therefore, encourage Alice to find out whether her school has a chess club, and to go along and try it, but do not force her to keep attending if she feels ill at ease. A good school club may inspire a life-long interest in the game, but a bad one, or one that places the player in an awkward position, may well have the opposite effect.

If Alice's school does not already have a chess club then the teachers, learning of her interest, may ask you whether you would be interested in forming one. In the first rush of heady excitement and gratitude that Alice has indeed chosen chess rather than lap dancing or the bobsleigh you may even be tempted to agree. This could be an excellent move, allowing you simultaneously to develop your own understanding of the game, see Alice in her school environment, take an unauthorized snoop around the staff room and assuage your guilt at not having made a single fairy cake for the past seven Summer Fetes. Alternatively, you may find yourself, every Wednesday teatime from now until eternity, wedged into a broken child's chair in a draughty classroom. Either no one at all will turn up, so that you and Alice play against each other, just as you would at home, only without the benefit of your usual large whisky, or twenty teenagers will crash through the door, throw chairs (including the one attached to your anatomy) at one another for twenty minutes and then leave, having taken careful note of every peculiarity of your figure, clothes and accent, news of which will be transmitted across the entire school by the following day's morning break. At best, as happened to me when I tried to run a chess club at a leading public school, they may courteously, charmingly, but utterly obdurately insist upon playing bridge. Alice, knowing you, her school, and her own toleration level for the humiliation of your public presence, is probably best placed to advise. (And remember, meanwhile, that a substantial raffle prize will atone for a multitude of failings in the fairy cake department.) Meanwhile, if you are really determined to make this most magnanimous of parental sacrifices, help is at hand, especially for American readers, on the US Chess Federation website, which publishes a comprehensive 'Guide to Scholastic Chess' which includes advice on running school clubs and tournaments, starting with the simplest 'quad' four player competitions.

In any case, as prisoners of war, foreign legionaries and families stranded in dilatory restaurants will know, one of the greatest advantages of chess is that it requires no particular equipment, venue, time or number of players. It may therefore be the case that Alice will learn and, most importantly, enjoy herself far more playing just with one or two friends than at a formal chess club. An informal club, meeting at your house, may cost you dearly in Coke and crisps (both, naturally, ground deeply into your carpet and soft furnishings), but the sacrifice is laudable, and you will at least have answers to the three great riddles of parenthood: Where is she? Who is she with? and What is she doing? (although the last may require you to leave the door slightly ajar, as it is not entirely impossible to combine chess with the other teenage vices).

The ideal solution, however, from your point of view and that of Alice and your carpets, will probably be a junior chess club, if you are lucky enough to find one nearby. Clubs of this type are aimed typically at juniors between eight and sixteen, although they will probably be happy to accept a younger child whose ability, self-reliance and behaviour are appropriate. Often the club will meet on school premises, most often on a Saturday, but it generally has no formal links to the school and the teaching staff is not usually involved. This gives the club immediate advantages in that it can draw from a much wider catchment area and avoid the artificial distinction between primary and secondary pupils. Most importantly it will contain, on the whole, only those who really want to be there, rather than those avoiding rugby or desperately currying favour after the debacle of their last maths lesson.

The junior club is usually run by a local enthusiast, or someone with a sufficiently well developed social conscience to mimic enthusiasm. Sometimes he (or occasionally she) will be a strong or strongish player in his own right, sometimes a former teacher or the parent of a junior player from the last generation. At this stage, a talent for organization and inspiration is generally more important than an impressive FIDE rating. The atmosphere at the club is generally relaxed but purposeful, and you should be able to hang around as long as your parental apprehension requires.

In the United States, young chess players can take advantage of the long vacation by signing up for one of the various chess summer camps, details of which are available from the USCF website. In Britain there is no such tradition of residential courses but you may be able to find a holiday chess club in your area, running for a week or two at a time and offering keen youngsters the opportunity for coaching, friendly tournaments and other chess-related activities. This game took place at such a event, one of several run by Sean Marsh in Cleveland, in the north-east of England. Gawain was only just seven, having begun to play competitive chess about a year before, and faltered before the experience of his opponent, a few years his senior and an old hand at Sean's tournaments.

☐ **Alex Fowler** ■ **Gawain Jones**
Easter Chess Extravaganza 1995
Sicilian Defence

---

1 e4 c5

The Sicilian Defence; my great passion in the first year or two although sometimes I found it easier to play than to pronounce (and certainly to spell).

2 Nf3 d6 3 d4 cxd4 4 Nxd4 Nf6 5 Nc3 a6

This is the Najdorf Variation of the Sicilian, a sharp[15] line which was advocated by Kasparov every time that he was Black in the World Championship match against Nigel Short. It was watching these games, and their subsequent analysis, which first really inspired me to play chess, and so they had a marked influence over my early games.

6 Be3 e6 7 Bd3?

Not good, as the bishop does nothing positive here but just gets in the way of White playing down the d-file. Playing the bishop to e2 would be better.

7...Be7 8 0-0 Nc6 9 Nb3 0-0 10 f4

---

[15] A 'sharp' line is one which leads to exciting but dangerous play as opposed to a 'quiet' variation in which fewer opportunities are available to either side and a draw is thereby more likely.

White tries for a typical attack on the kingside while I...

10...b5

...go for an attack on the queenside!

11 a3 Bb7 12 Qe2 d5!?

I am playing for an attack in the centre as well.

13 Bf2 h6?!

This move simply weakens my kingside. A move like 13...dxe4 or 13...b4 would lead to a level position, but here White is slightly better.

14 e5! Nd7 15 Rad1

White develops his final piece before deciding to go for an all out attack on the black king.

15...Nb6 16 Rfe1

16 Nc5! looks better, hitting my weak dark squares. At the moment White is not sure which is the better square for the rook, either e1 defending e5 or f1 helping the idea of an f4-f5 push

16...Nc4 17 Bxc4 bxc4 18 Nd4

White has a slight space advantage and is preparing his attack on my king. I, on the other hand, need to start a quick queenside attack.

18...Qc7

Trying to hold back the f4-f5 break for a few moves.

19 Qg4 Rfc8?!

The rook isn't doing anything on this square as the c-pawn blocks an attack. Instead 19...Rab8 or 19...Bc8! followed by ...Rb8 hitting the b-pawn looks more accurate.

20 Nxc6

White misses a fantastic chance. 20 Nxe6 would blow open my kingside and get three pawns for the piece[16] with a huge attack.

20...Qxc6 21 Bd4

The position is still about equal; it is simply a question of whose attack gets in first!

21...Bc5

Trying to get at White's king.

22 f5! (diagram 3)

Starting a big attack

---

[16] Values are often attributed to pieces as follows: queen 9, rook 5, knight and bishop 3, pawn 1. However, these values are elementary and often misleading, particularly towards the end of a game where, for example, three strong pawns can be significantly more powerful than a knight or restricted bishop.

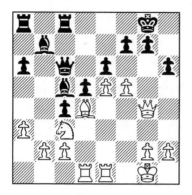

Diagram 3

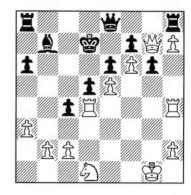

Diagram 4

22...Re8?!

Instead, 22...exf5 would stop White's attack from being so serious.

23 f6!

Now White has an extremely dangerous assault.

23...Bxd4+ 24 Rxd4 g6 25 Qh4!

White is clearly better with a strong attack while I have been left with a bad bishop[17] and no counterplay whatsoever.

25...Kh7

25...h5 is weaker on account of 26 g4.

26 Re3

Moving another piece into the attack and threatening Rh3, mating.

26...Rh8!

The only move, indirectly defending the h6-pawn and giving the black king squares to escape to.

27 Rh3 Kg8 28 Qf4 h5 29 g4! Kf8

I continue to bring the king to the safety of the queenside, avoiding 29...hxg4 30 Rxh8+ followed by Qh6 and Qg7 mate.

30 gxh5 Ke8

I am still running with my king. By now both players were very short of time and so naturally the standard of play deteriorated.

31 h6 Kd7?

---

[17] Nothing to do with Father Ted, just a position in which the majority of the pawns are on the same coloured squares as the bishop, thereby hindering his free movement. Perhaps rather like Father Ted after all, with the Craggie Island priests as the obstructive pawns.

Here I missed 31...Rh7 which would have stopped the pawn and it is difficult to see a way through for White.

32 h7 Qb6 33 Nd1

The only move to defend the b-pawn.

33...Qd8 34 Qh6 Qb6

I have run out of any defensive ideas and have no time left.

35 Rhh4 Qd8 36 Qg7!

Hitting the weak f-pawn.

36...Qe8 (diagram 4) 37 b3

Opening up the queenside for the rooks. Now White has total control.

37...cxb3 38 cxb3 Rc8 39 Rhg4 Qf8?

39...Kd8 was forced in order to get the king off the dangerous seventh rank.

40 Rxg6!

I was still trying for counterplay, but it was hopeless. I cannot recapture because my king is pinned.

40...Rc1 41 Kf2 Qc5

Still trying!

42 Qxf7+ Kc8 43 Rg8+ Rxg8 44 hxg8Q+ 1-0

With mate next move, even the optimism of a seven-year old was exhausted, and I resigned.

Where, particularly in an urban area, there are several Saturday clubs within reasonable travelling distance of one another, a small league may have been set up, with matches between teams drawn from the various clubs and a trophy presented at the end of the year. Playing in such matches can be an excellent introduction to competitive team chess while helping the juniors to forge valuable friendships. This may be particularly important to a younger but talented child, who may find it difficult to share her enthusiasm at school and could benefit greatly from friendships with slightly older juniors at the club. Often, when the weather permits, the children will round off the session with a game of football, albeit perhaps a slightly less boisterous one than among non-chess players.

Alternatively, a junior club may have been established under the auspices of an existing adult chess club, meeting, generally, in a community hall or social club either at the weekend or on a weekday evening. Here participants may have the benefit of more input from talented and experienced members of the senior club. One particular advantage of such an affiliated club, especially for the older or particularly talented junior, is that it will smooth the path when she comes to join the adult club.

Whichever type of club is available in your area (or as far beyond as you can face providing a taxi service) it will probably be well worth your investigation. Not only will Alice enjoy the benefit of innumerable games with opponents who actually want to play chess but she will also have the opportunity to develop an accurate assessment of her own strengths and weaknesses, to be initiated into the mysteries of openings, tactics and endgames and so to begin the constant process of improving and honing her own playing skills. Most importantly of all, she will have the opportunity to develop friendships with like-minded contemporaries, those for whom a talent for chess is a matter for open congratulation, rather than a dark and sinister secret. Meanwhile, the organizers of the club will be able to provide you with invaluable information about local tournaments, teams and championships. Finally, many well-established clubs will have had at least one player of international standard pass through their doors and, while you will want to take any specific predictions with a large tablespoonful of salt, they may be able to give you a pretty fair idea of Alice's true potential and of the adventures awaiting her in the brave new world of competitive chess.

Chapter Three

Pawnstorming: How to Invade your Local Chess Club)

At this moment the Unicorn sauntered by them, with his hands in his pockets. 'I had the best of it this time!' he said to the King...and he was going on, when his eye happened to fall upon Alice: he turned round instantly, and stood for some time looking at her with an air of the deepest disgust.

'What – is – this?' he said at last.

'This is a child!...We only found it today. It's as large as life and twice as natural!'

'I always thought they were fabulous monsters!' said the Unicorn. 'Is it alive?'

If:

1. Despite months of detective work, you can trace no junior chess club within a seventy-mile radius of your house.

2. You have found a junior club, but Charlie, nearly twelve and dangerously cool, flatly refuses to go near the place, suspecting that it may harbour eight year olds in kagouls.

3. Charlie's teacher has sent a note home complaining that he has filled his exercise book with twenty-seven variations of the Scandinavian Defence and that RE lessons have been terminally disrupted by his insistence that the proper place for a bishop is at the head of a violent diagonal attack.

4. You are so tired of being dragooned into playing chess every evening that last night you offered him twenty B&H and half a pint of cider if he would go back to Pokemon, or,

5. The flasher in the local park has turned himself in to the police rather than be blackmailed into yet another game behind the tennis courts.

then you are probably in desperate need of your Local Chess Club.

Unfortunately, although most major towns and cities have their own club, it may be a little tricky to locate, few chess players being in the habit of flyposting bus shelters or of leaving alluring little cards in smelly phone boxes. The library may be able to help, if the information desk hasn't been demolished to make way for a multimedia genealogy facility. Otherwise you could try the local paper, which may have a chess column tucked away somewhere between the obituaries and the car boot sale adverts.

If you have access to the Internet then you can use it either to search for a club in a particular location, using a general search engine, or to log onto your national federation website and view its list of affiliated clubs. These lists are usually also available by post. If you live in a major city, there may also be a club specifically for blind or deaf players. Details of such clubs in Britain are available from the Braille Chess Association and English Deaf Chess Association. Websites for all these organizations are listed in Chapter Nine.

The information that you first track down will probably consist of a name and contact telephone number. I suggest that you prepare yourself carefully before dialling it. While most clubs are keen to welcome juniors, recognizing that they constitute the club's own future, some may be a little wary. The chess club, however cold, damp and grimy (as we shall come to very shortly) is nonetheless a blessed haven for its members, a soft cocoon of pure thought and disinterested conflict away from the less rational demands of jobs, wives, and, most particularly, children. It is not surprising, therefore, that they are nervous of anything (and 'anything' in this case can consist of one lone and studious sixteen-year-old) which could portend an influx of chess-playing toddlers and the obliteration of their masculine paradise. That, at any rate, is the charitable explanation for their grunts and grimaces.

Your own Local Chess Club, of course, will be nothing like this, but will open its arms enthusiastically to young Charlie, helping him to hone his openings to perfection and rejoicing in the reflected glory of his future success. Most clubs these days are like this; the miserable ones, inevitably, dying out with their superannuated members. All the same, it does no harm to prepare yourself before speaking to the club chairman or secretary; remembering to say 'My son', rather than 'My little boy' and if in doubt rounding his age up, rather than down. If Charlie is really young then it might be advisable, if a little mendacious, to feign a mild interest in the game yourself as a first step, only later bringing Charlie along and quietly dropping out yourself. If you are male this will attract significantly less attention than otherwise, (unless, of course, you have happened upon a ladies' chess club). In any case, you will probably want to stay with Charlie for some time, at least on the first occasion, to get some idea of the place and people and to check that someone has even noticed he is there (chess-players, mid-game, not being among the keenest observers of the world around them). Don't, however, overdo the introductions. Charlie will learn a great deal simply by wandering around the room watching the other games and, being already a chess-player himself, and therefore a member of this eccentric sub-species, he may well prefer the side-long, grunt-of-recognition-after-forty-five-years mode of discourse over the brash immediacy of ordinary mortals.

As Charlie paces the room, checking out the latest intricacies of the Latvian Gambit you, unless you have taken the wise precaution of bringing an unusually gripping paperback with you, will slowly and uncomfortably be becoming aware of the more tangible attributes of the club. If in England, you are probably either in a community hall, of the type used for teenage parties and bearing the scars thereof, in the function room of a working men's club or in an unreconstructed urban pub. In the first two cases there is probably no heating at all, other than a couple of glowing red bars suspended some thirty feet above you and providing, according to elementary laws of physics, a comfortable degree of warmth exclusively to the roof. The floor will be constructed of bare boards or covered with a crude prototype linoleum, circa 1930. Nails will have been carefully inserted, the wrong way up, in precisely the right position to tear Charlie's school trousers and send you rushing down to Casualty for an emergency tetanus jab. Alternatively, if the club meets in a pub, then the heating provided will be, to say the least, surplus to requirements. Again, elementary laws of energy distribution state that if forty full-grown men (and some grown significantly further than that, usually in a horizontal direction) squeeze themselves into a room measuring less than twelve feet square, there will be little necessity for artificial heating. Nonetheless, heating is included in the rent, and the landlady is determined that you should get it.

Before criticizing your local club, however, for its ineptitude in choosing a meeting-place, take a moment to consider its position. Almost certainly it has virtually no financial reserves whatsoever, charging its members only the absolute minimum necessary to ensure some rudimentary roof over its collective head. When you go on to consider the large proportion of its membership who will be retired, unemployed, junior or in some other way eligible for a substantial discount, you will see why the option of a suite in the Ritz would always be something of a non-starter.

Of course, in your town or city things may be completely different. The club may benefit from a benevolent local employer, the bequest of a deceased member, the sympathetic landlord of a respectable public house or simply from the general prosperity of your neighbourhood and the ability of local chess-players to pay a moderate subscription in order to enjoy an evening's congenial company and entertainment.

Incidentally, most chess clubs, and virtually all tournaments now ban smoking in the playing hall, to the relief of most juniors and their parents. Not only are they liberated from the potential dangers of passive smoking but also from the more immediate danger of being assailed by a fit of coughing during the most critical endgame moves. The murky tactics of strategic smoking, once commonplace, by which the losing player, wafting clouds of smoke across the board, could endow a completely lost position with the confusion and uncertainty of a Napoleonic cannon engagement, are therefore now a dying art.

In any case (and you will be surprised at how quickly these minor details of comfort cease to be significant) the important thing is the welcome offered to Charlie himself. If, after watching Charlie play his first blitz[18] game, the entire club gathers around him, acclaiming him as the next Kasparov and pulling loose threads off his jumper to take away as souvenirs, you can be sure that (in ascending order of likelihood):

---

[18] Blitz: A quick game of chess, in which each player usually has five minutes or less to complete all the moves.

1. Charlie in fact *is* the new Kasparov, destined inevitably for world championship status, immense fame and riches and an excellent line in menacing scowls. However, before telephoning CNN and your Auntie Iris, you should remember that somewhere in the world a new Kasparov is discovered approximately once every 27 seconds. Even if, by some fluke of probability and genetic superiority (from your side of the family naturally) Charlie is in fact the sole and legitimate heir to the Kasparovian mantle, it is probably unwise to let him know it, if you have any hopes at all of surviving his adolescence.

2. You are not at a chess club at all, but at a gathering of the Balfian Brotherhood, a little-known religion founded by Kevin Balf in November 1973 while he was waiting for his mother to come out of the fishmongers. Principal among the tenets of the Brotherhood is the belief that immortality can be achieved by collecting sufficient loose pieces of second-hand wool to knit a ladder to heaven. Chess club, by the way, has been moved to Wednesday evening; today is Tuesday.

3. The chess club is desperate for new members, no one having joined since 1954, and would cheerfully declare any casual visitor to be the new Messiah, never mind the new Kasparov, if it might possibly induce him to stay and reduce their average age to less than 97.

4. The members of the chess club are simply pleasant, enthusiastic individuals, keen to encourage youngsters, to set Charlie at his ease and to demonstrate their faith in the next generation of aspiring players. Should Charlie turn out, in fact, to be WC (World Championship, naturally) material, they will of course be delighted, but scarcely more so than were he to win the junior grading prize at the next local congress.

In England, of course, this welcome will probably be demonstrated rather less effusively, probably limited to a nod, grunt and arm waved in vague invitation towards an unoccupied board. In general you should not expect any great display of emotion from a chess player, particularly one of Anglo-Saxon origin, but after a few weeks of regular attendance, he will become indubitably one of the lads, (even if female) and rewarded by their lifelong loyalty and friendship.

If, by any chance this should not happen, and you should find yourselves in one of the last bastions of middle-aged misery, then please do not let this put either you or Charlie off the game for life. Try a different club in the same town, a club in a different town or even the same club a few months later, when one or two of the die-hards may have done just that. There will always be a welcome somewhere, and the club that turned its nose up at Charlie while he was in short trousers[19] will be kicking itself when he does, after all, turn out to be the next Capablanca[20]

Charlie's first games will be 'friendly', either against other club members or against reserves or supporters of a visiting team, as in this early game of Ga-

---

[19] Metaphorical. See notes on club heating above.
[20] South American World Champion of the 1920s, notable for being handsome, charming, outgoing and, generally, er, South American. A rather more alluring role model than some...

wain's, played when he was six years old and had just joined Guisborough Chess Club[21].

☐ **M Shaw** ■ **Gawain Jones**
Guisborough 'B' v Whitby Friendly Game 1994
Sicilian Defence

---

1 e4 c5 2 Nf3 d6 3 c3 Nc6

This is not the most accurate move. The normal move in this position would be 3...Nf6, after which White would simply develop his bishop to e2. In such a position, I would not be able to take the pawn on e4 because of Qa4+! winning the knight. After White has played d2-d4, however, I can safely take on e4 as the white pawn is blocking the queen's path to the knight.

4 d4 cxd4 5 cxd4 Nf6

An immediate 5...d5 would be better.

6 Nc3 Bg4

Here, again, 6...d5 is probably more accurate.

7 d5 Ne5?!

Instead 7...Bxf3 would be better as here there is a cunning trap for White, which, fortunately for me, he missed.

8 Be2?!

Instead he should have played 8 Nxe5!, tempting me into 8...Bxd1?, taking the queen (the less glamorous 8...dxe5, taking a mere knight, is in fact forced and leaves White much better) 9 Bb5+! Nd7 10 Bxd7+ Qxd7 11 Nxd7 leaving White, at the end of the bloody skirmish, a clear piece up!

8...Nxf3+ 9 Bxf3 Bxf3 10 Qxf3 g6 11 0-0 Bg7 12 Qh3

An odd move. Perhaps simple 12...Be3 was better but Black is fine.

12...0-0 13 Bh6 Qd7!

Stopping any ideas of an attack by White.

14 Qxd7 Nxd7 15 Bxg7 Kxg7 16 b4!? (diagram 5)

Preventing me from being able to play my knight to c5.

16...a5!

Undermining white's queenside.

17 a3 Rfc8 18 Rfc1?

Missing my tactic. The best response here would probably be to move the knight but I am still better.

18...axb4! 19 Nb5

---

[21] where, incidentally, he received an unreservedly warm welcome and quantities of generous and invaluable help and support.

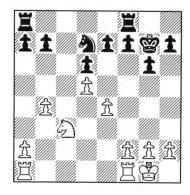

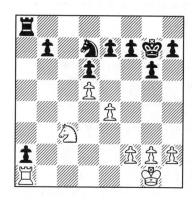

| Diagram 5 | Diagram 6 |

If, instead, we had played 19 axb4? Rxa1 (19...Rxc3! is even better!) 20 Rxa1 Rxc3 then I would have been a piece up.

19...Rxc1+! 20 Rxc1 bxa3

By now I was two pawns up but I still had to be careful

21 Ra1 a2! 22 Nc3 (diagram 6) 22...Rc8!

Forcing White to take with the knight. The alternative 22...Nc5 23 f3 should be a win but is still tricky. 22...Ra3! also wins comfortably.

23 Nxa2 Ra8! 24 Kf1 b5!

White's king is too far away.

25 Ke2 b4 26 Kd2 b3 27 Kc3 bxa2 0-1

Here White decided to call it a day as he would have been at least a piece down in the ending.

However, once you have demonstrated, by assiduous attendance at the 'Rat and Piecrust', that Charlie is a Serious Chess Player, members of the club may begin muttering into their beer glasses mysterious incantations like 'County League B', 'double Swiss' and 'Minor Championship', summed up in an ominous promise to 'give the lad a proper game'.

A proper game, in this context, means one that is Graded (in Britain) or Rated (in the U.S. and the rest of the world). The mystery of why Britain alone should choose not only a completely different system of classification but also to call it by a different name, is simply another national enigma to join the inexplicable habits of driving on the left, drinking dusty bilgewater in place of coffee and having no discernable constitution. Let us pander to this attention-seeking insularity and deal with it first.

Every half-serious British chess player has a grade, and many who are only around two-nineteenths serious have a grade as well, which plays havoc with the averages. Even the feeblest (notably the parents of chess players) will find themselves saddled with a couple of infinitesimal and embarrassing digits should they be lulled by a misplaced sense of family solidarity into trying an odd (frequently very odd) tournament or two.

A grade is obtained, and adjusted in an upward or downward direction, as a direct consequence of the player's results against other graded players. Crudely speaking (and there is always a small but regrettable amount of crude speaking when the annual grading list is published each summer) the winner of each game receives his opponent's current grade plus 50 points, while the loser's grade for that game is his opponent's minus 50. In the event of a draw each player is awarded the other's grade. For example, if Cedric, graded 110, played Egbert, graded 80, and won (as he would hope to) then the grades for that game would be as follows:

Cedric: 80 + 50 = 130   Egbert: 110 − 50 = 60

However, if by some intensive opening preparation, clever tactics, endgame manoeuvring or simple luck, Egbert managed to win, the grades would become:

Cedric: 80 − 50 = 30   Egbert: 110 + 50 = 160

while in the case of a draw:

Cedric = 80   Egbert = 110

As you will see, the rewards of victory against a more highly graded player are considerably greater than those of beating one who is already graded below you, and, conversely, the effects of losing to a player with a lower grade are statistically as well as personally humiliating. In order to meliorate the severity of this phenomenon, and to prevent highly graded players from flatly refusing to play against their inferiors, a further rule has been introduced by which any grading gap of over 40 points is limited to only 40 for grading purposes.

For example, Godric, who has a grade of 180 and is therefore a Pretty Serious Chess Player, the kind who knows more than one opening, deigns, in the course of the Annual Club Championship, to play Hubert, a keen young beginner with a first grade of 55. Alas! Godric's attention is diverted by a passing fire engine/ rustling scoresheet/impending cold[22] and the game, which, in normal circumstances, he would have won easily, is snatched from him by an incredible fluke on the part of the undeserving Hubert. Without the maximum 40 point gap rule, the effect of this reversal would be catastrophic for Godric and so beneficial to Hubert that he might well be overcome by all the excitement and give up chess for good,

---

[22] Excuse to be refined during the post-game analysis and subsequent evenings of brooding misery.

believing that he has now reached the pinnacle of his achievement and that it will inevitably all be downhill from here.

Godric: 55 – 50 = 5   Hubert: 180 + 50 = 230

But, fortunately for Godric and for Hubert's blood pressure, the game is instead graded as follows:

Godric: 140 (Hubert's nominal grade, being Godric's own grade less 40) – 50 = 90

Hubert: 95 (Godric's nominal grade, being Hubert's own grade plus 40) + 50 = 145

Those of you who are of a mathematical bent (my own mathematical having been bent out of all recognition by a nasty encounter with a chunk of trigonometry some twenty-five years ago) will have deduced a Rule from all this, whereby your grade can never go up or down more than 90 points, however exceptional or appalling your play. Believe it or not, this can, on occasion, be a source of comfort, as well as giving you some backup for your scepticism when Charlie comes running in from the playing hall shouting, 'I've worked out my tournament grade and it's 397!' (He has probably forgotten to divide it, which we will come to shortly.) In any case, it is a core parental duty to work out grading performances, and so you had better get some practice in. What would be the effect upon Godric and Hubert if:

1. Godric's attention had been drawn back to the game almost in time, so that he managed to escape with a draw?[23]

2. Hubert's inviting sacrifice hadn't been quite as sound as he had hoped, so Godric won after all, albeit not without a distinctly damp feeling under the armpits?[24]

Well done, if you managed those, and we will know who to call upon next time the Tower at Pisa feels like leaning a bit further and requires the odd bit of calculation to prop it up again. Not that anything actually changes immediately, grade-wise, that would be a bit too exciting. All Charlie's amazing victories (and his unmentionable defeats) simply get recorded by the championship/league/tournament secretary (if he remembers), sent to the County Grading Officer and thereupon to the National Grading Officer. The grades from the year's games are added together, divided by the number of games and an average

---

[23] Godric 140, Hubert 95 – sounds unfair but as you will have worked out, the ninety point rule becomes a forty point rule in the case of a draw.

[24] Godric 190, Hubert 45 – yes, you have seen those figures before – their original grades are retained, a little bruised but otherwise completely unchanged by the encounter.

is produced. This average is then tinkered about with a bit, to allow for the fact that infrequent or new players, such as Charlie himself, have no grade to begin with and so require special treatment. Extra points are also added to junior grades, to reflect the velocity with which their energetic little brain cells go popping about their skulls and lead them to improve with disturbing and inequitable rapidity.

The whole question of grading, regional variations, junior bonuses, official efficiency and premeditated in- or de-flation is one of immense emotional complexity, and its discussion can while away long hours in the parents' waiting room until someone snaps tearfully 'Well, it's all right for you in the North/Greater London Area/South-West isn't it?' and flounces off to check the pairing list[25]. Quite enough has been said about it now, except to point out that Charlie's actual grade will never quite tally with your private calculations, and you will never be able to work out why not, so there is little point in getting worked up about it. The BCF grading book often incorporates lists for each age-group[26] showing the top ten or twenty children in grading order which is, of course, very pleasant if Charlie appears in it, and a complete waste of paper if he doesn't. Console yourself with the thought that no one at all will remember in twenty, or even two years' time, who was the country's top seven year old in 2004, except perhaps the parents of the child in question.

In the United States, USCF ratings are similarly calculated according to the player's performance and his opponents' ratings. However, there are some significant differences in the way that ratings are awarded and in how they subsequently develop. As soon as Charlie has played four or more eligible games against rated opponents he will receive a initial rating, based on the formula:

$$\frac{\textbf{average rating of opponents + 400 (wins – losses)}}{\textbf{number of games}}$$

For example, if Charlie's results in his club championship were as follows:

loss against Aaron rated 1400

loss against Betty rated 1450

draw against Chuck rated 1300

win against Don rated 1150

win against Ellie rated 1200

---

[25] Pairing List: Not a lone chess parents' lonely hearts column (though there might be money to be made there) but details of who is playing whom in the next round of a tournament. Hold your horses, all will be revealed in the next chapter.

[26] Junior only, for some reason, although who would not be fascinated to know the identity of the seventeenth best forty-four year old British chess player?

then the formula would be:

$$\underline{1300* + 400\ (0**)}$$
$$5$$

(* 6500 divided by 5)

(** 2 wins minus 2 losses, disregarding the draw)

giving an initial rating of 1300. This would be shown as 1300/5, the second figure indicating that it is based upon only five games and is therefore not so reliable as a rating calculated from a wider-ranging performance.

Alternatively, the initial rating may be worked out game by game, in a similar fashion to the British system, simply by adding 400 to a defeated opponent's rating and subtracting 400 for a loss. Again, in the case of a draw, Charlie would merely adopt his opponent's rating. Using this formula, the championship games are rated as follows:

v Aaron:	1400 – 400 =	1000
v Betty:	1450 – 400 =	1050
v Chuck:		1300
v Don:	1150 + 400 =	1550
v Ellie:	1200 + 400 =	1600
Total		**6500**
divided by no of games		/5
Initial rating		**1300**

Charlie's first twenty games will be rated according to this method, and the rating thus obtained will be a provisional one. After this initial period, however, his rating will be considered as established, and will vary according to a rather different system, albeit based upon the same principles. Rating changes are not calculated according to the total ratings of the players concerned but only according to the differences between them. At its most simple, where two equally-rated players meet and draw, there is no rating change for either. If one wins, then his rating increases by 16 points while his opponent's goes down by the same amount.

The system becomes more complicated where, as is usually the case, the players' ratings are not the same. A difference of eleven points or less is disregarded, but in the case of any greater gap, adjustment points are used. These adjustment points, which vary from 1 for a difference between 12 and 33 to 16 for a difference of over 715, are subtracted from the basic 16 point change in the case of a win by the higher-rated player, and added to the basic 16 point change if the lower-rated player wins. If the game results in a draw, then the ratings change only by the amount of the adjustment points.

For example, if Charlie, rated 1380, played Frank, rated 1500, and lost, then the changes would be calculated as follows: (The adjustment points for a rating difference of 120 are 5.)

Charlie's new rating: $1380 - (16 - 5) = 1369$

Frank's new rating: $1500 + (16 - 5) = 1511$

If Charlie had won, then the changes would be:

Charlie's new rating: $1380 + (16 + 5) = 1401$

Frank's new rating: $1500 - (16 + 5) = 1489$

and if the result had been a draw:

Charlie's new rating: $1380 + 5 = 1385$

Frank's new rating: $1500 - 5 = 1479$

The system has one or two refinements: slower changes for higher rated players, and rating floors to stabilize existing ratings, but these will not affect Charlie at this stage. Full details of the rating system for the US and for other countries are of course available from the appropriate national chess federation. Meanwhile it may be helpful to note that a quick way to compare British grades with American ratings is to multiply the former by 8 and to add 700, so that an English player with a grade of 120, would be roughly equivalent to an American with a USCF rating of 1660. National federations should be able to supply similar formulae for comparing other national and FIDE ratings, although these should be used with care. Foreign tournament organizers should of course be supplied with Charlie's actual home grade or rating, although it may be helpful if you enclose an estimate of its equivalent.

If Charlie has joined a chess club then his first proper graded game is likely to be for a club team or an individual game in the club's championship.

A small chess club will probably have one championship into which all its players, regardless of ability, are automatically or voluntarily entered. This is perhaps the least stressful initiation for Charlie, since he has only himself to play for, and no team to be let down by a dodgy performance. It will, however, be his first opportunity to show his chess skills in a semi-formal setting, and his games may attract considerable attention. The championship trophy may be a battered piece of base metal, small plastic shield or mere certificate, but it will, nonetheless, be the object of tense and deadly combat, particularly if one player has won it consistently for the past twenty years and views it therefore as virtually his own property. However brilliant Charlie's results in his early 'friendly' games at the club, championship matches are a different matter and his opponents will be prepared to fight hard, with all the weapons at their legitimate disposal including the war of attrition (especially powerful against the player with a fixed bedtime and yawning parent). You should expect, therefore, not to have to shift your ornaments along the mantelpiece to accommodate this particular objet d'art for at least a year or two. This game of Gawain's was played a few weeks after the previous 'friendly' one, but in the cut and thrust of the championship, no prisoners, even six year old ones, were going to be taken.

☐ A.Lockhart ■ Gawain Jones

Guisborough Club Championship 1994

Sicilian Defence

1 e4 c5 2 Bc4

This is an odd line, played regularly at club standard yet hardly ever seen at the top level.

2...e6 3 Nc3 Nf6 4 d3 Nc6 5 Bg5 Be7 6 Nf3 0-0

I have just developed my pieces sensibly and have a comfortable position.

7 h4!?

White tries for an attack as, if he doesn't do so, I have the advantage.

7...h6 8 Bd2 Qc7?!

8...d5 seems a lot more sensible, leaving Black looking better.

9 g3 b6 10 Nb5 Qd8 11 Qe2 d5!

Opening up the centre where White still has his king, having not castled yet.

12 exd5 exd5 13 Bb3 a6 14 Nc3 b5 15 a3 Bb7?

The alternative 15...Bg4! would be very uncomfortable for White to defend. He would not be able to stop ...Nd4 as after either 16 Be3 or 16 Qe3, 16...d4 would win the c3-knight!

16 0-0-0?!

Getting the king out of the centre looks natural and would be okay, were it not for the fact that Black has already started an attack on the queenside. In the circumstances, I think that castling kingside would be safer, although this leaves Black in a very comfortable position.

16...c4!?

Locking White's light-squared bishop out of the game.

17 dxc4 dxc4 18 Ba2

18 Bxh6? Qa5! and White loses one of his bishops.

18...Re8?

Missing White's reply.

19 Bxh6! Bd6?!

This move looks natural, but I now think Qa5, keeping up the attack, is better.

20 Be3 (diagram 7)

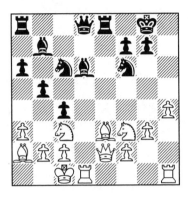

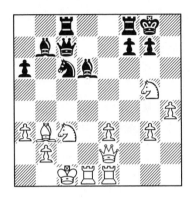

| Diagram 7 | Diagram 8 |

20...Ng4?!

Again, attacking on the queenside is a better option.

21 Rhe1?!

A move that doesn't do anything. Instead 21 Ng5! seems to be almost winning for White e.g. 21...Nxe3 22 fxe3 Nd4 and:

a) Not 23 exd4?? Rxe2 24 Nxe2 Bxh1.

b) But 23 Qh5!! or 23 Rxd4 Bxh1 24 Qh5!.

21...Nxe3 22 fxe3 b4?

Trying to attack but this just unleashes White's a2-bishop. Instead 22...Qe7 and Black's position still seems okay.

23 Nb1?

At this level both players are liable to make mistakes, and this time it is White's turn. Instead 23 axb4 or 23 Qxc4!! would be much better for him e.g. 23 Qxc4!! bxc3 24 Qxf7+ Kh8 25 Qh5 mate.

23...b3?!

Trying to open the c-file to get at White's king, but failing to appreciate how substantial White's attack will now be. 23...Qe7 would have kept Black slightly on top.

24 cxb3 cxb3 25 Bxb3 Rc8 26 Nc3 Qc7

I miss 26...Na5! when, after 27 Ba2 Rxc3+! 28 bxc3 Bxa3+, Black is attacking.

27 Ng5 Rf8? (diagram 8)

An attempt to defend f8 which unfortunately just assists my king into the trap. Instead, Ne5 would be a better way to defend.

28 Qh5! Rfd8

This is forced as Qh7 mate was threatened.

29 Bxf7+ Kf8 30 Nh7+! Ke7 31 Nd5+ Kd7 32 Qf5 mate

A well played attack by White.

A larger chess club may in fact hold two or more club championships, imaginatively named Major and Minor or A and B. In this case Charlie has a much greater chance of victory, entered, as a newcomer, in the lower section, although even here a particular player of modest ability may have marked out the minor trophy as his personal domain. In addition there may be special tournaments, particularly in the summer or at Christmas time. These will probably comprise games with a shorter time limit than usual, rapidplay[27] or blitz, which are generally easier for juniors, at least once they have the experience to recognize basic patterns and positions.

If in doubt, and if he has any choice in the matter, Charlie should probably enter any club tournaments for which he is eligible. His disasters, of which, inevitably there will be some, will be contained in a relatively private environment and he need not suffer the anguish of feeling that he has let an entire team down by his less than flawless play. It will also, on the positive side, give him the opportunity to develop his own skills, to demonstrate his incipient talents and most of all, actually to play the game that he joined the club for in the first place. It will also allow him to get to know the more peripatetic, generally younger, club members who hold no office but usually turn up half an hour late, play a quick game or two and vanish before last orders.

Meanwhile you are being introduced to a new and novel experience, but one with which, over the years, you will become intimately familiar: that of waiting for Charlie's game to finish. While he was only playing friendly matches, you could confidently (albeit silently) march into the club at half-past nine and drag him home. However, once he is playing a Serious Graded Game, you are pretty much stuck until the end of it, which may be well past ten o'clock and his (and your) Officially Designated Bedtime. This will be a constant feature of your life as a chess parent and, as yet, no known cure has been found. Expert opinion merely advocates that you avoid exacerbating the symptoms by ensuring that you have a good book and a warm jumper and that you haven't parked on double yellow lines. On the other hand, if bedtime is a serious physiological issue, so that Charlie is actually too tired to play chess in the late evenings, then you may be better off looking again for a daytime junior club or at least delaying his club championship debut for a year or two. The sight of a young child nodding into sleep over the board is a tender, but ultimately pointless one; he would be far better properly asleep and dreaming of his future victories.

---

[27] All a player's moves to be completed in 30 minutes. See Chapter 5

Not all the middle-aged and elderly men (and possibly even young men, and, oc-casionally, women) gathered around Charlie's board at the club are simply disin-terested observers, dispassionately watching the emergence of a new chess tal-ent. Some will be on a secret mission as talent scouts for a club team. They have neither the financial muscle, the generous salaries or the corporate backing of Arsenal or Manchester United, but in their own scruffy and hesitant way they can be just as determined. Most areas of Britain are covered by a local chess league, made up almost exclusively of amateurs, whose games, sometimes re-ported in the chess columns of the local paper, extend across the winter season, generally from October to May or June. If your club is a small one, it may pro-duce only one or two teams, but in the case of a larger club, virtually the whole local league may be drawn from its membership, with competition between the various teams to sign up new talent. The advantage of the latter situation is not only that Charlie may have the opportunity to choose which team to join, perhaps one containing other young players, but that most of his 'away' games will in fact be played at the club. Otherwise he will have to travel to other clubs to play against their teams, not only at different venues (often some distance away and generally impossible to find) but often on a different night of the week. In this way Charlie's chess club, which you had thought to be a discrete activity occur-ring in a defined and accessible location for three hours on a Wednesday night, becomes a ridiculously moveable feast, encompassing practically all your free evenings for nine months of the year and covering the majority of the land mass within the seven adjoining counties. Of course he may be able to travel with the team, just don't make the mistake of thinking that chess and driving are inter-changeable abilities... On the positive side Charlie will have lots of experience in playing different opponents, making a positive contribution to a team and meet-ing the junior players who will be his future colleagues, rivals and friends. In this game, for example, played in the Cleveland League when Gawain was nine years old, he met an opponent whom he was to play several times in the next few years, in tournaments right across the country.

☐ **Gawain Jones** ■ **John Garnett**

Middlesborough A v Elmwood A (Cleveland League) 1997

English Opening

---

1 c4

The English opening, which I often played at this time. This was not for patriotic reasons but because the theory was reasonably manageable.

1...e5 2 Nf3 d6 3 g3 g6 4 Bg2 Bg7 5 Nc3 Nc6 6 0-0 Nge7 7 Rb1 0-0 8 b4 Bg4 9 d3

I have simply developed my pieces and gone for a queenside pawn offensive.

9...Bxf3?!

Black is trying to get the d4-square for his knight but 9...Qd7 followed by ...Bh3 is more accurate.

10 Bxf3 Nd4?!

Giving up the b-pawn for an attack, but it doesn't really seem to be sound. Instead perhaps 10...a6, halting White's attack for a few moves, would be better.

11 Bxb7 Rb8 12 Bg2 f5 13 Nd5 Ne6 14 a4

I keep on with my queenside attack while Black tries to get enough for his pawn on the kingside.

14...Kh8 15 e3

Trying to discourage ...f5-f4.

15...Nxd5 16 Bxd5

Maybe 16 cxd5!? would be better, getting control of the c-file and forcing Black's knight from the e6-square without moving the well-placed bishop on g2.

16...Ng5 17 b5?!

Instead 17 h4! seems better – forcing the knight to the passive f7-square.

17...f4?!

Here 17...e4!, which would give Black the nice f3-square for his knight, seems better and gives him adequate compensation for the pawn.

18 h4!?

This looks good but it would be interesting to know what Black would have played if I had taken on f4, e.g. 18 exf4! exf4 19 h4! (the difference being that now 19...fxg3 is impossible due to 20 Bxg5!) 19...Nh3+ 20 Kg2 and Black does not have enough after 20...fxg3 (20...Qd7 21 g4) 21 Kxh3.

18...fxg3!

The only move to keep up the attack. If I now take the knight then Black plays 19...gxf2+ 20 Rxf2 Rxf2 21 Kxf2 Qxg5 and has a dangerous attack. It may not be quite enough to win, but it is not a nice position to try to defend.

19 fxg3

Simply recapturing the pawn, leaving White looking a lot better.

19...Nh3+

This is the only square that the knight can go.

20 Kg2 Qd7 21 Bf3

Trying to trap the knight. If instead 21 g4?! then Black can play 21...Rxf1 and his position looks fine. (I cannot recapture with the queen because this leaves the g4-pawn en prise.)

21...h5 22 Ba3

Simply developing the final piece. White cannot win the knight yet as after 22 Rh1? Rxf3! Qxf3 Rf8! Qe2 Rf2+ and Black has good compensation with his active queen.

22...Bh6

Hitting my weak pawn.

23 Qe2 Rf6?!

Trying to double rooks on the f-file but missing an idea.

24 Kh2?!

24 Bc6! was possible, stopping any idea of a black attack and giving White a winning position as after 24...Qe6 25 Rxf6 Qxf6 26 Kxh3 and White has won a piece. Instead Black can try after 24 Bc6 Rxf1 but 25 Bxd7 Rxb1 26 Bxh3 is good for White.

24...Rbf8 25 Qg2 (diagram 9)

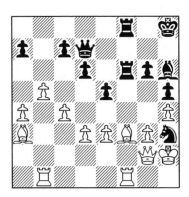

Diagram 9

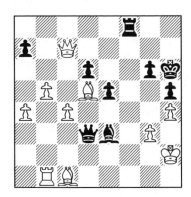

Diagram 10

25 Bc6 was possible, trying to exchange some of Black's dangerous pieces.

25...Bxe3

Grabbing the pawn but 25...Qf7!! looks better, possibly allowing Black to gain equality, as after 26 Kxh3 Rxf3 27 Rxf3 Qxf3 28 Qxf3 Rxf3, he wins back his pawn.

26 Bc6! Qg4 27 Rxf6

The knight on h3 is immune for now, as after 27 Qxh3 Qxh3 28 Kxh3 Rxf1 Black has won a rook.

27...Rxf6 28 Qxh3

Finally managing to take the knight but Black still has play.

28...Qe2+! 29 Bg2

Bringing back pieces in an attempt to defend.

29...Qxd3 30 Qc8+ Kg7 31 Bd5?!

Instead 31 Qxc7!+ Rf7 32 Qxd6 Qxb1 33 Qxe5+ would have won Black's bishop as well as stopping his attack.

31...Rf8 32 Qd7+?!

It would have been better to take the pawn.

32...Kh6 33 Bc1? (diagram 10)

33 Ra1 was the only move to keep in the game as after 33...e4! 34 Bf7 Qe2+ Kh3 White has escaped Black's attack.

33...Bxc1?

This should still be better for Black but in fact 33...Rf2+! leads to mate in six: 33...Rf2+ 34 Bg2 Rxg2+ 35 Kh3 (35 Kxg2 Qe2+ 36 Kh3 Qf1+ 37 Kh2 Qg1+ 38 Kh3 Qh1 mate) 35...Rh2+ 36 Kxh2 Qe2+ 37 Kh3 Qf1+ 38 Kh2 Qg1+ 39 Kh3 Qh1 mate.

34 Rxc1 Qd2+ 35 Kh3 Qxc1 36 Qe7?!

Again, I have to try and take the c-pawn!

36...Rf1 37 Kh2 Qd2+

37...Rf2+ 38 Bg2 Qxc4 looks like a simple win for Black.

38 Kh3 Rf2 39 Bg2

The only move to stop mate! 39...Qc2 looks more accurate for Black but he plays...

39...Qe2

If 39...Rxg2 then 40 Qf8+ would give a perpetual check.

40 Qd8

Now White starts threats as well!

40...Qg4+ 41 Kh2 Rxg2+

This is just a draw. The only way to play for a win was Kg7 although after Qxc7+ it is no longer clear that Black is better. If 41...Rf7 then 42 Qh8+ Rh7 43 Qf8+ which is perpetual check.

42 Kxg2 Qe2+ 43 Kg1 Qe1+ 44 Kg2 Qe2+ ½-½

Black continues to check and so the game becomes an inevitable draw. In this position it is too dangerous for Black to try to play for the win as he cannot both stop mate and also defend the c-pawn.

While Charlie is immersed in all this character-forming activity, you, for your part, will enjoy copious experience in pacing up and down, examining the clock and wishing you hadn't let him travel in the car driven by his team captain, whom God obviously intended to be one of the dedicated pedestrians of the world. Alternatively, you may be in your own freezing car cruising the industrial waste-lands in search of the Winklers and Tissue-Makers Benevolent Social Club. When you get there you can spend the next three hours listening to late night jazz programmes, scraping the bubble gum off the steering wheel and wishing you'd brought a sleeping bag. What do you mean, you thought it was a nice quiet pastime? Wait until you get into tournaments...

Chapter Four

The Vanished Centre[28]:
Where did the Weekend Go?

Alice had no more breath for talking, so they trotted on in silence, till they came in sight of a great crowd, in the middle of which the Lion and Unicorn were fighting. They were in such a cloud of dust, that at first Alice could not make out which was which...

...There was a pause in the fight just then, and the Lion and the Unicorn sat down, panting, while the King called out 'Ten minutes allowed for refreshments!' Haigha and Hatta set to work at once, carrying round trays of white and brown bread. Alice took a piece to taste, but it was very *dry.*

It will not be long after Alice joins her chess club that she overhears, with thudding heart, her fellow players whispering, in hushed and mysterious voices, of 'congress', 'sudden death' and the iniquities of the accelerated Swiss. After some initial perplexity, during which you may spend a sleepless night or two wondering which branch of the White Slave Trade the innocuous club is concealing, she will discover that they are talking about a chess tournament.

Alternatively, the cart may come before the horse, and you may somehow, by a type of psycho-social osmosis, learn about the existence of the tournament before even setting foot in a chess club. In either case, there is no better way to experience the unique flavour of Western chess than to take the plunge.

The traditional type of tournament in Britain and the United States since the Second World War has been the weekend tournament (or, to the very slightly raffish, the 'weekender'). This, as its name suggests, generally takes place from Friday evening until late Sunday afternoon, with a prize-giving ceremony to follow. It thereby occupies every scintilla of time between one week and the next and leaves no opportunity whatsoever for homework, supermarket shopping, discos or the prosecution by any other means of what might be described as a life. This may well be why chess players like them so much.

---

[28] Literally, a position where both players' central pawns have gone AWOL, so that the grown-up pieces have to rush around doing all the work. Sounds familiar?

There are normally five rounds; the first on Friday evening from around 7pm, and the remaining four on Saturday and Sunday, beginning at around 9.30am and 2pm. Games may take up to four hours to complete, each player being allowed around two hours for all his moves, although many games involving juniors are completed in not much over an hour. Occasionally an extra round will be added on Saturday evening or, on a holiday weekend, the event may stretch into the Monday.

Most weekend tournaments are divided into three or more sections, open to players of differing grades. The lowest section in a British tournament is normally known as the Minor, for players with a grade of under 100, and in the U.S. as a Section E for players rated below 1200. Ungraded players will also normally play in this section, although dire warnings are given of the consequences of failing to reveal a previous grade. The next category up in a US tournament, Section D, for players of 1200-1399 strength, will also normally fall within the British Minor category. These sections generally contain a large number of young junior players and so will help Alice to get to know her local contemporaries as well as giving you the opportunity to chat with other hovering parents.

Gawain began to play in weekend tournaments within three or four months of joining his first chess club. This game took place in a local Minor section a few weeks after his seventh birthday.

□ **N.Pearce** ■ **Gawain Jones**
Redcar Congress 1995
Sicilian Defence

---

1 e4 c5 2 Nf3 d6 3 d4

The Open Sicilian, which normally results in sharp tactical positions.

3...cxd4 4 Nxd4 Nf6 5 Nc3 a6

Kasparov's favourite Najdorf Variation.

6 a4 e6 7 Bc4 Be7 8 0-0 0-0 9 Be3 Qc7 10 Bb3

10 Bd3 is possible.

10...Nbd7

10...Nc6 may be better as the text move allows 11 Bxe6! fxe6 12 Nxe6 leaving White clearly better.

11 f3

White decides against 11 Bxe6, contenting himself with defending the e4-pawn.

11...b6 12 Qd2

Again, 12 Bxe6 would be possible.

12...Bb7 13 Rad1

At the risk of getting monotonous, White ought to consider 13 Bxe6!.

13...Rac8

Both sides have developed normally and the position seems to be about equal.

14 Rfe1

Going, going, gone... That was the last opportunity to take on e6.

14...Nc5!

Putting the knight on a nice square to simultaneously attack the bishop and defend e6.

15 Ba2 e5?!

A typical move in these positions, but here it seems wrong as it gives White the f5- and d5-squares and weakens d6. Instead, 15...Rfd8 with the idea of ...d6-d5 at some point seems fine for Black.

16 Nf5 Rfd8 17 Qf2 Bf8 18 Qg3

18 Bg5 looked good.

18...Kh8 19 Rd2?! (diagram 11)

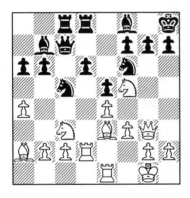

Diagram 11

Diagram 12

Trying to double on the d-file but 19 Bg5 would leave White considerably better.

19...Bxe4!

A good move! This destroys White's bind as well as winning a pawn.

20 Nd5?

It was critical for White to take the bishop with 20 fxe4. This would be met by 20...Ncxe4 and 21 Nxe4 Nxe4 after which White would not be much worse.

20...Bxd5?

My turn to play a bad move. Instead I should have chosen 20...Nxd5! which would be almost winning as after 21 Bxd5, I would have 21...Bxf5 and after 21 fxe4 I could play 21...Nxe4 which forks[29] the queen and rook.

21 Bxd5 Nxd5 22 Rxd5 Qc6 23 Red1 Qxa4

23...Nxa4 is more accurate, winning another pawn and preventing White from finding any attack.

24 Rxd6?!

24 b3 or 24 Qf2, defending c2, would be better here.

24...Rxd6

I managed to avoid the trap 24...Bxd6?? which would have been followed by the immediate 25 Qxg7 mate.

25 Nxd6 Bxd6 26 Rxd6 Qxc2 27 Qg4 Rg8 (diagram 12)

This move simultaneously slides the attacked rook out of danger and also defends against any of White's further threats.

28 Rxb6?

Letting my queen and knight in to wreak havoc, but it was already hopeless for White.

28...Qd1+ 29 Kf2 Nd3+! 30 Kg3 Qe1+ 31 Kh3 Qxe3 0-1

Black is now a piece up and threatening both the rook on b6 and ...Nf2, forking the king and queen. My opponent, some twenty years older than me and later a friend and fellow York player, resigned with grace and generosity.

The middle section in a British tournament, usually called the Major, is for players of approximately 100 to 150 strength and will usually include some relatively good junior players as well as many adults. Approximate equivalents in the U.S. are Sections A to C, for players with ratings of below 2000. Strong juniors typically move up to these sections after a couple of years in the Minor categories. Gawain in fact played in only a few Major sections, including this one in Hull Congress which he won at the age of nine.

☐ D.Strauss ■ Gawain Jones

Hull Congress 1997

Stonewall Attack

1 d4 Nf6 2 e3 g6 3 Bd3 Bg7 4 f4

The so-called Stonewall Attack. White sets up a solid position and then goes all out for a kingside attack.

---

[29] A fork, when it isn't the one you knew you had in the car somewhere which would have saved you from having to eat your salad with a pencil, is a simultaneous attack by a single piece, often a knight or pawn, on two or more of the opponent's pieces.

4...d5!

This move prevents White from playing e3-e4 and thereby getting himself a space advantage.

5 Nf3 Bg4!

Another good move, stopping the white knight from jumping into e5.

6 h3 Bxf3 7 Qxf3 e6 8 Bd2 c5!

Hitting White's centre and starting a queenside attack.

9 c3

Taking the pawn might be better although this move would be contrary to the inclinations of most Stonewall players as it releases the tension in the centre. After 9 dxc5 Ne4! 10 Bc3! (10 Bxe4 Bxb2 is good for Black) 10...Qh4+!? 11 g3 Nxg3 12 Qf2! leads to a wild position. No hot-blooded nine-year-old would object to a wild position but if Black wants to play safely then he can opt instead for the calmer 10...Nxc3 11 Nxc3 Qa5 which still leaves him slightly better.

9...Nc6

Perhaps 9...Qb6 hitting the b-pawn and defending the c-pawn would be better here.

10 0-0

Instead, maybe 10 dxc5 would be more positive, trying to unbalance the position, as here White's bad bishop gives Black a definite advantage.

10...0-0

Again, 10...Qb6 or 10...Nd7 would leave Black feeling comfortable.

11 Be1

As in the last move, White should have taken on c5. He is trying to improve the position of his bishop via h4 but unfortunately it takes too long.

11...Qb6! 12 b3? (diagram 13)

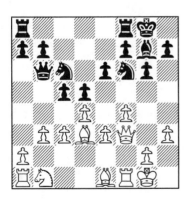

Diagram 13

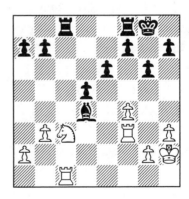

Diagram 14

12 Rf2 would be better, defending the b-pawn or instead 12 Nd2!? when White gets good play if I take on b2 as 13 Rb1 unleashes the white rook.

12...cxd4!

The start of a tactical sequence.

13 exd4 Nxd4! 14 cxd4

Perhaps 14 Qf2 would be better though Black is extremely comfortable after 14...Ne4! 15 Bxe4 dxe4 as White cannot take on d4 due to 16...Bxd4 pinning the queen.

14...Qxd4+ 15 Qf2

Instead 15...Kh1 may be better as after 15...Qxa1 comes 16 Bb4! Qd4! (anything else is met by 17 Nc3 and the black queen finds herself very short of squares) 17 Bxf8 Rxf8. Black is still two pawns up but at least this is better for White than the game. Alternatively, if 15 Rf2 then Black could play 15...Ne4! (not 15...Qxa1 as 16 Bc3! traps the black queen) and White would not be able to save the rook on a1 without losing heavy material as 16 Bxe4 is met by 16...dxe4 17 Qc3 Qd1!.

15...Qxd3 16 Bc3

Black is now two pawns up and still has play along the all-important a1-h8 diagonal despite White's attempts to stop it.

16...Ne4! 17 Qf3

This is the only possible move to keep hold of the bishop.

17...Bd4+!?

17...Qxf3 could be better, followed by18 Rxf3 Nxc3 19 Nxc3 Rac8 20 Rac1 d4 and leaving Black two pawns up in the ending with the further and decisive advantage of connected passed pawns.[30]

18 Kh2

The only move as after 18 Bxd4 Qxd4+ wins the rook on a1 and 18 Kh1 Ng3+! wins the f1-rook.

18...Qxf3 19 Rxf3 Nxc3 20 Nxc3 Rac8!

Black is now in an ending two pawns up with active pieces.

21 Rc1 (diagram 14) 21...e5?!

A mistake, as it weakens the d-pawn.

22 fxe5 Bxe5+ 23 Kh1

23 Kg1 looks better, keeping the king nearer the centre

23...Rfe8!

Playing the rook to the open file.

24 Ne2 Bd6

---

[30] i.e. a pawn which cannot be prevented from queening by any pawn of the opponent's colour. 'Connected' means simply that there is another pawn which can defend the first (as opposed to an 'isolated' pawn which has no such support).

Exchanging rooks followed by ...Bc7! also looks good.

25 Rxc8 Rxc8 26 Rd3 Rc2!

Hitting the a-pawn and the knight.

27 Rxd5

This results in a rook and pawn ending where White is two pawns down. Instead 27 Nc3 may be better as after 27...Be5! 28 Nd1 (not 28 Nxd5?? as 28...Rc1+ is mating.) 28...d4 and White can still play on for a while.

27...Rxe2

This should be an easy win but 27...Bc7! was better as after 28 Rd7! (28 Ng1 Rc1 followed by ...Bb6 is winning) 28...Kf8! followed by ...Ke8 is winning.

28 Rxd6 Rxa2

Now I am two pawns up and this should be easy.

29 Rd8+ Kg7 30 Rd7 b5 31 Rb7 a6 32 Rb6 Rb2 33 Rxa6 Rxb3

Black has managed to create a passed pawn and also has an extra pawn on the kingside.

34 Kg1 Rb2!

Slowing down the king in its attempts to stop the b-pawn.

35 Kh2 b4 36 Kg3 b3 37 Rb6 Rb1 38 Kf2 b2 39 Ke2?

This just lets Black get an easy win with a tactic. Again 29 Ke3? allows 29...Re1+ followed by ...b1Q winning. Instead if White does nothing with a move like 39 h4 then ...Kf8 and ...Ke8 is followed by bringing the king out to defend the b-pawn.

39...Rg1! 0-1

Now after 40 Rxb2 Rxg2+ wins the rook and anything else allows b1Q so White resigned.

The top section in a British tournament is generally an Open, meaning that there is no grading limit, either upper or lower, although Alice would be unwise to enter such a section until she has a few years' experience of tournament play. In the United States there may be more than one section for this level of player, from the Expert (2000-2199) to the Master (2200-2399) and Senior Master (2400+). Many Open sections, particularly those in or near major cities, attract titled players, grandmasters or international masters, and the top boards may be separated from the rest of the players, sometimes raised on a stage or dais, in order to facilitate spectators. If Alice has been reading chess books, magazines, web sites or columns she may be familiar with the names and games of some of these players, and she may enjoy watching them in action. (From a reasonable distance, please, and although a professional player may be flattered to receive an autograph request, especially on a newly bought copy of his own latest book, Alice should be careful to make sure that his game is really over before approaching him. A player on his way to the bathroom with a complicated and critical sequence of forthcoming moves running through his head will not appreciate being obstructed by a small child brandishing a ball point pen.) A few tournaments operate an upper limit of around BCF 200 (USCF approximately 2300) or a 'stars barred' policy, excluding titled players. Although such a policy may benefit local amateurs, it reduces the excitement of the whole event and rather perversely keeps out the one group of players who, as professionals, may actually rely upon the prize money for their basic income.

Gawain, like many other junior players, was keen to enter Open sections as early as possible, and began to play in this category just before his ninth birthday. For the first year or two he found them very tough, and accumulated considerably more experience than actual points. After a while, however, the challenge began to pay off and he was able to enjoy games such as this, played when he was thirteen.

☐ **Gawain Jones** ■ **H Li**

Manchester Open 2001

Sicilian Defence

---

1 e4

By this stage I'd switched from my earlier, slightly off-beat openings to the mainstream 1 e4.

1...c5 2 Nc3 Nc6 3 Bb5

An interesting line and one that was becoming rather fashionable at the time.

3...Nd4 4 Bc4

Retreating is best as I don't want Black to take the bishop without incurring some kind of disadvantage in return (e.g. doubled c-pawns).

4...g6

Perhaps 4...e6 would be better although it is hardly in the style of a Sicilian devotee, accustomed to playing a line such as the Dragon (where Black plays an early ...g7-g6).

5 Nf3 Bg7 6 Nxd4! cxd4 7 Qf3!

I don't bother to move the knight but instead threaten mate on f7.

7...e6?!

Instead 7...Nh6! would be the best move, defending against the threat on f7 without creating any holes in his position.

8 Nb5!

I have my eye on the d6-square.

8...d6 9 Qa3! (diagram 15)

Hitting the d6-pawn to which Black has no good defence.

9...Ke7!?

Finding an interesting way to defend against the threat to the d6-pawn. Instead 9...Bf8 would allow 10 Nxd4 as after 10...d5, 11 Bb5+ gives me time to move my queen. Another way of defending against it is 10...Be5 though a simple move like 11 d3, threatening f4 looks good.

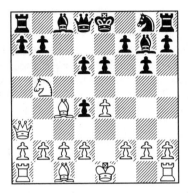

Diagram 15

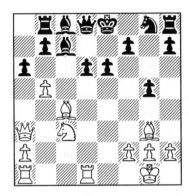

Diagram 16

10 c3

I have to try to get my knight out or a6 will come as a bit of an embarrassment: where does the knight go?

10...dxc3

Now if 10...a6 then 11 Nxd4 leaves White a pawn up.

11 0-0!?

Sacrificing the pawn in an attempt to get swift development. Perhaps not absolutely the best move but, over the board – in the time pressure of an actual game – it is almost impossible for either player to find and play the ideal moves.

11...a6

Black simply gives back the pawn to stop White's attack. The alternative is taking another white pawn on either b2 or d2, but that would give White very good compensation.

12 Nxc3 Rb8

Black moves his rook off the a-file so that he can play ...b5 followed by ...b4, winning a piece.

13 e5!?

Giving up further material to attack the black king.

13...Bxe5

Black takes the pawn. Instead he could play 13...b5 14 Ne4!, sacrificing the bishop but getting a huge attack after 14...bxc4 and 15 Nxd6.

14 d4!?

Another pawn is sacrificed for the attack.

14...Bxd4 15 Rd1

The critical position has been reached. Black is two pawns up but with just one piece developed and his king stuck in the centre.

15...Bc5

Black has to make a decision about where to move the bishop or how to defend it. This is not an easy task in view of the fact that there are nine different moves that would keep Black two pawns up. After most bishop moves White would play Bf4 and Ne4 to gang up on the d-pawn 15...Be5! is probably the best, defending the pawn and making it hard for White to prove compensation for the two pawns. After 15...e5 or 15...Qb6 again 16 Ne4 looks like the right sort of move keeping up the pressure on Black's king.

16 b4 Bb6 17 Bf4!

White must pile on the pressure.

17...Bc7 18 b5!

Unleashing the queen and also attacking with the pawn. 18 Ne4 was an interesting alternative.

18...g5!?

Black tries to give up a pawn to stop White's attack. The point is that after 19 Bxg5+ f6 20 Bf4 e5 Black has a blockade around his king. Notice that Black cannot play 18...e5 immediately as White would simply take it and a move like 18...Nf6 would allow 19 b6.

19 Bg3!

Keeping the bishop on the line of attack.

19...Ke8 (diagram 16)

Moving the king out of the fire of White's pieces. Black is hoping that White will simply take off the d-pawn when my attack subsides a little...not so!

20 b6!

Forcing the bishop off the defence of the d-pawn.

20...Bxb6 21 Bxd6 Bd7

Black tries desperately to defend. If 21...Ra8 then 22 Be5 would have won the other rook.

22 Bxb8 Qxb8 23 Ne4

White now has material equality (rook for bishop and two pawns) while maintaining the attack.

23...Bc7 24 Nd6+ Bxd6 25 Rxd6 b5 26 Rad1!

Bringing up the last piece.

26...Nf6 27 Qg3?!

Maintaining the threats though 27 Rxa6 looked to be best, giving Black no good defence to Ra8 winning the Queen.

27...Qc8

Instead 27...bxc4 allowed 28 Rxe6+! winning the black Queen: 27...bxc4 28 Rxe6+ Bxe6 29 Qxb8+.

28 Qe5! Ke7 29 Qxg5! Rd8

If Black takes the bishop with either the queen or pawn then 30 Rxd7!+ crashes through for White.

30 Bxe6!

Ripping off the last shred of cover for the black king. 30...Bxe6 31 Rxd8 or 30...fxe6 31 Qg7+ both win.

30...h6 31 Qg7

31...Qxh6 was also possible while 31 Qxf6+! Kxf6 32 Bxd7 Ke7 33 Bxc8 Rxd6 34 Rxd6 Kxd6 35 Bxa6 is an attractive way to win.

31...Rf8? 32 Bxd7 1-0

After 32...Nxd7 33 Rxd7 Qxd7 34 Rxd7 Kxd7 35 Qxf8 White is a whole queen up.

Tournament categories, and in particular their grading or rating limits, are by no means universal and, especially when Alice has a grade or rating, you should check very carefully to ensure that she has entered the appropriate section. In America, Novice Tournaments are held, for new players with no rating while British congresses sometimes include a Novice section, for players who have played in very few, if any, previous tournaments. Additionally, in Britain, an Intermediate category may be inserted between the Minor and the Major or, as in the Redcar congress referred to above, there may be two minor sections. Often, especially where the tournament is sponsored by a commercial enterprise, the sections may have particular names; the Grimthorpe Valve Minor, for example or the Yummy Yoghurt Open. Read the entry form carefully and try not to wince too visibly; chess needs all the sponsorship it can possibly get.

Entry forms are usually to be found at other tournaments and chess clubs or are available by post from the tournament secretary or organizer. Lists of forthcoming tournaments with contact telephone numbers appear on Teletext, in the back of chess magazines and on national chess federation websites. Occasionally it may be possible to enter the tournament by telephone, email or on the day itself but it is normally safer to do things in the traditional way by returning the entry form by post, with a cheque, well before the closing date. This date is usually only a few days before the tournament but, especially in the case of events organized by a local authority, may be several weeks before.

There is invariably an entrance fee for the tournament which goes towards the hire of the venue and provision of prize money. Often this is set on a sliding scale, so that the Minor has the lowest entry fee and there may be a further reduction for juniors. In Britain there is also a small reduction available to direct members of the British Chess Federation (BCF) representing that part of the entry fee which is paid to the BCF in order for the games to be officially graded. It may therefore be worth considering joining the BCF, either individually or as a family, at an early stage, especially as this will entitle Alice to receive the official magazine, 'ChessMoves', a printout of her graded games and reductions on BCF publications including the grading list and yearbook.

Prizes vary greatly between tournaments, depending upon the numbers of players, sponsorship available, cost of the venue etc. In some cases there is a considerable amount of prize money to be won, sometimes only in the top section but on occasion even in the Minor or Category E. Elsewhere trophies may be awarded, either to be kept until the next year or permanently. In some British tournaments the winner of the Open section, or the highest placed non-titled player, may be entitled to a place in the prestigious British Chess Championships, sometimes with an accompanying bursary towards the costs of entry. Prizes are normally awarded to the first three or four players in each section although in the case of a large tournament the list may extend as far as the top ten. Generally, where there is more than one player with a prize-winning score, the prize money is amalgamated and divided among them, e.g.

Prizes		Final Scores	Prize Money
1st	£100	Atkins 4½	£100
2nd	£80	Bruce 3½	£60
3rd	£60	Crabbe 3½	£60
4th	£40	Dodds 3½	£60

However, where a trophy or a championship place is at stake, a tie-break system will normally be used. These systems are often immensely complex, and another source of vigorous coffee-room debate, but the commonest use either the sum of the player's own progressive score or the sum of her opponents' scores.

Most tournaments also offer grading or rating prizes. These are awarded within sections, to players whose grade is significantly lower than the maximum for that section but who have achieved the highest score within their particular grading band. For example, a minor section with a top limit of 100 might have a grading prize for the highest-scoring player below 75 and below 50. These prizes serve to assist players whose grade or rating is slightly above the maximum for a particular section, allowing them to play in a higher category with the hope of still winning a prize, and they also encourage players to try their luck in a higher section than usual. There may also be particular prizes or trophies for specific categories of players: e.g. juniors, women or local players. The wall charts usually show who is eligible for such prizes.

Finally, some weekend tournaments have abandoned the old prize structure altogether in favour of a system whereby anyone who achieves over 50% (i.e. 3/5 or 3½/6) receives a modest recompense of at least their entry fee returned, rising to a more substantial prize for a perfect or near-perfect score. The merits or otherwise of this system are still bubbling beneath the grill of current debate.

Without further procrastination, we must now scale the heights of the Swiss system, which, when it is not a method for chocolate manufacture or a way of cluttering your windscreen with motorway permits, is the normal organizational basis of the weekend and most other open tournaments. You can quite happily continue for many years as a fully-fledged Chess Parent without knowing anything at all about any other system, other than the all-play-all, the details of which are refreshingly self-evident.

In the Swiss system each player's score begins, logically enough, at zero (except in the case of byes, which we will come to as soon as humanly possible). At the beginning of the first round the players are listed in grading order, with the top half of the list playing against the bottom half. This means that, very roughly speaking, if Alice is in the top half of her list she would expect to win her first game, and if not, not. As you might anticipate, this is one of those rules often outweighed by its own exceptions.

At the end of the first round points are awarded: one for a win and half for a draw, except in the occasional attempt to introduce soccer-type scoring to encourage decisive play. For Round 2 each player will be paired, as far as possible, with an opponent on the same score; so that, were Alice to win her first round, she would play her next game against another equally successful player. The players on the highest points play on the top boards with the rest in descending order. For example, in the case of a hypothetical and extremely small section:

Round One

Board 1:	Alice v Bertie	1:0	(Alice wins)
Board 2:	Charlie v Diana	½:½	(draw)
Board 3:	Egbert v Fran	0:1	(Fran wins)
Board 4:	Gilly v Hubert	½:½:	(draw)

Scores at the end of Round One

Alice	1
Fran	1
Charlie	½
Diana	½
Gilly	½
Hubert	½
Bertie	0
Egbert	0

Round Two

Board 1: Fran v Alice

Board 2: Diana v Gilly

Board 3: Hubert v Charlie

Board 4: Bertie v Egbert

This continues throughout the tournament; so that the winners of the earlier rounds are forced to play more difficult games against one another, while the losers similarly, play increasingly weak opposition until they manage to increase their score. Thus, at least in theory, each player finds his own natural position during the course of the tournament and the final scores provide a reasonably accurate snapshot of the relative strengths of the weekend's play.

The system generally works well although, as in most aspects of chess organization, it manages to create a fairly constant low murmur of disapproval. The principal difficulties in this case surround the issues of up- and down-floats and of the distribution of colours.

An up-float, and its concomitant partner the down-float, occurs where there is an odd number of players on a particular score, and one is required to play an opponent on a higher or lower score. During the early rounds of a tournament this difference is usually slight, generally only half a point, but later, especially where there are a lot of rounds and only a few players, the difference may be far more substantial. Generally speaking players grumble about getting an up-float, although they can be valuable for players on the top boards in the final rounds, affording the chance of taking a full point from a slightly more successful rival. Similarly, a down-float, to play an opponent on a lower score, is usually welcomed as heralding a slightly easier game, except where the person concerned particularly wanted to play a higher-scoring opponent.

Colours, or in other words whether the player takes the black or white pieces, are distributed in the first round according to a fixed pattern, with, for example, the highest graded player taking White on the top board and the second highest Black on the second. Thereafter, where possible, players are given alternate colours so that if Alice was White in the first round then she would expect to be Black in the second. As you will anticipate, during later rounds, as the scores separate and the nasty little spectres of up- and down-floats hover into view, it becomes increasingly difficult to ensure that players in fact have alternate colours. Generally speaking, though, the organizers (or the computer program carrying out the pairings) will make sure that the number of games as White (with the advantage of the first move) and as Black are roughly equal.

We can't put it off any longer: you must be put out of your misery regarding byes, which you strongly suspect of being a type of mountain sheep, though you cannot be completely sure. In fact there are two types of bye, the half and the full point, and they have very little to do with sheep, other than the strange baaing noise made by players receiving an unexpected one when they were hoping for a grandmaster opponent.

A half point bye is, as its name suggests, half a point awarded to the player at her own request in respect of one game in which she chooses, before the tournament, not to play. (Only one game, normally, so your cunning plan of entering a prestigious Open Section, taking half point byes in every round and, with a respectable score of 2½/5 walking away with the under 120 grading prize is unlikely to succeed.) Half point byes are normally taken in the first round of a weekend tournament, on the Friday evening, by players travelling a long distance, working late, or whose concentration is not at its best late at night. If either Alice or you, as her probable chauffeur, fall into this category then it may be worthwhile taking the Friday night bye and starting fresh, with her duck already broken, on Saturday morning. There is usually a box to tick on the entry form to indicate that you want to take this bye, and it is common for a large number of players to do so. Sometimes it may be possible to take a half point bye in another round, especially early in the tournament. If this is important to you, for example if Alice has another commitment such as a music lesson on Saturday morning, it may be worth making enquiries of the organizers, even if there is no provision on the entry form. Byes, of course, have no grading or rating significance.

A full point bye, on the other hand, is awarded where there are an odd number of players in a particular round and so one player is left without an opponent. Normally this is granted to the lowest scoring player, provided that she has not already received such a free point and can therefore be an act of charity to a struggling contestant. However, there is some fundamental force within any tournament organizer which abhors a vacuum, even on a Saturday morning, when most of us are obliged to resume acquaintance with at least a Dyson, and they have a consequent tendency to arrange some game, any game (though usually chess) for the odd (often extremely odd) player at the bottom of the table. Should Alice, therefore, find herself in this undignified position (and virtually all players do at some time so it is much less embarrassing to get it over with early) she may find herself playing the odd man out from another section, one of the organizers themselves, one of the organizers' small sons, girlfriends, mothers-in-law, Yorkshire Terriers, food processors..... (all right, maybe not the last one or two, though a food processor can be a formidable opponent in a tricky endgame).

Should her opponent simply not turn up, which is relatively common, especially on Sunday morning among the lower boards, Alice will not automatically win by default. She can start his clock[31] at the official start of the round and so, if he arrives up to around half an hour late he will simply have a shorter period in which to make his moves. After half an hour, according to most tournament rules, 'players will be re-paired if possible'. This sounds extremely uncomfortable, as well as far from feasible in most cases, but in fact simply means that two players, both with absent opponents, will play one another instead. Obviously this is not ideal, and undoes much of the painstaking work done by the organizers and/or their computers, but no better way has been found. It does, however, explain why players who regularly pull out of tournaments for no better reason than that they aren't doing as well as they hoped, and feel like a lie-in instead, are universally despised and may even find themselves banned from future events.

As you will appreciate, the business of pairing players for each successive round, with the careful balancing of colours, up- and down-floats, byes and absent players is not an easy one, even with a computer program to help. It becomes increasingly difficult towards the end of a tournament when the leaders may all have played one another (it is not permitted to play the same opponent twice in a Swiss tournament) and the prizes are tantalizingly within sight. In a high-level tournament there may be the additional complicating factor of players seeking

---

[31] See Chapter Six if you don't know what this means.

norms[32] and therefore needing to play sufficiently high-rated or titled opponents. It is in everyone's interests, particularly the organizers themselves, who are probably desperate for a coffee and a cheese sandwich, for the pairing to be carried out as quickly and efficiently as possible. Speed and efficiency are not normally enhanced, however, by having seventeen young men, and three younger men's mothers, breathing down one's neck muttering, 'I've already had three blacks in a row', 'Don't make me play old Jim' or 'Could you put Joshua on a table near the window so that his Auntie Sharon can watch him on her way to Bingo?' Just don't do it, please, and try to make sure that Alice doesn't either. The pairing will be put up as soon as it is finalized (sometimes this is delayed by a very long game), either as a computer print-out stuck up on the wall, or on a special pocketed board containing index cards for each player, usually propped on a chair. Obviously, if there is a real problem with Alice's pairing, for example if she has accidentally been paired with a player she has played in an earlier round[33], you should tell the organizers immediately, especially if there is very little time before the round is due to begin.

The pairings will also normally be shown later on a wall chart, displayed either in the playing hall or in an adjacent room or corridor. This chart (usually one for each section) will be put up at the beginning of the tournament to show each player's name, home town, club or school and grade or rating. As the tournament progresses, it will show the players' opponents in each round (indicated by a tournament number in the corner of the appropriate box) and her progressive score.

For example, the following wall chart:

1.	DEE, Tweedle	BATTLE	101	0 [3]	0 [4]
2.	DUM, Tweedle	BATTLE	99	½ [4]	1 [3]
3.	RABBIT, White	BOROUGH	95	1 [1]	1½ [2]
4.	WONDER, Alice	OXFORD	u/r*	½ [2]	1½ [1]

* unrated

shows that in the first round Tweedledee played the White Rabbit and lost, while Tweedledum drew with Alice. In the second round Tweedledee again lost, this time to Alice, while Tweedledum drew with the White Rabbit. The third round has not yet taken place, but Alice and the White Rabbit, as the leaders with scores of 1½ each, would normally play one another, leaving Tweedledum and Tweedledee to continue their own hostilities. Normally, the small numerals indicating the opponent are written in red where the player is White, and black... (I'll leave you to work that one out for yourselves)

---

[32] Not wandering ex-ministers from John Major's cabinet, but steps on the way to becoming a titled player. See Chapter Eight.

[33] In tribute to tournament organizers, I should say that I have never seen this actually happen.

These wall charts are a source of great wonder and fascination, especially to parents who have very little else to do (other, obviously, than reading this book). Apart from the really significant research: who has the silliest/most appropriate name in each section, what would be the most amusing pairing and will the organizers dare make it, you can collect all sorts of minor information about local players, chess clubs, schools etc. both from the chart itself and from eavesdropping on the other parents and players discussing these matters, often in the frankest possible terms. Until Alice is well known, and often beyond, especially if the back of your head is not particularly distinctive, you will, if you hang around the wall charts for long enough, probably hear her being discussed from somewhere in the vicinity of your left shoulder. You have two alternatives when this happens: either to remain rigidly motionless, trying your best to impersonate a random passer by who has wandered in under the impression that a cheese tournament is afoot, and hoping to pick up a prize-winning Double Gloucester, or to turn around and introduce yourself. If you choose the latter (and it is normally to be recommended, many lifelong friendships having been forged in front of a tournament wall chart) then please try to time your turn correctly, preferably just after the voice has finished saying:

'This little Alice is doing very well, isn't she? I haven't seen her name before...'

without waiting for it to continue the sentence,

'...but she's bound to be one of these dreadful hothoused brats who've been trained to try a fool's mate and think they're Judit Polgar.'

Turning around at that point, even to ask what Judit Polgar and a fool's mate are[34], is not the best basis for a beautiful and lasting relationship, though they have been known to survive worse.

Clearly, if you see a serious error on the wall chart you should let the organizers know as quickly as possible, particularly if the result of one of Alice's games has been recorded incorrectly. At the end of each game the players must advise the organizers of the result, normally using a slip of paper or copy score sheet, and it has been known, particularly with young juniors for this to be illegible, contradictory (both players recording wins or even losses), non-existent (with the results slip having been shoved absent-mindedly into a player's pocket) or just plain wrong. Similarly, if her grade is shown wrongly (and this will usually have been copied from her entry form) the organizers will need to know early, as this may affect pairings and prizes.

In Chapter Six we will look at the games themselves, and in Chapter Seven to what extent it will be helpful or otherwise for you to stay at the venue while these are in progress. Whatever your decision about this, you will almost certainly, unless the player is a teenager and the venue already familiar, need to provide transport to and from the tournament and possibly to be around for meals etc. Sometimes, where the venue is isolated and some distance from your home, you will have little alternative but to remain there all day in any case.

---

[34] One is a way of checkmating an ingenuous opponent in two moves and the other is the world's greatest female chess player. Your homework for the weekend is to work out which is which.

Similarly, if your child is young and the rounds are likely to be short, you may not have time to go anywhere else if you want to be able to see her between each game.

Tournament venues vary enormously in terms of location, physical conditions for the players, and facilities available to spectators and accompanying families. At one end of the scale you may find a hotel, with a pleasant airy playing hall, heated or even air-conditioned as the weather dictates, with comfortable chairs, enough space for the player to record the game and keep a drink beside him, a quiet carpeted floor and good, reasonably priced food and drink. A large room, or several, may be provided for accompanying parents, spouses etc. and for the players themselves to relax in between games, with comfortable chairs and sofas, coffee tables and space for toddlers to spread out their Fisher Price empires. Ideally, the hotel will either have facilities of its own such as a swimming pool or games room, which can be used by players and their families, or will be close to a pleasant beach or town centre. Even a basic playground, with a couple of swings and a bench for you to sit on may make the difference between a successful weekend and long hours of tedious bad temper.

At the other extreme, a few weekend tournaments are still held in run-down schools and seedy working men's clubs where the facilities for children, if they ever existed, have long been vandalized out of all recognition. Refreshments may be non-existent, or limited to identically-coloured mahogany-brown tea or beer and greasy burgers from a van outside. Sometimes there is nowhere at all, or at least nowhere warm and clean to wait, and you may be reduced to skulking in the Ladies (or Gents, which is probably even worse), staring desperately at your watch and wishing yet again that Alice had taken up some more salubrious hobby, like potholing through sewers ....

The secret is that you don't actually have to do it. Or, to be strictly honest, you don't have to do it many times. Right at the beginning, when Alice is new to the whole chess scene, she will probably want to enter as many weekend tournaments as you can track down, especially if they are relatively near at hand. It is not always easy to find out about events, (before you find yourselves on everybody's mailing list and are bombarded with entry forms in every week's post) and even less easy to tell which are likely to be worth going to. In these very early days, too, before Alice has made the vast hordes of chess friends whom she will soon be e-mailing day and night, you may feel that you ought to stay at the venue, however unprepossessing. Later, however, and not much later, you will be able to be more discriminating. Look for tournaments in pleasant places, at pleasant times of year, or at least those where you have friends or relatives nearby who don't mind being descended upon at unlikely intervals. Often, where the tournament is held at a hotel, rooms are available at special rates for entrants and their families. A room of your own in the venue can make an enormous difference to the success of the weekend.

Be a little careful, however, not to assume that a chess tournament in a holiday resort will inevitably be a holiday. Unless the chess player in the family is old enough to fend for herself during the day, your time will be very much curtailed by the demands of the playing schedule and by the perpetual uncertainty about what time each game will actually finish. This latter difficulty may be alleviated somewhat by the judicious use of mobile phones (though NOT in the playing hall!) but it will still be difficult for you to make any kind of plans in advance. Remember, too, that although Alice is there to play chess, and probably more than happy to do so, she will not necessarily be overjoyed to hear of her siblings' trip to some long-awaited theme park while she has been slaving over a tricky and perhaps ultimately doomed game. For she will lose sometimes, and lose badly or stupidly, and hate herself, and chess, and all the rest of you, so that the grand celebratory lunch at the expensive restaurant turns into a costly and snarling ordeal. It needn't happen; it is possible to combine a tournament with a species of mini-break, but it takes sensitivity and tact and most of all flexibility. It may, therefore, be less stressful for only one parent (or grandparent, aunt, uncle...anyone foolish enough to offer) to accompany Alice, while the other stays at home with the other children, the ironing and the gin bottle. You can always stake out the territory and make it a family trip next year, if you feel brave enough.

Of course, if Alice is old enough, and confident enough, she may well not want you hanging around at all, so that you can simply drop her off in the morning with a five pound note or a packet of sandwiches and collect her again in the evening. If the venue is too far away for you to travel there and back in a day then you may have to stay overnight with her, though eventually, as an older teenager, she will be able to stay by herself or with a friend (location and company suitably vetted).

But if Alice is still on the Flowerpot Men side of her seventh birthday, the only weekend tournaments remotely within reach are held in the kind of sink schools that even the taps have fallen off, and all your known relatives have emigrated to distant corners of the Commonwealth, please don't throw this book at the nearest arbiter in despair. There is an alternative.....or rather several.....

Chapter Five

Accelerating the Dragon[35]:
Rapidplay and other Tournaments

'We must *have a bit of a fight, but I don't care about going on long' said Tweedle-dum. 'What's the time now?'*

Tweedledee looked at his watch, and said 'Half past four.'

'Let's fight till six, and then have dinner.' said Tweedledum.

A popular alternative to the weekend congress, sweet to the ears of a long-suffering parent, who, by Sunday evening, has miniature knights hopping in front of his chess-crazed eyeballs, and a distant nostalgia for *Songs of Praise* and the washing-up, is the Rapidplay Tournament. This normally operates in the same way as the weekend congress, using the Swiss system and dividing the entrants into categories according to their playing strength. However, rather than each player being allowed between two and three hours for all his moves, he is given only thirty minutes. Those of you with mathematical leanings will quickly deduce that, under this system, the maximum length of each game is only an hour and that it is thereby possible to play six or seven rounds in a day while still allowing a fifteen minute break between each and an hour for lunch. Rapidplay tournaments therefore usually take only one day (with a few exceptions such as the British Rapidplay Championships), thus leaving a substantial chunk of the weekend free for mundane non-chess activities such as work (both home- and house-), catching up on the Archers, reintroducing yourself to your spouse and investigating the possibilities of what you used to know as a life.

Apart from this substantial benefit from a parent's point of view, rapidplay events also have advantages for the junior player. As anyone who has foolishly challenged their offspring to a Tetris match will testify, a child's mind and fingers can move with preternatural and almost frightening agility (though not, oddly enough, when called upon to tidy away a couple of Coke cans). Charlie and his friends will therefore probably be able to assess their positions and make

---

[35] The Accelerated Dragon, when not a piece of fantasy science fiction, is a variation in the Sicilian Defence, involving a kingside fianchetto. A fianchetto, by the way, is a bishop placed on b2, g2, b7 or g7, ready to exploit a long diagonal, as well as an opportunity to show off your Italian pronunciation (hard 'c').

their moves more quickly than their aged opponents. (They can also mis-read positions and make ghastly blunders more quickly than their elders but somehow they usually manage to wriggle their way out of the consequences.) Charlie will also, unless by some quirk of the space-time continuum you have given birth to a reincarnation of Job himself, have a considerably shorter attention span than his senior opponents. The baleful effects of this phenomenon, potentially devastating in a full-length game[36] are less acute within rapidplay time controls, where he has a shorter period in which to drift off into a reverie of Wolves winning the European Cup and to forget altogether that his knight is *en prise*.

The effect of these advantages, combined with parental enthusiasm for an event lasting only a day, is that rapidplay tournaments usually receive a dispropor-tionate number of junior entrants. These players and their parents will tell one another about other rapidplay tournaments, which in turn receive a dispropor-tionate....you get the idea. There are also often more titled and professional play-ers in these events, especially in London. Indeed, if it is at all feasible, you might consider travelling to London for a prestigious rapidplay or two. Charlie gets the opportunity to meet (and possibly even to play) one or two of his heroes and to inhale the heady atmosphere of metropolitan chess (well, there are worse things he could inhale), while you, if you dare, can sneak off to the V&A or whichever other institution caters for your particular variety of secret vice.

This game of Gawain's was played on one of his first trips to the London Chess Centre, a few weeks before his seventh birthday.

□ R. Wellington ■ Gawain Jones
Chess & Bridge rapidplay 1994
Sicilian Defence

---

1 e4 c5 2 Nf3 d6 3 d4 cxd4 4 Nxd4 Nf6 5 Nc3 a6 6 Bc4 e6 7 Bb3 Be7 8 0-0 0-0 9 Qf3 Nbd7 10 Qg3

It seems odd to move the queen twice in the opening but here White wants to pressurise the g7-pawn.

10...Re8

Sidestepping the rook so as to be able to defend g7 more easily.

11 Bh6 g6

11...Bf8, to defend the g7-pawn, was also possible.

12 Rae1 Bf8 (diagram 17)

Offering the exchange of bishops which White should probably agree to.

13 Bg5?!

13 Bxf8 would be better.

13...Bg7?

---

[36] See Chapter Seven

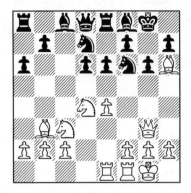

Diagram 17   Diagram 18

The bishop fianchetto looks natural but White can simply capture the pawn on d6!

14 Qh3?

Why not take the pawn?

14...b5

Expanding on the queenside to get some play and to develop the pieces.

15 Bh6

White decides that he was mistaken not to swap Bishops before and accordingly offers the exchange now.

15...Qc7

Activating the queen. If instead 15...Bb7 then 16 Bxe6!! looks good for White as after 16...fxe6 (16...Bxh6 17 Bxd7!) 17 Nxe6 forks queen and bishop.

16 Bxg7 Kxg7 17 Nf3?!

Moving the knight from the active d4-square to the passive f3-square. Instead 17 Bxe6! was interesting as after 17...fxe6 18 Nxe6 Rxe6 19 Qxe6 I cannot move my knight on d7 owing to 20 Qxf6+!! Kxf6 and 21 Nd5+ winning the queen back with interest.

17...Bb7 18 Ng5?!

White misses the threat. Instead better was 18 a3 stopping ...b4.

18...h6!

Forcing White's knight back.

19 Nf3 (diagram 18) 19...b4!

Forcing the other knight back.

20 Ne2 Bxe4

Black is a pawn up and looks to have a good position.

21 Ned4 e5! 22 Ne6+?

Sacrificing the knight but White gets nothing in return.

22...fxe6 23 Bxe6 Bxc2?! 24 Bxd7?

White misses a chance with 24 Rc1! pinning the bishop after which it would be hard for Black to keep the piece advantage. 24 Bxd7 also gives up White's best attacking piece.

24...Qxd7 25 Rc1 Bf5

25...Qxh3 was simpler, leaving Black a piece and a pawn up in an ending.

26 Qg3 Rac8

26...Ne4! was good, as White would rapidly lose any squares for his queen, e.g. 27 Qh4 g5 28 Qh5 Nf6 when White has no good square for the queen.

27 Qh4 Rxc1 28 Rxc1 Rc8 29 Re1 Qc7

29...Ne4 looks very good for Black as after 30 Rxe4 g5! White cannot play 31 Nxg5 due to 31...Rc1+ mating.

30 h3 e4 31 g4

White wants to try for tricks.

31...g5

31...Bxg4! would be even better.

32 Qg3 Bxg4 33 hxg4 exf3 34 Qxf3 Qd7 35 Kf1 Qxg4 36 Qb7+

White tries for something but he is completely lost.

36...Kg6 37 Qxc8?

A mistake that can be safely attributed to White's having very little time, as confirmed by his next move.

37...Qxc8 38 Re6? 0-1

Having read so far, and considered, no doubt, the additional advantages to a developing player of being able to try out his new openings in more and faster games, the comparatively spectator-friendly nature of rapidplay games and the savings to be made on the cost of Friday and Saturday night accommodation, you may now be wondering why anyone under fifty ever bothers with the hassle of playing in a long play tournament at all. Some don't, in fact, and if Charlie's interest is likely to be short-lived or to compete with many other commitments, then he might be happier competing only in rapidplay events. However, if he is serious about his chess development, and aspires to selection for important teams, rapidplay tournaments alone are unlikely to be sufficient. In Britain rapidplay games are graded, using the same criteria as full-length games, but the two systems are kept separate, so that a player who competes in both types of game has two separate grades; a standard (long-play) and a rapidplay grade. Unfortunately for many juniors, it is the standard grade which is overwhelmingly considered from the point of view of selection for teams etc. It is therefore essential that Charlie, if he has aspirations to play at county level or above, should have sufficient experience of long-play games. These need not, of course, necessarily take place within a conventional weekend congress, although most serious young players, even those who belong to a junior club and play mainly in junior tournaments, find it beneficial to play adult opponents from time to time, either in weekend or longer tournaments or in a local or national league. A balance between long- and rapid-play chess is best for most players, with the proportions tweaked to suit Charlie's individual needs and the resources of your time, patience and wallet. Usually, as we have seen, juniors prefer to play rapidplay games, although many older players studiously avoid them. If Charlie himself is wary of the rapidplay time control then he should perhaps be gently encouraged to try it, as this form of chess is quickly growing in status and significance (now being used by FIDE in stages of their official world championship) and he is likely to handicap himself if he does not acquire the particular skills involved. Junior players tend to play very quickly in any case, and to slow down as they grow older and more experienced. This means that, if Charlie is already using most of his two or three hour allocation in a long-play game, he is either exceptionally disciplined and mature, or he is playing too slowly, perhaps out of excessive caution and a reluctance to rely upon his intuition and instinct for the game. It is difficult at first for new players to adjust to playing within such different time controls, but most soon adapt, developing discrete strategies and methods of dealing with each type of game.

Occasionally an important rapidplay event will last more than the one day blissfully alluded to above, though it is unlikely to take more than two. One example is the British Rapidplay Championships, where strong junior players frequently draw with and defeat titled adult players. Inevitably, it is also common for young players to be paired against one another, as in this game from the 1999 Championships when Gawain, then eleven, played against a talented junior, some four or five years older, and already his friend and international team mate.

□ **Gawain Jones** ■ **D. Tan**

British Rapidplay 1999

Sicilian Defence

---

1 e4 c5 2 Nf3 d6 3 c3

One of the many variations played against the Sicilian. The idea of this line is that after d2-d4 you can recapture with the pawn. Another bonus is that there is not a lot of theory to learn.

3...Nf6 4 Be2 Nbd7

Black cannot take the pawn as 4...Nxe4 5 Qa4+ wins the knight.

5 d3

Now White must defend the pawn as the d7-knight blocks the check.

5...c4!? 6 Be3

The theory of this opening recommends the move 6 d4! with the idea that after 6...Nxe4, 7 Bxc4 leaves White slightly better.

6...cxd3 7 Bxd3 b6 8 0-0 Bb7 9 Nbd2 e6 10 Re1 Be7

Both sides have developed their pieces and now have to find a plan.

11 Bd4!? 0-0 12 e5

White improves the range of his pieces.

12...dxe5 13 Nxe5 Nxe5 14 Rxe5

White cannot take with the bishop as it leaves the other bishop hanging.

14...Bd6 15 Rg5?!

Going for the attack but leaving the pieces rather offside. Instead, 15 Re1 would have left it about equal.

15...e5! 16 Be3

I can't take the pawn as Black swaps bishops and then goes on to take the bishop on d3.

16...Bc7 17 Nf1 h6 (diagram 19)

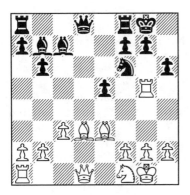

Diagram 19

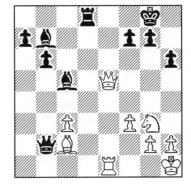

Diagram 20

18 Rf5

Missing a chance. The alternative of 18 Rxg7+!!(?) Kxg7. 19 Bxh6+! would give tremendous play in exchange for the piece. A draw is then possible after 19...Kxh6 20 Qd2+ Kg7 21 Qg5+ Kh8 22 Qh6+.

18...Qd5

This looks very good for Black but another possibility would have been 18...Bc8! winning the white rook.

19 f3 Rfd8!

Here 19...Bc8 doesn't look as good as White has 20 Rxf6! when the initiative has suddenly switched to White.

20 Bc2 Qe6 21 Qe1 Nd5 22 Rh5

Somehow I have survived the onslaught and am only slightly worse. This is the problem (or advantage depending on the way you look at it!) with rapidplay chess: one side may get a decent advantage but then has only a short period of time in which to try and find a way to exploit it.

22...Nxe3 23 Qxe3 Bd6 24 Kh1

Fortunately I don't fall for ...Bc5 winning my queen.

24...Re8 25 Ng3 Rad8

Black still seems fine but White is no longer so passive and the rook doesn't look out of place on h5.

26 Re1?!

Probably a mistake as it gives Black the a-pawn, although in rapidplay it may not matter much... it being more important to go for the king!

26...Bc5?!

Here it was critical to take the a-pawn after which it doesn't look as though I have enough for victory.

27 Qe2 Qxa2?!

He takes it now but the critical difference is that I can recapture the pawn on e5 and simultaneously bring the rook back into the game.

28 Rxe5 Rxe5 29 Qxe5 Qxb2?! (diagram 20)

This is perhaps not actually a mistake but it means that Black has to defend very accurately against my attack. Unfortunately by this time he has only around five minutes left and so this defence proves impossible.

30 Nf5!

Starting up the mate threats.

30...Bf8

The only move.

31 Ne7+! Bxe7 32 Qxe7 Rb8??

Now he is missing White's threats whereas the alternative of 22...Rf8 23 Bh7+! Kxh7 24 Qxf8 still looks approximately equal.

33 Qe8+! 1-0

Oops! Black resigned as after 33...Rxe8, 34 Rxe8 is checkmate.

If Charlie enjoys rapidplay chess, if he needs a kick-start into trusting his own instincts, or if you simply wish you could watch a game of chess without having to wait half an hour for a single pawn to move, then you should look out for a blitz tournament. Blitz is rapidplay gone hyper, a very fast form of the game with a short time control. Technically, anything under fifteen minutes is blitz, but the most popular limits are five, three, or for the really frenetic, one minute each. At the moment there are few actual blitz tournaments, although the form is growing in popularity and many chess clubs organize their own friendly five minute events. Blitz is, as you would imagine, enormously popular with juniors, who will play it constantly before, after, and between rounds in other events. It is a great way for Charlie to practice openings, to experience success and failure when both will be wiped away in an instant, to see and play a myriad of positions, tactics and strategies, to make friends without artificiality or embarrassment, and to destroy the delicate balance of chess clocks. For the latter reason, combined with the unrestrained shouts of joy which often accompany a blitz victory, it is usually strictly forbidden to play blitz with tournament equipment or in the playing hall. If Charlie has his own portable set and clock, he may therefore wish to bring them with him to such events and to seek out suitable playing spaces and opponents. The fact of his having paid for the clock himself, or at least being obliged to bear the cost of a replacement, may help to ensure that neither he nor his friends thump it too enthusiastically.

Wherever four or more junior chess players are gathered together, one thing can be guaranteed; that sooner or later they will begin playing exchange. Exchange, or cross chess in Britain, Bughouse or Siamese chess in the United States, is a peculiar variation of the standard game which combines the speed and excitement of blitz with the co-operative skills of bridge and the physical restraint of all-in wrestling. It is the subject of an odd mid-Atlantic transformation, arousing a strange and atavistic fury in British coaches and organizers alike, and banned even more strictly than blitz, but attaining respectability and honour in America, where it even has its own tournaments and trophies.

Two games take place simultaneously, next to one another, with the two White players sitting diagonally opposite each other, as follows:

Archie (White)	Bernie (Black)
□	□
Charlie (Black)	Danny (White)

Archie is playing against Charlie, while Bernie is playing against Danny. However, Archie and Bernie constitute a team, as do Charlie and Danny. The games are played as normal until a piece (or pawn) is captured, when it can be given to the capturing player's partner. For example, if Archie took Charlie's black queen, he could then hand it to Bernie, who could place it anywhere he liked on his own board, even if he already retained his own queen.

There are of course countless other chess variants with differing degrees of adult approval, from 'lightning' or 'buzzer' chess, where an electronic bell rings every thirty seconds upon which a move must be played immediately[37], rather like Pavlov's dog, albeit without the rewarding Winalot, through 'suicide' games, where the object is to lose, to weird and Byzantine games with cumulative numbers of moves. Generally their function is social, rather than educative, and probably none the worse for that. It is easy for parents to underestimate the pressure cre-

---

[37] Particularly prestigious in Australia and New Zealand.

ated by an important match or tournament, and to forget that children and teenagers are just that, and need some relatively boisterous way of letting off steam between rounds. Given the choice between exchange chess and cocaine, one minute blitz and gang warfare...?

But back to tournaments. If you live in an area where junior chess is strong and able to attract organization and resources, you may be fortunate enough to find a local junior tournament. These are normally one day events using a rapid-play format or occasionally a mid-range time control of one hour per player. Entrants will normally be divided into categories according to their age rather than grading strength, although it is usually possible for a particularly strong player to enter a higher category than his chronological age would warrant. Most such local tournaments are open to all junior players, including beginners, and can provide a pleasant and sociable introduction to tournament chess. The atmosphere at these events is often very relaxed, with other parents and organizers keen to welcome new players and able to give assistance to novices in the niceties of tournament play such as the use of clocks, scoresheets etc.

Do, however, read the entry forms and leaflets relating to these tournaments particularly closely as there are important points upon which they may differ from adult tournaments and also from one another. There may be a strict closing date for entries, so that, unlike the majority of weekend congresses, it is impossible to enter on the day of the tournament. There may also be geographical, as well as age, limits, particularly with regard to eligibility for prizes and trophies. It is a good idea to check these well in advance, subtly, if you are concerned not to appear pushy, and to make sure that Charlie is aware of any limitations. The prize-giving ceremony is a rather late and public occasion at which to discover that, after a perfect score, he cannot after all stagger away under the weight of the enormous champion's cup because of your negligence in giving birth to him half a mile outside the city boundary. Provided that he is eligible to enter at all, there is of course no reason why he should not play in a tournament for which he cannot win the principal trophies. Should he, relaxed by the small stakes or spurred on by the pride of the outsider, do exceptionally well, most organizers will usually ensure that there is something for him to take away in recognition of his achievement.

In 2002, for example, when Gawain was fourteen, he played in the Italian Under-16 Championship. We had been living in Italy for only four months and did not expect that he would be eligible for any actual title, so the event was a relaxed occasion, an opportunity to spend time with his new friends from the Lucca chess club and to meet his contemporaries from the rest of the country. In the end, he came a tactful second in the tournament so no awkward decisions had to be made.

□ **Gawain Jones** ■ **A.Pulito**

Italian Under-16 Championship 2002

French Defence

---

1 e4 e6 2 d3

The normal move against the French is 2 d4 but the text is perfectly respectable.

2...d5 3 Qe2

3 Nd2 is also possible and it is slightly more popular but there is nothing wrong with the text.

3...Nf6 4 Nf3 c5 5 g3 Nc6 6 Bg2 Be7 7 0-0 b6

7...b5 or 7...0-0 are slightly more usual but there is nothing wrong with this.

8 e5 Nd7 9 c4 d4 10 h4

White trying to limit Black on the kingside and to start attacking on that flank should he choose to castle.

10...Bb7 11 Bf4

Bringing the bishop out to defend the e5-pawn.

11...h6

Perhaps preparing a ...g7-g5 push at some point.

12 h5

Cutting out ...g7-g5 and limiting any expansion on the kingside for Black.

12...Qc7 13 Nbd2 0-0-0!?

Instead 13...0-0 would leave White with a pleasant edge as it would be hard for Black to come up with a good plan.

14 Rfe1 Rde8 15 Bh3

Stopping ...f7-f6.

15...Kb8 (diagram 21)

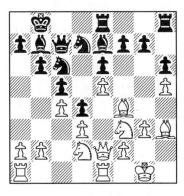

Diagram 21

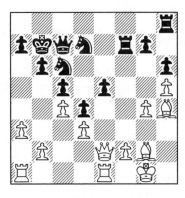

Diagram 22

Simply sidestepping the king out of the line of fire of h3 and also defending the a-pawn should it ever come under attack.

16 a3

Starting an offensive on the queenside.

16...Bf8

Black is trying to defend the e-pawn so as to permit a ...g7-g5 break. At the moment after 16...g5 17 hxg6 fxg6 18 Bxe6 would win a pawn. Instead though 16...Nd8 looks better, defending the pawn and freeing the b7-bishop.

17 Ne4

Bringing the knight into the centre of the board. Black can't take on e5, e.g. 17...Ndxe5 18 Nxe5 Nxe5 19 Nxc5 when White is better.

17...Qd8

Carrying on with the plan of ...g7-g5. Playing ...g7-g5 immediately gives up the f6-square.

18 g4

Making an escape square for the bishop down to g3 and h2 as otherwise it starts to get very short of squares.

18...Ka8

Black continues to play safely, taking the king off the diagonal h2-b8 though it wasn't really necessary to be so cautious. Perhaps an immediate 18...g5 would be better.

19 Bg2

Bringing the bishop back to a more active square as now the pawn on g4 blocks that diagonal to the bishop.

19...f6

Finally Black starts an offensive. After 19...g5 20 Bg3 was possible which leaves White slightly better.

20 Ng3

Trying to defend the pawn on e5 but 20 b4! would be interesting as after 20...fxe5 21 Bg3 Black has no real attack.

20...Be7

Black now had to move very quickly. He only had four minutes for his twenty moves before the next time control so it is not surprising that he missed the best move here. Instead 20...g5! would leave Black slightly better.

21 exf6 Bxf6 22 Ne4!

The knight returns to the centre to hit the weak d6-square.

22...e5

Trying to block the bishop out of the game, though now White is comfortably better as it is hard for Black to continue his attack.

23 Nd6!

Now Black can't take the bishop on f4 as 23...exf4 24 Qxe8! swaps off the pieces after 24...Rxe8 25 Rxe8 into an ending where White is the exchange up.

23...Re7 24 Bg3 Qc7

Black has no way to keep his b7-bishop as 24...Ba6 allows 25 Nxd4! followed by Bxc6+ so he has to allow the swap.

25 Nxb7 Kxb7 26 Nh4 Bxh4

Black does not want the knight to jump into either f5 or g6 but now with the two bishops and more active pieces White is clearly better.

27 Bxh4 Rf7 (diagram 22) 28 b4!

Finally. Now Black has no compensating attack on the opposite flank.

28...Re8??

Black blunders immediately. Retreating the king was forced though White would still have a pleasant advantage.

29 b5

Black cannot move the knight as it is pinned to the king by the bishop on g2.

29...e4

Desperately trying to block out the bishop but it is useless.

30 bxc6+ 1-0

He is going to be at least a rook down after 30...Qxc6 31 Bxe4.

Gawain always enjoyed playing in local junior tournaments, where most of the entrants were friends and the atmosphere was relaxed and yet, at moments, thrilling. This game was played in Middlesborough when he was nine, and his opponent four or five years older.

□ Gawain Jones ■ O.Gill

Cathedral Software Tournament 1997

English Opening

---

1 c4 c5 2 Nf3 b6 3 g3 Bb7 4 Bg2 Nf6 5 0-0 e6 6 d4 cxd4 7 Qxd4 Nc6 8 Qd3

A typical position where White has slightly more space.

8...Rc8 9 a3

After 9 Nc3 Nb4 White would not be able to defend the c-pawn as 10 Qd4 fails to 10...Nc2.

9...Na5

Black tries to exploit the weakness of the c-pawn.

10 Nbd2

The best move to defend the pawn as after 10 Ne5 Black can swap bishops, followed by ...d6 winning the c-pawn while 10 b3 allows 10...d5 after which Black is better.

10...Ba6 11 b3

Again, this is the only move to defend the pawn.

11...d5

Trying to exploit the pins on the queen.

12 Bb2?!

Instead 12 Rd1! would keep it about equal as after 12...dxc4 13 bxc4 Nxc4 14 Nxc4 Bxc4 15 Qxd8 Rxd8 and 16 Rxd8 Kxd8 17 Ne5! hits the bishop and the pawn on f7.

12...dxc4 13 Qxd8+ Rxd8 14 b4!

White is a pawn down but has some compensation with more active pieces and better development.

14...Nb7?!

14...Nc6 looks better.

15 Nb1?!

A very strange move, I was trying to manoeuvre my knight round to c3 but it's rather slow. Instead 15 Rfc1 looked better, hitting the weak c-pawn.

15...Nd5

Bringing the knight into the centre of the board.

16 Nc3 Nxc3 17 Bxc3 Nd6!

Putting the knight onto a better square and trying to bring the bishop back into the game.

18 Nd4 (diagram 23)

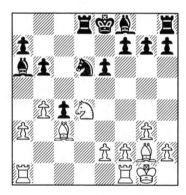

Diagram 23

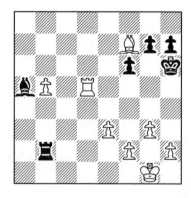

Diagram 24

Again the knight looks better on e5.

18...b5?

18...Bb7 swapping off the light-squared bishops is preferable.

19 Bc6+ Ke7 20 a4!

Blowing apart Black's weak queenside.

20...e5!

The alternative of 20...bxa4 21 Rxa4 would be very good for White as the bishop is forced to retreat to c8.

21 Nxb5 Bxb5

21...Rc8! would be interesting when 22 Nxa7 Rc7 23 b5! (the only move to keep bishop and knight) 23...Rxa7 24 bxa6 Rxa6 leaves White with only a slight edge.

22 axb5!

Better than 22 Bxb5 as this allows the rook into the game.

22...Nc8

The only way to keep the a-pawn. This is essential as otherwise White's b-pawns would be too strong.

23 Bxe5

Now White is a pawn up with more active pieces and it will still be hard for Black to develop his bishop and the rook on h8.

23...Rd2!?

Black needs to try and get some play.

24 e3 f6 25 Bd4! Kf7

Black has no way to defend his pawn on a7 so tries to develop his pieces at last.

26 Bd5+ Kg6 27 Bxc4 Bxb4 28 Bxa7 Nxa7 29 Rxa7 Rc8

Black has finally managed to develop all his pieces but is two pawns down. White has to be careful though as if the rooks are exchanged then the endgame, with opposite coloured bishops, will be very difficult to win.

30 Bf7+ Kh6 31 Ra4 Rb2 32 Ra2?

32 Bd5 trying to help the b-pawn through would be preferable as this move loses the b-pawn.

32...Rcc2?

Instead 32...Rxa2 33 Bxa2 Rc5 would win the b-pawn, resulting in a position which is very difficult to win.

33 Rxb2 Rxb2 34 Rd1 Ba5 35 Rd5 (diagram 24)

Defending the b-pawn. This should be a win for White but it is still quite difficult.

35...Be1??

Missing the other purpose behind Rd5. Instead he could have played 35...g6, giving the king a way back into the game.

36 Rh5 mate

In some cases, you may find that entry to a junior tournament is not open to all, but requires some initial qualification. A principal example in Britain is the London Junior Championships, which, despite its name, is really a national event, although players need some link with London (birth, residence or education) in order to win the designated London trophies. Normally, junior players qualify to play in London by competing in various regional tournaments and achieving a particular score. Exceptionally, if Charlie can demonstrate otherwise (e.g. by a high grade for his age group, or by outstanding tournament performances) that he is of sufficient strength to hold his own among such competition, he may be permitted to enter without prior qualification. The championships, with categories from Under-8 to Under-21, take place during the Christmas period and typically last several days, using a long-play format, although both the time control and length of event are shortened proportionately for the younger sections.

Playing in the London Championships can be enormously exhilarating and satisfying for a talented junior, knowing that he is playing against at least a good proportion of the very best of his peers, his games overseen by the coaches, arbiters and organizers who have been responsible for nurturing the talents of two or three generations before him. He will also find himself, perhaps for the first time in an environment where junior chess is taken seriously and where his ability gives him a passport to camaraderie and long-standing future friendships. It can, however, be a somewhat stressful experience, for you and Charlie alike, particularly if you do not live in the London area and have had to travel a considerable distance, leaving the remnants of your family to deal with the fallout of Christmas and New Year. The atmosphere can be a little tense, particularly among the parents of the younger age groups, who may be relying upon a creditable score in this event to bolster a school entrance application. Most parents, of course, will be welcoming and level-headed, and you too will be able to make friends for the future, but it is difficult, as you will find yourself, to remain perfectly calm and Confucian when your child is entangled in a tricky endgame, particularly if there are educational prospects at stake. The tournament organizers are, however, unfailingly friendly, helpful and unflappable and succeed in reducing most impending mountainous crises into neat and manageable molehills.

Before his first London Junior Championships, most of Gawain's games had been against adults and teenagers, or at least against boys and girls several years older. It was reassuring, therefore, to discover that his remarkably talented opponent in the third round of the London Under-8's, was even younger – exactly a year younger – than Gawain himself.

□ **Gawain Jones** ■ **T.Thiruchelvam**
London Under-8 Championship 1994
London System

The day on which this was played was very important to both of us. Why? Because it was our birthday of course![38] I was seven and he was just six. Considering the ages of the players this is a very well played game.

1 d4 d5 2 Nf3 Nc6

---

[38] Obviously an auspicious day for chess players, as it is also the birthday of Viswanathan Anand, the Indian super-grandmaster!

This move is okay but it would probably be better to leave the queenside knight where it is on b8 for the time being to develop the other pieces as the knight doesn't yet know where it wants to go[39] and Black may want to play his pawn to c5 or c6.

3 Bf4

The London System. A simple solid line which I played before the English.

3...Nf6 4 e3 h6 5 Bd3

Perhaps 5 c3 first would be better, cutting out Black's reply.

5...Nb4!?

Forcing the bishop back as White doesn't want to swap the good bishop for Black's knight.

6 Be2 Bf5! 7 Na3

This is the only move which defends c2.

7...e6 8 0-0

I would have been better off playing 8 c3, forcing the knight back immediately.

8...Bd6

8...c5! would be interesting, after which Black looks to have equalised.

9 c3!?

After 9 Bxd6, 9...cxd6!? looks okay for Black.

9...Bxf4!?

Doubling the white f-pawns.

10 exf4 Nc6 11 Bd3?!

Moving the bishop once more in the opening. Instead 11 Ne5! would use the f4-pawn and retain a very slight advantage for White.

11...Bxd3 12 Qxd3 Qd6

Black delays castling and instead attacks the f-pawn although he is forcing it to where it wants to go anyway. Castling kingside would be better, leaving the position approximately equal.

13 f5!

Getting rid of the doubled f-pawn and also weakening Black's pawn structure.

13...0-0-0 (diagram 25)

Black decides that he wants an ultra-aggressive game with the kings on opposite flanks, though it would have been safer to castle kingside.

---

[39] In other words, Black doesn't yet know quite how the opening will develop and which square would be best. However, there is something about the knight which seems to encourage this kind of anthropomorphic musing. Perhaps the first signs of chess delirium come when the knight finally makes up its mind and the player bends low over the board to listen. You have been warned...

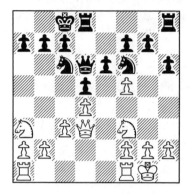

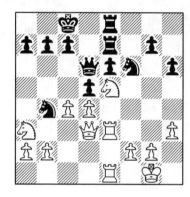

Diagram 25   **Diagram 26**

14 fxe6 fxe6?!

14...Qxe6 looks better, keeping Black's pawn structure solid, Now Black has a backward e-pawn[40] which is a weakness.

15 Rfe1 Ng4?

Black is determined to attack but at this point there are too many weaknesses in his position.

16 h3?!

Forcing the knight back from whence it came. However, 16 Qg6 hitting the knight, e- and g-pawns would have been better, and would have won at least a pawn.

16...Nf6 17 Re3

Preparing to double rooks (put both rooks on the same file) against the weak e-pawn.

17...Rhe8 18 Rae1 Re7 19 Ne5!

Getting the knight into the e5 outpost (an outpost is a square which cannot be defended by any of the opponent's pawns).

19...Rde8 20 c4!?

Starting an offensive against Black's king but 20 Nb5! also looked good, forcing 20...Qd8 after which White could weaken Black's queenside with 21 Nxc6 bxc6 22 Na3 (not 22 Nxa7+? when 22...Kb7 traps the knight), leaving it very weak.

20...Nb4!? (diagram 26)

---

[40] Nothing to do with its intellectual achievement: a backward pawn is one which stands one rank behind an adjacent pawn of the same colour and cannot therefore be protected by this second pawn. This usually implies that a 'hole' has been created just in front on the backward pawn, which may well become a useful outpost for an opposing piece. Here, for example, the backward pawn is on e6, its colleague is on d5 and the 'hole' is on e5.

Still refusing to defend passively, Black keeps up his threats.

21 c5!!

What a weird position! Both queens are now attacked, but I think that I am practically winning as Black has no good move.

21...Nxd3?

The most natural move though probably not the best. The problem here for Black is that he has no good square for his queen as after 21...Qd8 22 Qb5 Na6 23 c6! is winning for White and after 21...Qa6 I can simply swap off queens with 22 Qxa6 Nxa6 23 Nb5! Kb8 24 Ng6 winning the e-pawn and having an overwhelming position. Instead 21...Qxe5!? 22 dxe5 Nxd3 23 exf6! Nxe1 24 fxe7 traps the black knight but Black can continue to play on with two pawns for the knight after 24...Nxg2 25 Kxg2 Rxe7.

22 cxd6 Nxe1 23 dxe7

Here's the problem: Black has no square for his knight on e1.

23...Rxe7?!

Better was 23...Nxg2 when Black at least gets two pawns for the knight.

24 Rxe1 Nd7 25 Nxd7 Kxd7 26 f4

Trying to bind Black down.

26...g5 27 fxg5 hxg5 28 g4 Kd6 29 Nc2,

Rerouting the knight to a better square although 29 b4! would probably be better, keeping Black tied down.

29...c5!

Forcing the creation of two connected passed pawns (two pawns that are next to each other which cannot be stopped by any of the opponent's pawns).

30 dxc5+ Kxc5 31 Kf2

Bringing the king into the game although missing 31 Re5! which wins a pawn as Black cannot defend e6 and g5.

31...Kc4 32 Ke3

Again Re5 looks good.

32...e5 1-0

Here the game record finishes, noting that White won. I presume that there were more moves; six year olds aren't in the habit of resigning early but I should have been winning easily with a knight for a pawn after a move such as 33 Rc1!.

The tournament becomes considerably calmer in the older age-groups, where teenagers are already settled at school and the mere fact of playing chess at this exalted level is impressive enough for university entrance tutors. There is also the enormous advantage of not having so many parents hanging about. In fact, once Charlie reaches adolescence, if he is sufficiently good to play in the London Championships at all, it may be possible for you to pack him off there without having to stir further than the station, as an excellent scheme is offered by which generous, London-based parents offer accommodation to lone provincial competitors.

An alternative or addition to the London event, for especially keen or talented players, is the British Chess Championships which includes a range of junior sections. The 'British' as it is universally known, despite murmurings about the continued eligibility of Commonwealth players, is the major chess event in the U.K. and is held for two weeks every summer, generally during the first fortnight in August. The venue changes annually, but is usually a leisure centre, entertainment complex or university in a holiday location or major city in England, Scotland or Wales. With serious prize-money (serious in chess terms, which unfortunately means derisory in comparison with snooker or almost any other sport) it attracts a good number of grandmasters and international masters every year, including several of the top ten British players. Because it is held in August, often on the south coast, it is more likely than any other British event to be accompanied by fine weather. Perhaps for this reason, it usually tempts several expatriate British professional players, often with their families and creates the nearest thing that chess-playing Englishmen can create to a carnival atmosphere.

Apart from the British Championship itself, a closed, mainly adult tournament, around twenty other events take place within the fortnight of the Championships, open to players of a wide range of ages and abilities.

The most significant for younger players are the British Junior Championships, which at the time of writing comprise separate tournaments for each year-group from Under-8 to Under-14, with Under-15s and Under-16s combined in a single event. A separate trophy and title are awarded to the highest scoring girl in each age-group but girls and boys play together in each tournament. There are no qualification requirements for these events other than age (the player must have been under the specified age on the previous September 1st, so that, for example, most Under-10s are, by the time of the championship, already ten) and British or Commonwealth citizenship or residence for the past three years. There is no bar upon players entering a category or categories above their own chronological age or to, subject to timetabling clashes, players entering more than one category.

The youngest section at present is the Under-8, although the idea of adding an Under-7 is mooted from time to time. The event lasts only one day, albeit a tiring, fraught and dramatic day, usually the first Friday in August. It is therefore feasible, if you live within a reasonable travelling distance of the venue, to attend for the day only and, indeed, there are often large numbers of local children taking part. The time control is that of a rapidplay event and many of the games are over within the first half hour. The standard of play varies considerably, from local near-beginners to veteran almost-nine year olds who may already have two or more years of experience in serious tournament chess. It is likely, therefore, that whatever Charlie's current playing level and experience, he will find himself matched with appropriate opposition. You should ensure, however, especially if he has played little competitive chess beforehand that he is fully familiar with the rules and the time control, that he can use a clock and record his moves and that he can deal with unexpected failure in a socially acceptable way (keeping his screeches of despair unhealthily internalised, at least until he is safely outside the building). There is no theoretical reason why a much younger child cannot play in this section, although, as discussed in Chapter One, the dangers are likely to outweigh the benefits until he is at least five or six. All the junior events, but particularly this one, involve a great deal of work by the organizers and arbiters, especially where, as here, they involve very different numbers of spectators, timescales and attitudes to the adult and teenage tournaments. It is therefore unfair upon these hard-working men and women, upon the other participants and most of all on Charlie himself, to enter him for the tournament when he is not really ready, or with unrealistic expectations. For his home club, where he may be the most promising seven-year-old they have seen for generations, his victory may be inevitable, but faced with opposition from all around the country, not to mention India, one of the strongest nations in junior chess, he may find the reality very different. On the plus side, however, as long as both he and you approach the event realistically and positively, seeing it first of all as a potentially enjoyable experience rather than as a trial of combat, you will all have a very good time. The atmosphere at the British is generally friendly and relaxed, parents are keen to exchange information, gossip and tips about the area and national and regional junior organizers are always on the lookout for new talent. Charlie may even come away with something, for certificates are normally awarded to entrants who achieve more than a 50% score while there are often several small book or other prizes in addition to the main trophies and cash sums.

The Under-9 championship normally follows immediately on from the Under-8, taking place on the middle Saturday and Sunday of the fortnight. Many Under-8 players, particularly those who have competed before, stay on for this event as well, and it is often the most frenetic of the entire Championships. The time control is double that of the Under-8's, each player having an hour to make all his moves, so that games can last for up to two hours each. This is a rate of play which Charlie may have to practice beforehand, falling, as it does, between the normal long- and rapid-play rates, and he may need to make a rapid mental adjustment if he has played in the Under-8 event the day before. Many of the same considerations apply as for the younger age-group but, with seven rounds over two days, the amount of actual chess played is obviously considerably more, and the abilities and experience of the top players even greater. You should note, incidentally, that the Sunday of the Under-9 Championship is normally a rest day in the main British Championship and so, if Charlie is hoping for a glimpse of his grandmaster idols, he should remember to look out for them on Saturday. Apart from a few complete monomaniacs, who insist on playing in the Sunday rapid-play tournament, all serious chess players will be staying well away from the venue on Sunday.

The other junior championships, from Under-10 to Under-16, each have seven rounds at the 'quickplay finish' rate of play in the Championships, which allows a game to last a maximum of four hours. It is essential that Charlie looks very carefully at the precise way in which this time allocation is made up. In the current year of writing (2002) it is as follows:

moves 1 to 40:   100 minutes (i.e. one hour and forty minutes)

moves 41 +:   20 minutes

but he must check, and check again on each occasion, in this and every other event, to ensure that he has understood it correctly. The British uses several different rates of play in different events (in the main Championship and Major Open games can last a mammoth seven hours) and so it is especially important that both he and you read the information provided for competitors very carefully.

Similarly, you should be absolutely certain, especially with these junior events, that you have correctly read the playing schedule. The odd-numbered age-groups (Under-11, Under-13 and under 15/16) normally play during the first week of the tournament with the Under-10, Under-12 and Under-14 events taking place in the second week. Within this framework, however, the precise timetable varies quite considerably, in order to allow a balance of one- and two-game days and to permit players to take a minimum number of half point byes to allow them to compete in more than one event. Full details of these are always given in the information brochure attached to the entry form.

In theory, it is possible for an eight year old child to play in all four of the Under-8, Under-9, Under-10 and Under-11 tournaments and from time to time the feat is indeed attempted by some precocious moppet or other. Before you rush off to post Charlie's bulging entry form, however, do consider that the complete marathon would involve him in twelve solid days of serious competitive chess, with twenty-six rounds to play and a possible maximum of seventy two hours sitting at a chess board (not including analysis, blitz, friendly games etc.) Even to compete in one event is extremely tiring and to play in the Under-8 and Under-9 is likely to leave him (and you) completely shattered by Sunday evening and better prepared for a quick round of hari-kiri than for yet more chess first thing on Monday morning. Of course, if you are travelling from a considerable distance, and Charlie is desperate to play as much chess as humanly possible, it may be appropriate for him to enter more events. You know your own child, and how much he can reasonably be expected to cope with before turning to tears, tantrums or the bottle. Bear in mind also, the other 'friendly' non-championship events (see below) which may give him valuable games and experience without being so fraught with tension and fragile hopes.

Because the Under-10 and Under-11 sections are played at the rate of only one or two games per day, the pace is a little more relaxed, although the games themselves are likely to be comparatively long and demanding. By now some of the players will have several years of tournament experience with established repertoires and a motley entourage of coaches. None of this need faze Charlie, although it is sometimes intended to. The additional time between rounds in these categories will give him time to prepare for his games, a discipline which he needs to acquire in order to compete at this and higher levels. This means not only revising and practicing his own openings, endgames etc. but also studying his opponents' likely moves and strategies. Most games in these sections take place in the mornings, and the pairing for each round will usually be available at the venue during the afternoon or evening before. This allows Charlie to find out who he will be playing the next day and to research the opening, or response to his own opening, which, on past experience, he would expect his opponent to play. Some clues may be given by the daily tournament bulletin, containing a transcript of all the games played in that category. By the last few rounds of the tournament, the bulletins will contain several games by each player, as Black and as White, and can therefore supply important information about his current repertoire. At the beginning of the tournament the bulletin is obviously of less help, although if the opponent has played in another event earlier in the British, you may be able to purchase copies of the relevant issues.

Additionally, if you have access to a computer during the Championships, you may be able to look up Charlie's opponent on ChessBase.[41] This is particularly useful when playing very experienced juniors who may have played at international or other important tournaments whose games are recorded as a matter of course.

Obviously you need to take all this information with a large pinch of salt, particularly older games from ChessBase. Be careful, too, of common or ambiguous names, which may in fact refer to a different player entirely. Juniors are encouraged to change their openings regularly and it can be dangerous to assume that whatever they played last year, or even last month, will be what they will play tomorrow. Even the current week's bulletin is not an infallible guide, especially if the forthcoming game is a significant one, as Charlie's opponent may have a newly-learned opening waiting to be uncovered. The converse is also true, of course, that the opponent will be studying Charlie's games in the bulletin, (and on ChessBase if possible) and will be preparing lines of play based upon what he anticipates that Charlie will do. The whole thing is a complicated game in itself; of bluff and double-bluff, the strategy of which is best left to professional coaches, who seem to enjoy that sort of thing. From Charlie's point of view, if he does not have a coach to advise him, it is probably best to keep things as simple as possible; finding out what he can about what his opponent is likely to play, but concentrating primarily upon his own game and upon facing the next round well-rested, calm and armed with his natural chess abilities and a good dollop of common sense.[42]

This game is taken from the 1996 under 10 section, in which Gawain, eight at the time, came joint first with K Chakraborty from India. He also played in the under 8 section which he won outright.

□ **Gawain Jones** ■ **J.Berlin**
British Under-10 Championship 1996
English Opening

---

1 c4 Nf6 2 Nf3 g6 3 g3 Bg7 4 Bg2 0-0 5 0-0 d6 6 Nc3 c5

---

[41] See Chapter Nine
[42] for more about preparing for games, see Chapter 6

The so-called Symmetrical English. Both sides have developed normally and it is approximately equal.

7 d4

Trying to get a space advantage.

7...Nc6 8 b3

White decides to fianchetto both bishops. A more conventional move here is 8 d5.

8...e5 9 d5 Ne7 10 Bb2 Bf5 11 Nd2 Qd7 12 e4 Bh3

Black offers the exchange of light-squared bishops.

13 Ne2 Bg4?!

A difficult move to explain. Black uses up a couple of moves trying to force a concession but ends up by just giving White more time to start an attack.

14 f3

Forcing the bishop back to h3 as 14...Bh5 15 g4! wins a piece.

14...Bh3 15 Bxh3

It may be better just to leave the bishops there and instead develop with 15 Qc2!? or to start an offensive on the queenside with 15 a3!?.

15...Qxh3 16 Kh1

White wants to play f4 but can't at the moment because of 16 f4 Ng4 when there is no defence to ...Qxh2.

16...Qd7

Black brings his queen straight back, perhaps because he was worried about it getting trapped after g4 at some point by White. However, instead he could have started an attack on the queenside with a move like 16...a6, or challenged on the kingside, e.g. with 16...Ne8 followed by ...f7-f5!?.

17 a3

Starting to give Black worries on both sides on the board.

17...Rac8

Black tries to stop any queenside expansion but instead he should have started his own attack, perhaps with 17...Nh5!? followed by ...f7-f5.

18 f4

Attacking on the other flank!

18...Ng4!

Black defends the pawn on e5 as well as trying to make some threats on his own account.

19 Rf3

With the idea of doubling rooks on the f-file.

19...Bh6?!

Black's bishop is bad here. Better would be 19...exf4, simply swapping off some off the dangerous pieces round Black's king.

20 h3!

Black's pieces start to look very exposed.

20...Nf6 (diagram 27)

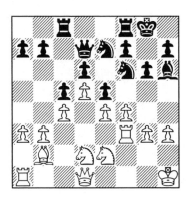

Diagram 27

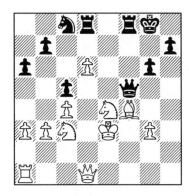

Diagram 28

21 fxe5?

This is a bad mistake, giving all the play to Black. Instead 21 Kg2 or even 21 g4! looks good for White as Black has no way to defend the pawn on e5 and after 21...exf4 22 Bxf6 nets the black knight.

21...Qxh3+

Suddenly Black has all the play.

22 Kg1 dxe5?!

However, this is not the most accurate move. After 22...Ng4! most of Black's pieces would be situated round my king and it would be extremely difficult to defend against all the threats.

23 Rxf6 Be3+ 24 Rf2 Bxf2+

An immediate 24...f5! would be better, still giving Black a slight edge.

25 Kxf2 f5 26 Bxe5?!

Another dodgy move from White, giving the play back to Black! After 26 Qh1! fxe4+ 27 Kg1 White would have fended off Black's attack and have a good position.

26...fxe4+ 27 Ke3?

A mistake, as the g1-square would be much safer for the king.

27...a6?

An odd move as Black needs to keep attacking the king. This delay gives White an extra move to coordinate. Instead 27...Nf5+! 28 Kxe4 Rce8 would have left White's king looking extremely vulnerable in the centre of the board.

28 Nxe4!

White nets another pawn and gives his king an escape route to the queenside.

28...Qf5 29 Bf4 Rce8!

Black is playing the best moves but he is a move down, after having played the unnecessary 27...a6. The pawn on a6 doesn't matter at all in this position.

30 N2c3! Nc8 31 d6?!

Instead 31 Kd3, just playing my king to safety, looks more sensible.

31...Rd8?! (diagram 28)

Black misses 31...g5! which would keep him in the game, as it wins White's dark-squared bishop.

32 Qd5+!

Swapping off the queens wins easily.

32...Qxd5 33 Nxd5 Rf5?! 34 d7! Rff8

After 34...Rxd7 35 Nef6+! would win the rook and after 34...Na7 35 Ne7+! would win the other rook.

35 dxc8Q Rxc8 36 Ne7+ Kf7?! 37 Nxc8

Black resigns, as after 37...Rxc8 38 Nd6+ wins the other rook.

Moving up from the Under-10 and Under-11 sections to the older championships, the skies seem to clear somewhat and the going gets more peaceful. Partly, of course, this is because the players themselves are older and in need of less parental supervision. During the day young teenagers can more or less be left to their own devices at the venue, to play endless games of blitz, consume huge quantities of Coke and, with any luck, remember to turn up to the next round on time. Their fortunate mothers and fathers meanwhile, rather than pacing the corridors and gnashing their teeth with the Under-8 parents, can be stretched out on the beach (or at least cowering under their kagouls) able to be summoned by mobile phone in a really dire emergency (such as the snack bar having run out of cheese & onion crisps). Partly, too, although these are the official British Championships, with titles fervently contested and richly deserved, the entrants do not necessarily include all the strongest players in these age-groups. To some extent this is of course true of all the junior championships, for there are always players who prefer not to compete in the British in a particular year, perhaps because it clashes with another tournament or family holiday or because that year's location is inconvenient. In addition, however, particularly among the older juniors, there may be the opportunity to play in the main British Championship, or they may prefer to play in the Major Open.

The Major Open is not a Championship event, and is therefore open to players who do not fulfil the citizenship or residence requirements for the events discussed above. However, it incorporates the British Under-18 titles, for which these criteria must be met. Other than that, it is open to all players except those who are automatically entitled to play in the British Championship, i.e. grand and international masters and those with very high FIDE ratings. The timetable and rates of play are the same as those for the British Championship, i.e. eleven rounds over twelve days, with a possible maximum length of seven hours per game. For many players, especially quickly improving teenagers, the Major Open acts as a kind of training ground for the main British Championship, while for others, particularly strong amateur players, it is their regular tournament of choice.

When Gawain was eleven, the British Championship was held, conveniently for us, in Scarborough, on the north-east coast of England, and attracted several of the best players in the region, including Gawain's opponent in this Major Open game.

☐ **N.Soloman** ■ **Gawain Jones**
British Major Open 1999
Benko Gambit

---

1 d4 Nf6 2 c4 c5 3 d5 b5

The Benko Gambit. Black sacrifices a pawn on the queenside in order to obtain fast development and open lines.

4 cxb5 a6 5 bxa6 g6

There is no need to take the pawn back immediately as it is not going anywhere.

6 Nc3 Bxa6 7 e4

This is the main line. White gives up castling to get developed.

7...Bxf1 8 Kxf1 d6 9 g3 Bg7 10 Nf3 Nbd7 11 Kg2 Nb6 12 Qc2 0-0 13 Re1 Ra6

Beginning to pressurise the a- and b-pawns.

14 b3 (diagram 29)

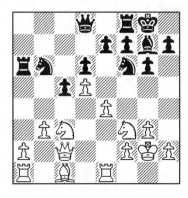

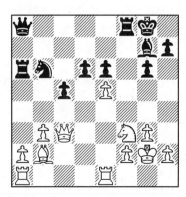

Diagram 29   **Diagram 30**

This is the way White normally plays in this opening, with b3 and a4 to try to blunt Black's queenside play.

14...e6!?

Deciding to open the centre. 14...Qa8 was also possible.

15 dxe6 fxe6 16 e5

White tries to exploit Black's central break.

16...Nfd5!?

Not 16...dxe5? when 17 Nxe5 would give White a very pleasant position.

17 Bb2

Maybe 17 Ne4! would be better.

17...Nxc3!

The problem for White now is that after 18 Bxc3 d5 (or even 18...Qa8) looks good for Black. Black clearly now has enough for the pawn.

18 Qxc3 Qa8! (diagram 30)

White is pinned everywhere; along the a1-h8 diagonal by the bishop on g7 and along the h1-a8 diagonal by the queen on a8.

19 a3?

This leaves White very poorly placed. Instead 19 Qd3 would be the best move when White is threatening to play Qe4 to block the pin on his king, leaving him only slightly worse.

19...Ra7!

Black plans simply to increase the pressure on the knight on f3.

20 Rad1 Raf7!

Now White has no good way to defend the knight on f3.

21 Re3

White tries to defend the knight but now Black wins easily. Instead 21 Rd3 would be better but after 21...Nd7! White has no good defence to ...Nxe5 followed by picking up the knight on f3.

21...Nd5!

Winning an exchange and keeping the pin on the a8-h1 file.

22 Rxd5 exd5!

22...Qxd5 would also be good but this is better, as now White has no defence to ...d4 winning at least the knight.

23 Qd3 d4!

Now, after the rook moves, ...Rxf3! wins the knight, e.g. 24 Re4 Rxf3 25 Qxf3 Rxf3 26 Kxf3 Bxe5 leading into an ending where Black is a queen for a rook up and even the rook will soon drop off.

24 e6!?

White tries to complicate the position but it is hopeless.

24...dxe3 25 exf7+ Rxf7 0-1

White resigns as he has no way to defend the bishop and the knight and after 26 Qxe3 Bxb2, Black will be a piece up.

The Major Open is a demanding event, both in terms of time and of the strength and experience of the entrants. It is not, therefore, a tournament which would generally be appropriate to inexperienced players or to young children, who would probably find it more satisfying to play in their own age-group championship, possibly combined with one of the other non-championship events.

There are generally several of these, including two five-day open tournaments, mainly aimed at adults who can only spend a week at the Championships and so do not have time to enter the Major Open. There are also weekend tournaments, divided into graded sections, and one day rapidplays, usually on the two Sundays of the fortnight, which are particularly popular with juniors. If this were not enough to assuage the enthusiast's thirst for constant chess, there is usually a crammed calendar of additional social events including junior blitz tournaments, a cricket match against local opposition, quizzes and the notorious Crazy Lightning Chess. Your principal difficulty will therefore be not so much finding entertainment for Charlie, but trying to prevent him simply from camping on the floor of the venue and attending absolutely everything. (Camping on the floor of the venue is, by the way, strictly forbidden.) Burning the candle at both ends can be a problem, especially for competitors in the junior events whose games, unlike the British Championship and Major Open, begin early in the morning. Think of it as a heaven-sent opportunity to demonstrate your finely-honed parenting skills of tact, negotiation and bellowing at the top of your voice.

Finally, of course, there is the British Championship itself, the central and major event which lasts for almost the whole fortnight, with eleven full-length rounds, one per day. Entry to this event is restricted to titled players, those with exceptionally high grades or FIDE ratings or those who have won qualifying places in regional, usually weekend, tournaments throughout the preceding year. There are always some junior players in the British Championship, including, generally, one or two very young and photogenic stars upon whom the Press focus their attention, but it takes several years, even for the highly talented, to reach this stage. Although the British rarely attracts the two or three strongest British players, the 'super-grandmasters', it is nonetheless a prestigious and challenging event and the privilege of competing in it is avidly sought by amateur and developing players.

Even if, by some alchemical combination of talent, hard work and luck, Charlie does eventually qualify, he should not expect, on the first few occasions, to play more than one or two games against serious titled opposition. Indeed, he might well have none at all, bobbing about at the bottom of the tournament along with the other flotsam and jetsam of young, struggling and qualified-by-the-skin-of-their-teeth players. So long as he anticipates this, he is likely to have an enjoyable, if exhausting two weeks, and to find his own chess in future games to be undoubtedly, if inexplicably improved. If, however, he believes whatever hype his local paper likes to gloss his entry with, and expects to take the British by storm, defeating all comers, he is likely to receive a rude shock. He may be a very big fish indeed in his small town chess club, but faced with real professional adult players he will soon be diminished to a small and sniffling stickleback.

In this game, played in Gawain's second British Championship, when he was fourteen, he is heavily outrated, confronted with an unfamiliar opening, hustled into time trouble and ultimately defeated, but somehow he manages to enjoy the experience.

□ **A.Wohl** ■ **Gawain Jones**
British Championship 2002
Bird's Opening

1 f4

An unusual opening move, the so-called Bird's Opening.

1...d5

A solid reply, taking the centre.

2 Nf3 Nf6 3 e3 Bg4 4 b3 e6 5 Bb2 Bd6 6 h3 Bxf3 7 Qxf3 Nbd7

Trying to force through ...e6-e5.

8 Nc3 c6

Black cannot play ...e6-e5 yet as the pawn on d5 would be en prise.

9 g4!?

White goes for an attack. If he doesn't then Black will play ...e6-e5 and stand well.

9...h6

Trying to block the pawn storm on the kingside. Instead after 9...e5, 10 g5 forces the knight back to g8, though in fact this is not too bad for Black.

10 h4 h5! 11 g5 Ng4 12 Ne2

White brings back his knight to uncover the bishop's attack down on the g7-pawn.

12...Rg8

Simply defending the pawn though 12...e5!? was also possible. I didn't want to castle kingside however as after 13 Ng3, hitting the h-pawn, White has a big attack.

13 Ng3 g6

The only way to defend the pawn on h5.

14 e4?!

A mistake as he misses a tactic.

14...Qc7!

Now the f-pawn is very weak due to the fact that 15 e5? doesn't work as I have 15...Ndxe5!! 16 fxe5 Bxe5! when both the bishop on b2 and the knight on g3 are attacked. After 17 Bxe5 (any other move loses a piece) 17...Qxe5+ wins the rook on a1.

15 Ne2

This looks like the only move but White also had 15 Bg2!!, the point being that after 15...Bxf4 16 0-0! the pawn on f7 is attacked after 16...Bxg3.

15...dxe4

Perhaps a very slight mistake. Instead 15...e5! was good for Black.

16 Qxe4 0-0-0 17 Bh3 Qa5 18 Qf3 Qf5

Hitting the c-pawn and defending the knight.

19 0-0-0 e5!?

Finally Black gets the central break in. Now it is probably about equal.

20 Rhf1 exf4

Perhaps 20...e4 was better as White now gets a lot of play down the f-file. However, I wanted to be able to defend my knight on g4.

21 Nxf4 Qa5!?

Getting the queen off the dangerous f5-square and hitting the pawn on a2.

22 Kb1 Nh2

Forking the White queen and rook.

23 Qd3

The only move. White hits the bishop so that after 23...Nxf1 24 Qxd6 gives White very good compensation.

23...Qc7! (diagram 31)

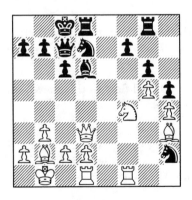

Diagram 31   **Diagram 32**

But this seems extremely good for Black, hitting the knight and still attacking the rook. Surely now White must lose material...?

24 Nxh5!!

A brilliant move leaving both pieces *en prise*. Now if 24...Nxf1 25 Nf6! leaves White with a good position seeing as both my knights and my rook are all attacked.

24...gxh5 25 Rxf7

White has only two pawns for the piece but has a strong attack and a powerful passed pawn on g5.

25...Rgf8

Trying to swap off the dangerous rook.

26 Rxf8! Rxf8 27 g6!

The pawn on g6 is too strong as Black's queen, knight on d7 and bishop are all tied down.

27...Ng4

Desperately bringing that knight back into the game and blocking White's bishop.

28 g7 Rg8 29 Qh7 Qd8

The only move to defend the rook as moving either knight to f6 allows 30 Bxf6 when Black cannot recapture owing to the h3-c8 pin.

30 Rf1!?

Bringing the rook into the game.

30...Kc7?!

Trying to move the king off the dangerous diagonal. However, 30...Qe8 defending the pawn was better, after which Black may still be in the game.

31 Qxh5

White now has three pawns for the piece with two of them being connected and passed. He also has very active pieces.

31...Ngf6?!

Finally bringing the knight back, but there is a tactical flaw in this move. On the other hand, after 31...Nge5 White is still much better.

32 Qf7?!

Missing a tactic that he had at his disposal. Instead 32 Bxf6 (or even 32 Rxf6! which is even better) leads to 32...Nxf6 33 Qa5+! Kb8 34 Qxd8+ Rxd8 35 Rxf6 when White has recovered the piece and is winning easily.

32...Qe7 33 Qxe7 Bxe7 34 Bxd7! Nxd7

Black cannot play 34...Kxd7 as then the knight on f6 would be hanging.

35 h5 (diagram 32) 35...Bg5

The only move to stop h5-h6.

36 Rg1 Bxd2 37 Rg6 Nf8

Desperately trying to give up the knight for the g-pawn.

38 Be5+

White gives an intermezzo check (intermezzo being a move played before the tactic, such as recapturing the knight).

38...Kd7??

A big mistake in time trouble. Instead Black needed to play 38...Kc8 when after 39 gxf8Q+ Rxf8 Black can struggle on although White should win.

39 gxf8N+ Rxf8 40 Rd6+

White wins the bishop and so is winning easily.

40...Kc8 41 Rxd2 Rf5 42 Bd4 c5 43 Bf2 Rxh5 44 b4 1-0

I resigned as after 44 cxb4 Bxa7 I'm a whole piece down and it's only a matter of time before White mops up my remaining pawns. If my opponent had been a weaker player then I might well have played on in this position, but against a stronger player there is no chance of his not being able to convert his advantage into a win and so it would be a waste of time. In addition, it is a breach of chess etiquette (i.e. in ordinary English, rude) to play on in a lost position against a stronger player.

In summary, therefore, the British Championships are undoubtedly a Good Thing, especially for keen juniors comparatively new to chess. If you can manage it, in terms of time, money and patience, it will almost certainly help Charlie considerably to compete in the appropriate championship, take part in the social events, make himself known to local and national organizers and most of all to make friends with other chess-players alarmingly like himself. On the other hand, if you find the idea of a fortnight, or even a week, in this year's cosmopolitan resort completely impossible to contemplate, then please do not spend the rest of your life racked with guilt. There are, believe it or not, several worse things that you can do to your child than deprive them of their annual fix of the British and even the most dedicated chess parents have been known to slope off abroad from time to time for a supposedly chess-free camping holiday (although watch out for those outdoor sets which have a nasty habit of looming up from behind the table football).

In addition to the British, there are other long (i.e. longer than a weekend) tournaments dotted about the calendar and in and around the British Isles. A disturbing number of them seem to take place on islands: Man, Jersey, Guernsey etc, possibly to make it difficult for accompanying parents to escape. Generally these tournaments are held in hotels, off-season, and special accommodation, meal and sometimes travel rates are offered which could, subject to all the caveats above, allow you to combine Charlie's chess with a reasonably priced and pleasant family holiday.

The main English chess event other than the British is the Hastings Chess Championships, a venerable institution enacted in the depths of winter, across the New Year, in the Sussex town which houses the offices of the British Chess Federation and one of the very few chess clubs in the country with its own premises, open daily. The principal tournament at Hastings is the Premier, an all-play-all, restricted to ten selected players, mostly grandmasters. This, like the main British, can be a spectator event if you (or more likely Charlie) are attracted by that sort of thing. Next down the ladder comes the Challengers, a nine round tournament for experienced players. This usually attracts a large number of strong juniors, mostly teenagers whose parents can somehow tolerate a brief separation during the barren post-Christmas wastes. The winner of the Challengers normally qualifies for the following year's Premier and/or for the British Championship. There are also a variety of shorter tournaments which take place over the weekends and New Year week, catering for general tournament players including novices and beginners. One day junior championships, with Under-18 and Under-12 Major and Minor sections are normally held in the town on the final Saturday of the congress.

Gawain has played twice at Hastings; once just after his eighth birthday, in the grandly-titled World Amateur and again as a gargantuan fifteen year old in the Challengers section, now despatching titled opposition.

□ **Gawain Jones** ■ **H.Mas**

Hastings Challengers 2003

Sicilian Defence

---

1 e4 c5 2 Nf3 d6 3 c3 Nf6 4 Be2 Nc6

This move is not the most accurate in the position as it allows White to play d2-d4. Instead moves such as 4...g6 or 4...Bd7!? (the point behind this being that the pawn on e4 is under attack as there is no longer a Qa4+ for White).

5 d4 cxd4

Black still cannot take the pawn on e4 as 5...Nxe4 6 d5! hits the knight away and is followed by Qa4+, picking up the e4-knight.

6 cxd4 Nxe4

Now Black can take the pawn and this is the critical test of White's opening.

7 d5! Qa5+

The only move, as if the c6-knight moves, White still has Qa4+ winning the knight on e4.

8 Nc3!? Nxc3 9 bxc3 Ne5.

Not 9...Qxc3+ as after 10 Bd2 and both the queen and the knight on c6 are attacked.

10 Nxe5 dxe5

The more normal move in this position is 10...Qxc3+ with the idea of picking up the knight without damaging Black's pawn structure.

11 0-0 Bd7

After 11...Qxc3 I would have 12 Bb5+ which is uncomfortable for Black.

12 Rb1!?

Hitting the weakened b-pawn.

12...b6 13 c4

Simply defending the pawn. It is too dangerous for Black to take the pawn on a2 as White gets so much play.

13...Rc8 14 Bb2 f6 15 Bg4!?

15 f4! would also be interesting, giving White a big attack and making it difficult for Black to develop his pieces on the king's wing.

15...Rd8

Defending the bishop. It is too dangerous to play 15...Rxc4 as after 16 Bxd7+ Kxd7, 17 Qd3! followed by Qf5+ leaves Black's king extremely exposed.

16 Bxd7+ Rxd7 17 Qe2 Qc5!

Bringing the queen back into the game and blocking f4.

18 Rfc1 g6 19 Rc3 Bg7 20 Ba3 Qd4 21 Re3!? Bh6!

If 21...0-0 then 22 Re4! Qc3 23 Bb4 wins the black queen.

22 Rh3 Qd2!

The best way to defend the bishop.

23 Qe4 0-0!

A move that looks dangerous though now Black has almost consolidated his extra pawn.

24 Re1!? Bg7 (diagram 33)

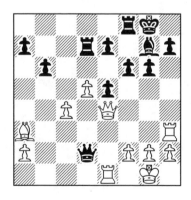

Diagram 33

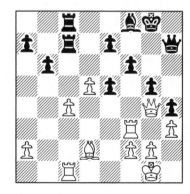

Diagram 34

25 Re2

Chasing the queen away from its good square on d2 and also defending a2.

25...Qd1+ 26 Re1 Qa4

Perhaps 26...Qd2 with a draw would be better as now White still has good compensation for the pawn.

27 Qh4

Starting to eye the weak kingside squares.

27...h5

Defending the pawn though 27...Kf7!? also looked interesting as White cannot take the pawn on h7 in view of ...Rh8 trapping the queen.

28 Qg3!? g5

This badly weakens the light squares. Perhaps better was 28...Kf7 when White still has to prove compensation for the pawn.

29 Qd3

Not 29 Rxh5 as 29...Qxc4 is a good reply.

29...h4

Defending the pawn, though now all Black's pawns are on the same coloured square as his bishop, making it a very bad piece.

30 Qf5!

Now White can slip the queen into the light squares around Black's king. Black can't capture on c4 as the rook on d7 would then be hanging.

30...Rf7 31 Rc1 Rc7 32 Rhc3 Qd7

Black brings his queen back in the hope of swapping queens as then he could try to make his extra pawn tell.

33 Qg6 Rf8 34 h3

Played in order to stop any back-rank tricks Black may have and also to allow Rf3 at some point without ...g5-g4 being a nuisance.

34...Rfc8 35 Rf3!

Bringing the rook to the dangerous f-file with ideas of breaking through with a d5-d6 advance.

35...Qe8 36 Qe4 Qf7 37 Bb4!? Bf8 38 Bd2 Qh7

Black has to move his queen as otherwise Bxg5 wins the pawn. He cannot recapture with the pawn as Rxf7 would leave White well on top.

39 Qg4 (diagram 34) 39...Rd8?!

Missing White's trick though Black's position was difficult as he had to stop the d5-d6 break.

40 Bxg5!?

Sacrificing the bishop to shatter Black's kingside pawns.

40...fxg5?

Losing. Better was 40...Qg6! after which Black can play on.

41 Qe6+! 1-0

Black resigned as there is no way to defend the rook on c7 after 41...Kh8 42 Qxe5+.

If you can bear the idea of stirring from the fireside, jellied fruits and family rendition of 'Auld Lang Syne', then a Hastings tournament may be a good opportunity for Charlie, whatever his level, to combine challenging games with a substantial immersion in the social world of chess. On the plus side, there are an awful lot of pantomimes within an afternoon's drive of Hastings. On the minus side, I mean an awful lot. And if the south coast seems less than enticing at this time of year, spare a thought for the players in the old days, some five or six years ago, when most of the amateur tournaments were held at the end of the pier, stretched out into the English Channel. Now *that* was chilly.

On the other hand, while appreciating the unique atmosphere and attraction of Hastings, you may prefer to leave sacrificial gestures in sub-zero temperatures to Captain Oates and his breed. It is in fact possible to combine your laudable concern to nurture Charlie's chess development with something approaching a normal human being's idea of a holiday, by the simple expedient of going abroad. Continental Europe offers a myriad of chess tournaments at a range of levels and at latitudes appropriate to each of the major skin types. Like the British island events, these are almost invariably held in hotels with reasonable terms and can provide an ideal opportunity to exploit a little of Charlie's talent for your own hedonistic pleasure. (After all those school corridors, you deserve it.) Actually, before your martyred parental alter ego whispers that you aren't here for hedonistic pleasure, and sends you back to the Whipper-Snapper Working Men's Club for another weekend of sweat and lard sandwiches, I might mention that the Euro-option is also rather good for Charlie and his chess. He is likely to be very warmly welcomed, to play in excellent physical conditions, eat seriously good food, make yet more friends among his European peers and, provided the tournament and section are chosen wisely, gain valuable experience and possibly even hard cash. The nature of chess means that language is unlikely to be a serious obstacle and it can be an inspiring sight to see two young players who know nothing of one another's language, analysing a game by gesture alone. However, the shaming ability of most Europeans to speak at least basic English, particularly in Germany and the Benelux countries, means that Charlie may well not even have to go this far. It is, of course, courteous to try to use the host's language for simple greetings and sensible to ensure that Charlie can translate the most basic chess terms – particularly the word for 'draw'. You should also, as always, make sure that he knows the tournament rules and especially time controls, which may be slightly different from those with which he is familiar in England. The list of websites in Chapter Nine will point you towards possible tournaments while recommendations from other parents and players will naturally be invaluable.

One such open tournament, combining serious opposition (the legendary Korchnoi played this year), a picturesque Alpine setting and the opportunity to blow Charlie's potential winnings at the town's casino is held annually in Saint Vincent in the north west of Italy. Gawain played here for the first time this year, at the age of fifteen, and expects it to become a regular fixture on his chess calendar.

□ **Gawain Jones** ■ **J.Van Den Bersselaar**

Saint Vincent Open 2003

Four Knights Game

---

1 e4 e5 2 Nf3 Nc6 3 Nc3 Nf6 4 Bb5 Bc5 5 0-0 0-0 6 d3

Here I missed a chance. Instead, 6 Nxe5! Nxe5 7 d4! (forking the bishop and knight) 7...Bd6 and now 8 f4! when, after the knight moves, White can play 9 e5 forking the bishop and the other knight and obtaining a useful space advantage.

6...d6 7 Bg5 h6

Otherwise White will play 8 Nd5! when the pin would be awkward and lead to a weakening on the black kingside.

8 Bh4 Nd4!

This is a good move – Black's pieces assume strong positions.

9 Nxd4

Taking the dangerous knight.

9...Bxd4 10 Bxf6 Qxf6 11 Nd5

The point of taking the knight. White gains a tempo while attacking the queen and thus giving Black no time to capture the pawn on b2.

11...Qd8

11...Qg5 was interesting but after 12 Nxc7 Bg4 (12...Bh3 13 Qf3!) 13 Qc1! White would successfully fend off Black's attack.

12 c3

Forcing the bishop back.

12...c6!

Leaving the bishop to be taken! If instead 12...Bb6 (12...Bc5 13 b4 Bb6 14 Nxb6) then 13 Nxb6 axb6 14 d4 gives White a slightly better position thanks to the space advantage.

13 cxd4 cxd5!

Another good move! The alternative of taking the bishop would have left Black with weak pawns and White's knight would be well placed on its central outpost. We now have an extremely odd but bizarrely balanced position in which White has the only developed piece – the bishop on b5 – but it is achieving so little that it might as well not be developed at all!

14 dxe5!

14 exd5 Qb6! would highlight the problem with the bishop as after it moves to either c4 or a4, ...Qxd4 would leave Black well placed.

14...dxe5

The alternative capture 14...dxe4 15 dxe4 dxe5 gives White a slight edge.

15 exd5

Anything else would leave Black with a very comfortable position.

15...Qxd5 16 Bc4!

This is the point of taking on d5: bringing the bishop back to a good square on c4 where it attacks the queen. Black has a better pawn structure here but White retains the development advantage and has more active pieces.

16...Qd4 17 Re1!

Ignoring Black's threat to the pawn on b2. If Black takes the bait with 17...Qxb2 then White's development advantage is hugely increased with 18 Rb1 Qd4 (18...Qc3 19 Rb3 Qd4 transposes) 19 Rb5! Re8 and 20 Qh5!

17...Bd7

Black wisely declined to take the 'poisoned pawn'!

18 Qh5?!

The text is very tempting but maybe 18 Re4! would have been better. Play could then go 18...Qxb2 (18...Qd6 19 d4! and 18...Qc5 19 Rc1, threatening Bxf7+ winning the queen, both look good) 19 Rb1 Qc3 (19...Qa3 20 Rxe5 looks good for White) 20 Rxb7! Bc6 21 Rc7!! as after 21...Bxe4 22 Bxf7+! wins Black's Queen.

18...Rae8 19 Re4!?

Time for a real sacrifice, even forcing Black to take the b-pawn.

19...Qxb2 20 Rae1 (diagram 35)

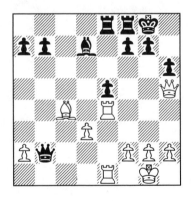

Diagram 35

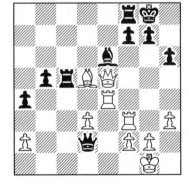

Diagram 36

White is a pawn down but with compensation thanks to the active pieces.

20...b5

An immediate 20...Bc6! might be better since I can't take the e-pawn in view of the fact that after 21...Rxe5 22 Qxe5 (22 Rxe5 allows back rank mate with 22...Qa1, b1 or c1!) 22...Re8!! I cannot play 23 Qxb2 as 23...Rxe1 is mate. If instead 21 Rg4, playing for mate, then 21...e4!! and my position is reduced to ruins after 22 Qxh6 (22 dxe4 Qc3! and I can't defend both bishop and rook) 22...exd3. So I should probably simply offer the exchange of queens with 21 Qe2! after which Black would not be able to defend the extra e-pawn but would still have a slight advantage due to his better pawn structure.

21 Bb3 Qd2

Again, 21...Bc6 was worth considering but now I can play 22 Rg4 safely since 22...e4 doesn't work – White can just take it. Black has no ...Qc3 hitting the bishop and rook and so I have enough compensation for the pawn.

22 R4e3 Qb4 23 h3!

Creating an escape square for the king. If 23 Rxe5?? instead then 23...Qxe1+! mating.

23...a5 24 Re4 Qd2 25 R1e3!

Now that there are no annoying back rank mate threats to deal with, White can bring the other rook into the game.

25...a4!

Moving the bishop from its secure position as well as keeping the pawns advancing ever closer to promotion.

26 Bd5 Rc8!

Black starts his own counterattack.

27 Rf3

Missing 27 Kh2!! which would keep White slightly better. The point is that after Black plays 27...Qxf2 then 28 Rf3!, and he can't defend against the threat to the pawn on f7. 27 Rg3 doesn't work, however, as Black has 27...Rc1+ 28 Kh2 Qxf2 when the threat of ...Qg1 mate is hard to meet.

27...Be6!

Saving the f-pawn and also putting the brakes on the White attack.

28 Qxe5 Rc5! (diagram 36)

Pinning the bishop. Short of time, I now miss the only defence.

29 Rg3??

Trying to go for the attack rather than bothering to defend the bishop. Another possibility, which I might have seen over the board with more time, is 29 Rd4! which keeps White in the game as after 29...Rd8 there is the superb 30 Be4!! and Black can't take the queen owing to 31 Rxd8 mate!

29...g5!

Not 29...g6, when 30 Rxg6+! fxg6 leads to 31 Qxe6! Kh8 (31...Kg7 32 Qe7+ wins and if 31...Kh7 then also 32 Qe7+) 32 Qe5+! Kh7 33 Qe7+ with mate after 33...Kh8 34 Qxf8 Kh7 35 Qg8.

30 Rh4

Trying to keep up an attack as now 30 Rd4 Rd8 31 Be4? doesn't work because the king has g7.

30...Bxd5??

It is Black's turn to blunder in time trouble. The alternative 30...Rxd5! 31 Qf6 Rf5! 32 Qxh6 Qxf2 33 Kh1 (33 Kh2 Qxg3+!) 33...Qe1+ 34 Kh2 Qxg3+! 35 Kxg3 gxh4+ would leave him with a winning ending.

31 Rxh6 f6??

Complete collapse. Better is 31...Qc1+! 32 Kh2 Qh1+!! 33 Kxh1 Bxg2+! 34 Kxg2 Rxe5 and White has only a slight advantage.

32 Qe7!

Threatening mate on h7 as well as the rook and Rg6+ with either Qg7 mate or Qxf8+ to follow.

32...Qc1+ 33 Kh2 Rf7

Stopping the Qh7 mate and Rg6+ threats but allowing a knockout from another direction.

34 Qe8+! 1-0

Black cannot stop mate next move: 34...Kg7 35 Qh8 mate and 34...Rf8 35 Qg6 mate. A very double-edged game!

In the United States there are, of course, a wide range of tournaments for all standards, ages and preferences. If Charlie is himself American then his eventual sights may be set upon the U.S. Chess Championships, in which the nation's strongest players, including a new generation of talented teenagers, compete for the national title. More immediately attainable are the large open tournaments including the World Open, held in Philadelphia in early summer with eight sections ranging from Open to unrated and with alternative schedules of between three and nine days designed to accommodate those with more or less time available.

Other regions hold their own, less ambitiously named championships, such as the New York State Open held in March, with seven sections while the Pan-American Amateur, held enticingly in Bermuda, is restricted to unrated players or those with a rating of under 2000.

Junior, often known as Scholastic, chess is thriving in the United States, encouraged by AF4C with its Classroom Chess Curriculum. There are a wide range of national and regional championships, including the National Scholastic K12 in December, catering for pupils from kindergarten to Grade 12, the National High School, Junior High School and Elementary Championships held each spring and the US Junior Open, with Under-21, 15 and 11 sections.

When Gawain was nine he travelled to the U.S. to play in the US Junior Congress South in Charlotte, South Carolina. As well as enjoying a warm welcome from the organizers, excellent accommodation and playing conditions, he succeeded in obtaining a perfect score in the 9/10 year old section and received a made-to-measure trophy to take home, being of course ineligible for the actual championship title.

□ Gawain Jones ■ T.Raney

US Junior Congress South 1997

English Opening

---

1 c4 e5 2 g3 Nf6 3 Bg2 Nc6 4 Nc3 Bc5 5 Nf3 0-0 6 0-0 d6 7 d3

This is a simple line that I used to play against everything. It is perhaps not the most critical variation but it gives White an easy position to play.

7...Re8 8 Bg5 Rb8?

This is a mistake by Black, who is really forced to play 8...h6 in order to dislodge my bishop.

9 Nd5! (diagram 37)

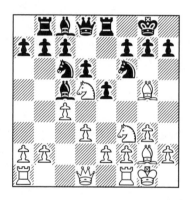

Diagram 37

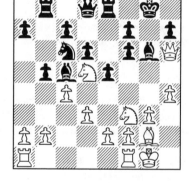

Diagram 38

Now Black has no way to stop White doubling his kingside pawns and thus leaving a perilous hole in front of his king.

9...Bf5 10 Qd2 b5 11 Bxf6! gxf6 12 Qh6

White's kingside attack has developed dangerously. Black tries to get counterplay on the queenside but it is not enough.

12...Bg6 13 h4! (diagram 38)

Now h5 by White is unstoppable within the next two moves, forcing the Black bishop away from its crucial defensive position. One possibility for Black is 13...bxc4! before the inevitable 14 h5. This might in fact be best for Black as after (13...bxc4 14 h5) 14...cxd3 15 hxg6 fxg6 16 exd3 Rxb2 he has three pawns in exchange for the lost piece. Black cannot play 14...Bf5? as then 15 Nxf6+ Kh8 16 Ng5 Qe7 17 Ngxh7 is winning for White. Black now blundered with...

13...Nb4?

...which, after...

14 h5 Nxd5

...allowed...

15 hxg6! fxg6 16 cxd5

... and now White is a piece for a pawn up.

16...Re7 17 Bh3! Qe8 18 Be6+ Kh8 19 Nh4 Rg7 20 Kg2! Rb6 21 Rh1 c6 22 Rh2 cxd5 23 Bxd5 Qf8??

The final blunder but the position was already hopeless for Black with Rah1 next move and an overwhelming offensive on the h-file.

24 Nxg6+! Rxg6 25 Qxh7 mate

Australia's premier event is the Australian Open Chess Championships incorporating Lightning, Rapidplay and a Minor event for players rated under 1600. The Australian Junior Championships, open to citizens and permanent residents of Australia, is held in January. The main sections are Under-18 and Under-12, each with a separate girls' category and the Championships also include lightning and rapidplay tournaments. In New Zealand separate open championships are held for the North and South islands, each including rapidplay events, while the Junior and age group championships take place on a national basis. Eire regularly hosts important tournaments including the Kilkenny Congress and Bunratty Chess Festival while Ulster holds a range of events including the Junior Championship.

Full details of these and other tournaments, both adult and junior throughout the world, are of course available from the national federations. The often precarious nature of chess funding and the inevitable timetabling clashes between events mean that tournament dates, venues and formats often vary greatly from year to year, with old events disappearing and new ones sprouting up in their place. It is therefore very important that you check the up to date situation as early as possible in order not to miss an important tournament or championship.

Alice, who has so far been taking a rest during this chapter, pops up now to point out that, in addition to the events mentioned above, she may also be eligible for a range of women's and girls' tournaments and titles. These include the U.S. Women's Championships and the British Women's Chess Association's Girls' and Women's Rapidplay Championships. Some girls like to play in women-only events while others prefer to concentrate on mixed tournaments. In either case, both you and Alice may find it beneficial, in the overwhelmingly masculine world of competitive chess, to take advantage of the insights and opportunities offered by women's chess organizations.

Finally, as Charlie and Alice progress up the perilous ladder of chess achievement, they may be invited to play in various closed tournaments, i.e. those for which an invitation is necessary. I will deal with these further in Chapter Eight.

Chapter Six

Outposts and Desperadoes[43]:
Playing the Game

'Oh, don't go on like that!' cried the poor Queen, wringing her hands in despair. 'Consider what a great girl you are. Consider what a long way you've come today. Consider what o'clock it is. Consider anything, only don't cry!'

Chess is a remorseless business. However carefully you help Alice to choose her tournament, provide her with the right pieces, board, clock, books, software and all the rest of the miscellaneous paraphernalia, ferry her dutifully into the middle of nowhere and back again, the game itself is what matters, and the game itself is Alice's own domain. If and when she loses, or, almost as bad, draws a game which she expected to win, she will have no one to blame but herself, no convenient team-mates, weather conditions or biased referees. That is not to say, of course, that it is unknown for chess players to blame external factors for their disappointments: impending colds, opponents' tapping feet, chlorine-scented playing halls or unreasonable time controls. From time to time one or more of these factors may indeed be partially relevant. Nothing, however, not even the wildest paranoia of colour-coded yoghurts[44] can take away the players' own fundamental responsibility for what happens across the board.

That is one side of it. The other is that, as the constantly quoted statistic records, there are probably more different possible chess games than electrons in the universe, and after only three moves more than nine million different positions can be reached. Faced with this enormity, there is inevitably a huge part to be played by chance in any but the most sterile game and certainly in encounters between relative beginners. To hear chess players in their post-game analysis, you might imagine that every move was made only after a comprehensive consideration of the position and in full and accurate apprehension of the moves that would fol-

---

[43] An outpost is a valuable square, while a desperado is a move made by a doomed piece, used to create as much mayhem as possible before its inevitable demise. The connections of both with the Wild West are not altogether coincidental, as anyone who has witnessed a two-minute blitz game can testify.

[44] for the significance of yoghurt in the development of world chess see *The Even More Complete Chess Addict*, referred to in Chapter Nine.

low. In fact, however, players often miscalculate, misunderstand or simply blunder. Faced with a near-perfect opponent, e.g. a strong computer program, these mistakes would of course lead to inevitable defeat. However, where the other player is equally fallible, they can often serve only to randomise the position. It has been said that the winner in a chess game is not necessarily she who makes fewer mistakes, but she who avoids making the final one and this is particularly true of encounters between young juniors.

The closest parallel experience for most of us to a serious chess game, especially in a long-play format, is probably the sitting of a formal exam, something like the ancient O level. Much, maybe most, as our teachers and parents reminded us, depended upon our own conscientious preparation during the course and revision period, our physical and mental readiness and proper reading of the exam paper. On the day itself, however, more than they would care to admit hinged upon chance; whether the passage chosen for close analysis was one that we had glanced at casually the night before, whether the Corn Laws came up that year, which bit of the periodic table happened to lodge itself in a corner of our brains. Once in the examination, as in the playing hall, it is too late to rush back to the text-books, to snatch a few hours' sleep or to trawl the teacher's experience for last minute advice.

So, how can you best arm Alice with the weapons she needs for her epic encounter, and try to ensure, so far as possible, that the odds are at least not stacked against her?

As in an exam, the first requirement is long-term preparation. Obviously, if this is her first tournament as a novice, she will have very little idea of opening theory, book lines, defences and gambits. Soon, however, she will need to start building up her own basic repertoire of at least one or two openings played as White, and defences when she is Black. If she has a regular chess coach, he or she will help Alice to choose the openings which best suit her style and stage of development, and to anticipate and answer the most likely moves of her opponent. Otherwise, the basic opening books referred to in Chapter Nine will help her to select and develop her principal openings. Having decided upon these, friendly games against family and friends, and particularly against an appropriate computer opponent, will give her opportunities to identify holes in her preparation to be plugged before the forthcoming tournament. Some players like to keep new openings under wraps before an important event, bringing them out as a surprise weapon. While this is probably not appropriate in the early stages of Alice's development, and later only with the advice of a reliable coach, it is common sense to dissuade her from demonstrating her entire repertoire in friendly games against potentially serious opponents.

As well as openings, Alice will also, of course, want to spend some time studying the main strategic and tactical ideas of the middle game and, very importantly, endgames; positions reached in the final stages when there are only a few pieces and pawns on the board. There are definite techniques for these positions; certain principles and sequences of moves which can ensure or avoid the queening of a pawn or final checkmate. It is important for Alice to know these techniques so that she need not waste valuable time trying to calculate them from scratch over the board, with her clock ticking away beside her. Similarly, she will need to be able to recognize a drawn position, to distinguish between one that is inevitable and one that still has winning chances for one or other player, and to act appropriately upon this understanding. Again, she can learn these from books and videos, with or without the assistance of a coach, and can practise upon her computer, parents, gerbil and anything else that stays still for long enough to have a pawn pushed in its direction.

Chess preparation is time-consuming, particularly if Alice reaches higher levels, and although computers can make it quicker and more fun, it can still assume the dimensions of a major chore, along with homework, bedroom tidying and thank you letters. The last thing you want, unless you are seriously twisted, is yet another thing you have to nag her about. Yet if you don't, and she loses a longed-for championship, are you not somehow to blame?

 On the whole, probably not. It was, after all, her decision to start playing chess in the first place[45] and her choice as to how seriously she wants to take the game. She is either too young to be doing any serious opening preparation at all (in which case it is probably up to you to be available for gentle practice games) or old enough to take responsibility for it by herself. What you can do is ensure that she has the necessary space, peace and resources (see Chapter Nine) and, where possible, the time, to do the job properly. The time factor may mean that your other standards have to slip. Ask yourself how untidy her room really has to be before it constitutes a major environmental hazard. If you can't stand the sight of it below that threshold then maybe you could close the door, or even tidy it yourself while she is away at a tournament. It would at least take your mind off worrying about how she is getting on. Similarly, how many of her great-aunts would mind, or even know, if you wrote the thank you letters yourself? Homework is a slightly trickier problem as many junior chess players attend intensely academic schools where piles of the stuff is heaped upon them, not to mention music practice. Fewer chess players, unfortunately, take part in other, more physical sports, but if Alice does then you are unlikely to want to dissuade her. There are, however, twenty-four hours in a day, and probably one or two currently devoted to expendable activities; television, Playstation, squabbling with siblings or sleep. Again, if Alice really wants to play chess then she will find time, with your co-operation (and maybe, occasionally, the quietest murmur of reminder), if not, then it is best to find it out now, before your whole lives are turned upside down.

If Alice moves up into serious tournaments, where the games are played at the rate of only one per day, she will need to carry out a different and more immediate kind of opening preparation, one geared to her particular opponents in that event. Where the tournament is closed, or very small, and the list of entrants known in advance, she may be able to do some of this work at home before she leaves, but most will be carried out at the event, usually during the morning before an afternoon game, after the draw or pairing list has been published.

---

[45] At least, I sincerely hope that it was. Any crazed lunatic who is actually trying to force a reluctant child to play competitive chess against her own inclinations might be best advised to turn his or her energies to something easier and more condusive to family harmony, like testing weapons of mass destruction over the breakfast table.

As we discussed briefly in Chapter Five, the publication of tournament bulletins and the existence of the ChessBase database allows Alice to investigate her opponent's playing history. In particular, she will be looking to find out what openings the other player most commonly employs and what defence she is likely to offer to Alice's own preferred opening. The tournament bulletin will obviously contain the most up-to-date, albeit limited, picture, while the database can also provide useful statistics such as the player's relative success as Black and as White, percentage of drawn games and a summary of the openings used, even if long abandoned, during the player's entire career.

This kind of pre-game analysis is essential to really high level, professional and international chess, but is dangerous ground upon which to venture without an experienced guiding coach. It is all too easy to get bogged down in the intricacies of a database, to waste valuable time and emotional energy in the frustrating business of trying to persuade a laptop to do what you want it to and to spend hours preparing a brilliant refutation of a line which the opponent jettisoned three years ago, or one played only by her indistinguishable namesake or second cousin. Be especially careful with Eastern European and Asian names, as characters from the Cyrillic and other alphabets are not always transcribed as the same letter (witness the early confusion over whether the rising star of the 1980s was in fact Gary, Garry or Harry Kasparov.)

Note also that however comprehensive your database, it will not include all of the opponents' games and that, at any moment, a hitherto untried line may be brought out from under its wraps.

Without professional help, therefore, it is unwise to attempt too much in the way of prediction or second-guessing the other player's plans. A quick but careful perusal of the tournament bulletin and straightforward check of ChessBase, if you have it, should give Alice a basic overview of what she is likely to face. Whether or not these details are available (and an absence from ChessBase can be a positive sign, suggesting that the player is relatively inexperienced), the bulk of her pre-game preparation will usually be a simple and commonsense revision of her own openings and defences.

From time to time an opponent will play something completely new, unrelated to her previous history, intending it as a secret weapon against Alice's preparation. No matter how unexpected this new line, with calm confidence and her natural talent for the game, Alice will usually be able to work out a playable, if not necessarily the best response. The unexpected, apparently unnatural move may be a brilliant one, but is more likely to be fundamentally unsound, a psychological attempt to wrong foot Alice's careful preparation and to plunge her into despair. If she considers the position rationally, using her general positional principles and tactical awareness, she has a good chance of discovering the flaw in her opponent's strategy, or the temptation or trap into which she is intended to fall. By thwarting her opponent here, Alice puts herself into a stronger psychological position and in fact increases the likelihood of her eventual victory. If she panics, on the other hand, as her opponent hopes that she will, the game may begin to slip from her grasp, and it will be a struggle to wrest it back again. Remember, though, that many players attack best from the back foot and that the game isn't over until the fat lady signs the scoresheet.

Finally, don't encourage Alice to overdo her preparation. Probably more games are lost in these events through rigid over-preparation, inflexibility and consequent desperation than through insufficient work beforehand. In particular, don't panic if you have lost the bulletins, blown up your computer and overslept to within five minutes of the game's commencement. It is far more important for Alice to be refreshed and relaxed than to have a meticulous evisceration of her opponent's repertoire.

Unfortunately, sleep and chess tournaments do not always combine to perfection, especially when you live a long way from the venue and when playing in junior sections, when more games are scheduled for the morning. It is no coincidence that, in events such as the British Championships, the higher level tournaments take place in the afternoons, allowing hard-working or high-living grandmasters to have a lie-in and leisurely breakfast.

Travelling the night before may help, subject to accommodation and travel difficulties, although you may be reluctant to spend even more time away from home. The alternative may be a very early start, particularly if you haven't been to the venue before. Frantic meanderings in and out of an unfamiliar one-way system three minutes before the first round are not guaranteed to create an appropriately calm and confident attitude on either Alice's part or your own. Whichever you decide, do not be surprised if Alice has difficulty in sleeping the night before an important tournament (or, for that matter, if you yourself do). There is of course little you can do to help (high dosages of sleeping pills not being advisable for the maintenance of her concentration next day) other than to make sure that both she and you have built up a reasonable surplus of sleep over the previous week or so, and to reassure her that, provided she is resting and relaxed, actual sleep isn't all that important. (I have no idea whether this is in fact the case, but it is what my mother told me, and I have always found it a source of comfort on these occasions.) Finally, unless you live on the outer rim of the Hebrides, your own travel difficulties may be put into perspective by a reading of Bill and Michael Adams' experiences with the Cornwall to London sleeper.[46] Since Michael Adams is now among the top ten players in the world, the long-term effects are presumably not invariably catastrophic.

Similarly, if you make a few tentative efforts to ensure that Alice has a reasonably healthy diet during the weeks leading to an important tournament, you need not be wracked by guilt and consternation when she doesn't feel like any breakfast before the actual game. Like any other endurance activity, a long chess game, or series of games, can be made easier by the right food, preferably a meal that releases a steady flow of energy, rather than a quick rush followed by a plunge into lethargy. However, shortcomings in the pre-match snack department can be made up by a judicious application of nutrients during the game, as we shall see shortly.

Confidence is always a tricky issue, and it is virtually inevitable that Alice will have the odd catastrophe when she slips down one side of the fence or other. Nerves may be a problem, particularly in the early rounds of an important com-

---

[46] *Development of a Grandmaster*, see Chapter Nine

petition, although the whole experience is unlikely to be as terrifying for Alice as it would be for you or I. However, there will be occasions, perhaps when moving up to a new section or level of tournament, where she feels herself to be out-classed by the opposition and is consequently unable to do herself justice.

The opposite temptation is probably more of a danger to many talented juniors who, after a successful run of games, feel themselves to be invincible. This may happen particularly where Alice, having been playing for a year or two, enters a tournament in which she is the highest rated player, and confidently expects to win it easily. Fortunately for the moralists, less so for Alice herself, pride in chess really does tend to go before a fall, and a nasty one at that. The experience is un-pleasant for Alice and for you, and this really is the dangerous time to be eaves-dropping on the conversations over your shoulder. There is, however, not much that you can do to avoid it, other than the gentlest of hints that chess is, after all, a funny old game and that it might not be wise to take anything for granted. (You could, of course, try carrying out a complete demolition job on your child's character before every tournament, reminding her that she is a mere worm in the compost heap of creation and that she would be lucky to defeat a small and aca-demically challenged stick insect, never mind a hall full of over-educated eleven year olds. On the other hand, if you prefer not to incur a lifetime of self-loathing and therapy bills, then you may have to accept that this is a lesson she must learn for herself, and make sure you are there to pick up the pieces.[47])

So, having followed the advice so far, you are happily approaching the tourna-ment venue, in plenty of time, accompanied by your happy daughter, glowing after her twelve hours' sleep and perfectly balanced breakfast of fruit and whole-grains. She is calmly expounding to you the fine details of the Najdorf Variation with the occasional interjection recalling that this is, after all, only her first proper tournament, and that she will be quite content to be defeated in every round, provided that she manages to play a decent game and learn from the ex-perience. She and you will then be appointed jointly to the chair of the United Nations, given until lunchtime to end world poverty and canonized on the spot in a bolt of specially modified lightning.

Or, in real life, you are driving past the same scrap heap for the seventh time, swearing terrible vengeance upon the Institute of Town Planners, the British Chess Federation and Great-Uncle Paul who bought the bloody chess set in the first place, counting the seconds until she will lose the first game on default. Next to you sits a tearful but belligerent small person, alternately whingeing that she doesn't know what to play against d4 and making elaborate plans as to which computer games she will buy with the first prize money she obviously considers to be hers by right. You try to remind yourself that she has only had half an hour's sleep, immediately before you dragged her into the car at 4am to set off down the M1. The car is littered with the wrappers of the Mars Bars which have

---

[47] metaphorically speaking, of course; the retrieval of knights flung across your hotel room not being within your job description, and knights flung across the tournament hall signalling, almost certainly, the immediate and abrupt cessation of Alice's chess career.

been her only source of sustenance for the past three weeks, a fair number of which are now steaming in a regurgitated heap in the last emergency layby.

In either case, now what happens?

Ideally (and I know how hollow that word sounds, echoing across the stationary lanes of the M25), you should aim to arrive at the venue around a quarter to half an hour before the first round starts. Alice will, of course, have committed all the round times, time controls and all other essential information to memory beforehand, or at least you will try not to lose the retained portion of the entry form which contains these details. Once at the venue you can check the location of the essentials: the playing hall, toilets, refreshment areas and analysis room. The draw for the first round may already be up, if not, it should appear shortly and she will be able to find out who she is playing in the first round, whether she is Black or White, and which board they will be playing on. Boards are numbered sequentially from 1, being the top board, through 2 the second, etc. Sometimes in a tournament of several sections one sequence of numbers is used for the entire tournament, so that there is only one Board 1, the top board in the top section. Elsewhere each section may have its own numbering so that there is a Board 1 in the Open section, Board 1 in the Major etc. If this is the case then you will have to check not only that Alice is at the correctly numbered board but also that she is in the right section. It is generally worth while finding the board straightaway, even if she doesn't want to sit at it immediately, as, particularly in unusual venues, the numbering can be confusing. If you cannot find the correct board then do not hesitate to ask. Sometimes, where there is no one playing hall large enough, the games may take place in smaller rooms, and you may have to walk some distance to a different part of the building or complex.

Shortly before the round is due to begin, Alice should sit down at her board, in front of the correctly coloured pieces and make herself comfortable. In an American tournament she may need to provide her own board, pieces and clock, and discuss with her opponent which set of equipment will be used. In default of agreement otherwise, Black's is usually used provided that it is of a standard type. There will often be a scoresheet next to the board; if not then she may need to collect one from the front of the room or use her own, brought from home. There may also be a separate results slip to be handed in at the end of the game. She will need a pen to complete the scoresheet and preferably a spare in case it runs out. Occasionally pens are given away by tournament sponsors but you should never rely upon this. An ordinary ball point pen is usually best, as there is often a carbon copy scoresheet attached to the top one and anything that writes too lightly may not show through. Generally, in this case, the top copy of the scoresheet is to be handed in and the carbon kept by the player.

While she waits for the round to start she can begin filling in her scoresheet, with the date, round number, her own name and that of her opponent. If the opponent's name is difficult, Alice is young enough to get away with it and you are not on hand to sprint back to the draw to check the spelling, then she can wait for the other player to arrive and then ask him to write his own name on her scoresheet. The scoresheet should then be placed conveniently somewhere in the vicinity of Alice's elbow (right, if she is right-handed, left ditto), near enough to be completed easily, and visible to her opponent but not so near as to impede her in moving the pieces. If she has a drink or snack, these too can be placed near the board if there is enough space. Unfortunately, especially in the lower sections of weekend tournaments, the boards are often placed so closely together that there is no room even to place a scoresheet between one pair of players and their neighbours. In this case the scoresheet may have to be tucked sideways into the gap between the player and her own pieces and turned around to be filled in after every move.

It is also wise, in view of this possibility, to provide Alice with a drink in a small screw-top or sports drink bottle, something with a secure top and small footprint, rather than a can or glass. Most young juniors drink water or a soft drink during the game and it is a good idea for Alice to have something like this with her at the beginning of the round, especially during summer games, when playing halls can get very hot. Older players may prefer a hot drink, and coffee and tea are usually on sale at most tournaments. If there is little space at the board, or if, as is often the case, Alice's mental dexterity is not matched by its physical counter-part, it may be a good idea to avoid taking these back to the board. Pouring lukewarm coffee over a tricky middlegame position is not guaranteed to elucidate its mysteries.

In a rapidplay tournament Alice will normally be able to get enough to eat be-tween rounds, although if there is little time and long queues, it may be advis-able for you to buy her a sandwich while she is still playing, to be eaten immedi-ately after the game. In longer play formats, however, she may need something while the game is still going on, especially if it is a long one and her energy is flagging. There is generally no prohibition against eating at the board within reasonable common sense limits. Obviously, it would be discourteous as well as contrary to the rules to do anything that might distract her opponent, so avoid excessively noisy food (crisps, crunchy apples etc.) and anything smelly or requir-ing large amounts of cutlery. Soft fruit such as grapes, conventional sandwiches, sweets and chocolate should all be fine at the board (subject to any particular rules of the individual tournament) while other, more anti-social foods can be eaten away from the playing area, provided that Alice has sufficient time to spare. Precisely what she should eat is up to you and she to negotiate but you should bear in mind that a serious game of chess is in fact much harder work than it looks, and that a quick fix of energy in the endgame can do wonders for a flagging concentration.

Normally, especially in a junior tournament, Alice's opponent will join her at the board shortly before the first round is due to start. They will greet each other politely (chess being a civilized sort of game) and, if necessary, help each other with the spelling of their names on the scoresheets.

At the beginning of the first round the tournament director or chief arbiter will usually say a few words of welcome to the players, often reminding them of the time controls and round times and pointing out the location of toilets, refresh-ments and the analysis room. This little speech is generally concluded by the immortal words;

'Start White's clock on all boards please.'

By now you have probably seen a chess clock; but in case you have managed to avoid it, I should explain. A traditional chess clock is a smallish box comprising two clock faces with a button on the top of each. When the button on top of one clock face is pressed fully, the other clock starts going and when both are slightly depressed then neither clock does anything. (The metaphorical implications of this are no doubt profound, and should occupy you in philosophical contemplation for at least a rapidplay round or two.) The clock is placed along one side of the board so that each player can easily see her own clock face (the one nearest to her pieces) and reach the corresponding button. Usually it is placed at the Black player's right hand side, or in a position which allows the director and arbiters easily to see all the tournament clocks. Each player moves while her own clock is ticking and, immediately after she has made her move, and using the same hand, presses the button above her clock to stop it, and to start her opponent's clock. The effect of this is that each player's allotted time is used only for her own moves. Obviously she will use her opponent's time as well to think about the game, but, without knowing exactly what move the other player will make, this time is less critical and more relaxed. Hanging above the number 12 on each clock face is a little piece of red plastic, known as the 'flag'. As the long clock hand passes the number 11, it lifts the flag up on its point, where it remains for the final five minutes, before swinging down again as the hand reaches 12. This is known as the 'fall' of the flag, and, at the end of a time control, signals the point at which a player's time has run out and she has therefore lost the game on time.

Before each round the clocks are set by the tournament organizers to show the time available until the first control. In a rapidplay game this is straightforward; for a thirty minute game the long hands are set to 6, for a blitz five-minute game they are set at 11. If the game has not finished, by a win or draw, beforehand, the player whose flag falls first has lost the game on time. There is no particular significance, so far as results, grades etc. are concerned, in a loss on time, which is treated in exactly the same way as any other kind of loss, by checkmate or resignation. However, some players feel less humiliated by this than by other forms of defeat. 'I only lost on time.' you will overhear, with the clear implication that, had the game been played at a more civilised pace, the outcome would undoubtedly have been reversed. There are, of course, instances, particularly in rapidplay, and even more so in blitz, when a player does indeed lose on time despite being in a clearly winning position[48]. However, it is generally more often the case that the player who wins on time was likely to win in any case and that it was the hopelessness of her opponent's position which led her to expend those desperate final seconds.

In a longer game there will probably be a more complex time control which involves the players in more than simply pressing their own clock buttons. There will usually be a time allotted for a certain number of moves, possibly a further time limit for another number, with a final allocation for the remaining moves of the game. For example, the time control in the 2002 British Championship and

---

[48] See Gawain's game against International Master Malcolm Pein, discussed in Chapter Nine.

Major Open was 40 moves in two hours, followed by 20 moves in one hour, and finally all the remaining moves in 30 minutes. For this time control the long clock hands will be set at the o'clock position for the first two hour control. The first time that the flag falls for both players will not have any particular significance, showing only that the first hour has passed. However, if a player's flag falls for the second time without her having made her 40th move, then she will have lost on time. Once this happens, the state of the second player's clock is irrelevant; it is no defence to a loss on time to argue that your opponent would similarly not have had sufficient time to complete the necessary number of moves. Even if there are only seconds, or less, between the two clocks, so that both flags are hanging precariously, the first flag to fall is all that counts, provided that the victor notices in time, and stops her own clock to signal the end of the game. This is done by pressing the button halfway only, so that both clocks stop ticking. The loser is under no obligation to point out that her own flag has fallen and players should therefore be keeping an eye on both clocks.

If both flags fall before either player points this out, and stops the clocks, then, if traditional analogue clocks are being used, the game is automatically drawn. In the case of digital clocks, however, it may be possible for the arbiter to determine whose time expired first and thereby to award a win to the other player.

The only time at which a player does not actually lose if her flag falls at the end of a time control is when her opponent does not have 'mating material' on the board. This has nothing to do with anything that might be available from vending machines in the Gents, but refers to the combination of pieces still active and their theoretical ability to deliver checkmate. A pawn, however solitary, threatened or impotent is always 'mating material' as is a queen or a rook. A 'bare king' i.e. a king with no supporting pieces of the same colour can obviously not deliver checkmate alone, and, for the purposes of this rule, neither can a king supported only by a single bishop or knight. In such a position, where a player 'loses' on time without her opponent having mating material then the game is deemed to be a draw.

If this situation arises, particularly where one or both players are comparatively young or inexperienced, it is always wise to stop both clocks and seek advice or confirmation from an arbiter. Certainly, if there is any dispute between the players as to the position, an arbiter's ruling should be sought immediately. Occasionally a position will arise which is difficult to assess, such as where the player claiming a win has only a pair of knights. In such an instance a senior arbiter or the tournament director may be called upon to give a definitive verdict. In most tournaments such a ruling is conclusive but in some instances an expert committee may form a court of final appeal.

Assuming, however, that both players have succeeded in making sufficient moves within the initial time limit, the clocks are adjusted after Black's final move. This involves the long hand on each clock face being turned back by the period of the second time control. In fact, in the example given above, of the British Championship time control, there is no need for the clocks actually to be adjusted after the fortieth move, as the second control is a complete hour. Time unused from the first time control is therefore available for the next part of the game. Both clocks are normally turned back by the same player, usually the older or more experienced, who shows the faces to her opponent to check that she has carried out the operation fairly. If neither feels sufficiently confident to turn back the clocks, then they can ask an arbiter to do it instead. Finally, the same thing happens for the third time control, in this case after Black's 60th move, when the clocks are turned back by half an hour.

A further rule relating to the time control provides that, where a player has less than two minutes on her clock she may, subject to the decision of the arbiter or Tournament Director, claim a draw if her opponent is making no effort to 'win by normal means'. This refers neither to the opponent's kicking her shins under the table nor to his bribing his big brother to glower at her, but only to his making moves with no discernable strategic or tactical purpose, merely with the intention of gaining a victory on time. This rule operates only in full-length games using the (confusingly-named) 'Quick Finish' rules and certainly not in rapidplay or blitz chess. It is therefore really vital to check at the beginning of each event exactly which rules are in force. The regulations governing the particular tournament will be displayed on the wall and may also have been previously published in the tournament programme.

Traditional chess clocks are operated by clockwork and so require winding from time to time. Usually they will have been checked before the tournament but occasionally problems can arise; one or both clocks failing to go or continuing after the button has been pressed. If this happens, or if there is any other difficulty, the players should stop both clocks if possible and raise their hands to signal that an arbiter is needed. Generally speaking, however, although it can be daunting to use a clock for the first time, juniors quickly get the hang of their operation and even resist the temptation to bang them too severely.

In the past few years an alternative to the mechanical clock has been developed in the form of a digital clock with a numerical display in place of the old clock face. This is now used in many high level tournaments although the cost of replacing the old clocks means that it has not generally filtered down to weekend and junior tournaments. One particular advantage of the digital clock, other than that of knowing exactly how many seconds you have to make a move and having an audible signal in place of the falling flag, is that it allows more sophisticated time controls to be used. One of these, known as the 'Fischer mode' adds several seconds to the player's remaining time after each move, so that, at least theoretically, provided she plays quickly enough she may never in fact run out of time.

Some of the rules relating to time controls have evolved in response to the advanced capabilities of the digital clock (e.g. the position discussed above, where both 'flags' have fallen). Again, therefore, it is advisable to check the precise rules that are being used for that tournament.

Despite the director's command, it is not polite for Black immediately to press the clock for White's first move, unless White has not yet arrived at the board. Instead, they begin by shaking hands and only then does Black start the clock. This shaking of hands can appear quaintly anachronistic on first sight, especially between two six year old girls, but it is an essential courtesy, carried out before every game from novice to world championship level. Where one player arrives late, with her clock already ticking, it is still customary to take a second or two for a brief handshake before moving.

The game proper now begins, with White making the first move and writing it down on her scoresheet. It is vital in all long play and most junior tournament games that both players record their own moves and those of their opponents. In rapidplay tournaments this is not normally required, although many players like to record at least the opening moves, for future reference.

Two forms of chess notation exist in British chess, known as descriptive and algebraic. If you have any old chess books in the house, or even a copy of *Alice Through the Looking Glass* then you will probably have come across descriptive notation. This system assigns a name to each piece and pawn, based upon their opening position, e.g. Queen's Knight or King's Rook's Pawn. The squares of the board are similarly named by reference to the pieces' starting positions, e.g. King Four, Queen's Bishop Six. This system requires that each square in fact has two names, one from White's side of the board and one from Black's. Generations of British chess players have mastered the code, but then British chess players are renowned for exciting code-breaking activities, although not necessarily involving trench coats and Kate Winslett. As far as you and I are concerned, descriptive notation is just one enigma too far.

You will be relieved to hear, therefore, that there is no urgent reason for Alice, or indeed you, to know anything more about descriptive notation. Sooner or later, after a bout of generosity or ruthless spring-cleaning, she may be given a pile of antiquarian chess books, most of which will be worse than useless, but may contain old but still inspiring titles such as Nimzowitsch's *My System*, using descriptive notation. If and when this happens, she will no doubt teach herself the arcane mysteries within about three minutes, like those breathtaking autodidacts who, assailed by a sudden urge to read the *Iliad*, master ancient Greek from scratch within five days. But as far as you yourself are concerned, it can safely remain a perpetual conundrum.

For now, however, all even Alice need worry about is algebraic notation, which, you will be extremely relieved to hear, has nothing whatsoever to do with simultaneous equations or the value of $4x^2$. Under this system each square has a constant name, no matter which player, piece or pawn is moving. This naming is carried out from White's side of the board, with the squares being designated horizontally from left to right as a to h and vertically from White towards Black as 1 to 8. The square upon which White's queen begins the game is therefore d1 and Black's king e8. Pieces are represented by capital letters: K (king), Q (queen), R (rook – again, try to remember not to call it a castle), B (bishop) and N (night, that is knight, the K having already been appropriated by a higher authority). Pawns are referred to by the column which they currently occupy, not necessarily that upon which they began the game (they capture diagonally, remember).

There are two basic forms of algebraic notation, long and short. In long notation the square from which the piece moves and the square to which it moves are both recorded, i.e. Bc1-d2 or, for a pawn move, f7-f5. In short notation only the second square is noted, i.e. Bd2 or f5. In some cases this will not give sufficient information, where there is more than one of the same type of piece which could move to the target square and so an additional letter or number needs to be added, e.g. R6d4 or Nbc5. (You are beginning to think now that simultaneous equations weren't so bad after all.) Players recording their games can use either the long or short forms, whichever they find easier, although most chess books, articles etc. only use the short.

Most introductory books and videos explain the algebraic system fully and so Alice should, by the time she plays in her first tournament, be familiar and comfortable with the system. It may, however, be worth her while practicing writing down her moves, so that it becomes second nature and doesn't distract her from the game itself. You should note, particularly if she is very young or has handwriting difficulties, that the spaces allotted to each move on commercial scoresheets are very small. If this is likely to cause her difficulties then you may be able to get hold of a few to practice on beforehand, either from your local club or from a chess supplier. In rapidplay and many junior and weekend tournaments there is no official scoresheet which has to be used and so, if she finds it difficult to reduce the size of her handwriting sufficiently to use ordinary sheets, you could try producing your own, larger format scoresheets for her to use. Introducing contrasting background colours for the White and Black columns is an additional help, particularly as many new players, inadvertently missing out a move, then transpose subsequent moves into the wrong columns. As time goes on, the size of these special scoresheets can be progressively reduced until they are equivalent to the commercial ones. You may well find, however, that importance of recording her games has a more swift and salutary effect upon her handwriting than months of workbooks, ergonomic pens and agonized parent-teacher interviews.

From the tournament organizers' point of view there are two principal reasons why moves should be recorded, apart from the value of preserving them for posterity, or at least for the tournament bulletin. The first, and usually most important is so that there is a clear record of how many moves have been played. This is obviously essential where a time control occurs after a certain number of moves. Many players circle this move number on their scoresheets at the beginning of the round, to remind themselves of its importance. (For this reason, it is vital that, if a mistake is made on the scoresheet, it is corrected in the margin and not in the space below.) Secondly, it may, in certain circumstances, be necessary for an arbiter to be able to recreate the moves of the game. This most often occurs where a draw is claimed based upon the repetition of a position but can happen in other situations, including where (purely hypothetically of course) a player ignores her parents' repeated warnings about swinging on two legs of a chair, topples over and sends the board and pieces crashing to the floor. I have never actually seen this happen, but find it impossible to believe that it hasn't.

Alice should write down her opponent's move as soon as he has made it and pressed his clock. It may be tempting to play her reply first but, unless she is in severe time trouble[49] this is likely to be counter-productive. Once a move is inad-

---

[49] Generally, during the last five minutes of a time control, a player may, if she does not have enough time to write down her moves in full, record them by means of a tick in the appropriate space showing how many moves have been made. If this is the case

vertently missed out, she will not know accurately how many moves have been played and therefore how she must apportion her remaining time. A missed move may also prevent the game from being properly recreated and preclude her from making claims for a win on time or draw by repetition. When precisely she should write down her own move is a matter of preference. Many players like to decide upon their move, write it on their scoresheet and then carry out a final mental check before actually touching the piece. This has the advantage of forcing her to double-check the safety of the move before playing it, and so to avoid the frequent catastrophes, particularly among juniors, invoked by the tempting blunder. One slight disadvantage of this sequence is that Alice's opponent, if exceptionally sharp-sighted and skilled in reading upside-down, may be able to see what she is contemplating and gain extra time to calculate his reply. A judiciously placed elbow may be called for here, while remembering that both players' scoresheets must, according to the rules, be visible at all times. There may also be more serious problems if Alice frequently changes her mind about her move after having written it down and so must mark the correction on her scoresheet. While there is unlikely to be any objection to the occasional change, where her final check reveals a flaw in her planned move, if this happens too often, her opponent can legitimately object. All calculations in the course of a game must be carried out in the player's head only, and the use, or apparent use, of the scoresheet as a notebook or aide-memoire, is strictly against the rules.

Similarly, Alice should get into the habit, as early as possible, of never touching a piece during a game unless she intends to move it. The 'touch-move' rule is rigorously enforced and provides a high proportion of tournament disputes and complaints, especially within junior sections. If a piece has been placed carelessly, or knocked, so that it is not properly within its square, then it can be straightened, but only after the words '*j'adoube*'[50] have been murmured by the player doing the tidying. *J'adoube* is not, as some juniors, and adults who certainly ought to know better, seem to think, a magic formula allowing a player who has picked up a piece and subsequently changed her mind, to put it down and choose another one, like crossing your fingers behind your back when telling a fib.

Some modifications to the general tournament rules apply where one of the players is blind or partially sighted. In such a case two boards may be used; a normal board for the sighted player and also a special board with pegged pieces for her visually impaired opponent. In addition to writing her move on the scoresheet, Alice must also announce it aloud and may have to make her opponent's move as well as her own on the normal board. The 'touch-move' rule for the blind or partially sighted player applies only to a piece actually removed from its hole in the board and a special clock may also be used upon which the position of the hands

---

then the full moves must be recorded by an arbiter and the player must use her own time, after the time control, to copy them on to her own scoresheet.

[50] Literally 'I dub' as in 'Arise, Sir Gawain', now used to mean setting a piece in the centre of its square, or, for the tidy-minded, turning the knights so that the horses' heads face forwards. Sometimes translated, by fervent Francophobes, into a grunted English 'Adjust'.

and flag can be felt. Obviously, these additional duties require time to complete, and if her opponent does not have an assistant to carry them out then Alice herself can request such help.

And so the game progresses, in a calm (or at least outwardly calm) progression of moving, pressing the clock and recording, to its final conclusion by win or draw. The most basic conclusion to a chess game is of course a checkmate and it is likely that many or most of Alice's first tournament and match games will end in this way. The winning player (let us assume this to be Alice) makes her final move, stops the clock and says, quietly but audibly, 'checkmate' or simply 'mate'. It may in fact not be necessary to say anything, as her opponent, anxious to get the whole thing over and escape, may say, upon Alice making the last move, something like 'Yes' or 'that's mate'. Alternative responses, meaning the same thing, include a nod, a grunt, a smothered curse and a cascade of sudden and disconcerting tears.

As Alice progresses in the game, and begins to play stronger opponents, fewer and fewer games will end in an actual checkmate. Instead, as it becomes clear to the losing player that defeat is inevitable, she may prefer to anticipate the outcome and resign the game. This not only avoids the agony of the final death throes but is, against a strong player, a practically obligatory sign of courtesy, once all reasonable hope[51] has gone. Among weaker players, however, where endgame technique is patchy, and mistakes still rife, it is quite acceptable, and indeed prudent, to force the winning player to continue and show that she can in fact deliver the threatened mate.

The traditional means by which a player indicates that she is resigning is to place her king on its side, so that it lies, as if dead or fatally injured, across the board. In practice, however, this histrionic gesture is rarely, if ever, seen in tournament chess. Instead, the player resigning should stop the clock, offer her hand and say, clearly, ' I resign'. The words are often in fact omitted among the experienced, but are best used, among newer players, in order to avoid any confusion with the offer of a draw.

A game can end in a draw either by the operation of one of the relevant rules or by agreement between the players. A stalemate leads to an automatic draw, as it is impossible for the game to continue, but in the case of the three-fold repetition of a position, it is necessary for one of the players to claim the draw when it is her turn to move. There is no obligation upon either to point out that the situation has arisen and if neither player wishes to do so then the game continues as usual. As in a resignation, the player claiming the draw, or whose turn it is to move in a stalemate, stops the clocks and briefly explains to her opponent why she is doing so. If the other player agrees that the right to a draw has arisen then the game ends there, if not then an arbiter must be called to investigate the position.

It will make Alice's life, and by extension your own, considerably simpler, albeit less thrillingly unpredictable, if she can make sure, preferably before her first

---

[51] 'Reasonable hope', of course, includes the prospect of the dominant player losing on time.

tournament, that she is familiar with all the varieties of draw and their vicissitudes as well as with other tricky areas such as castling, *en passant* capture and promotion. To learn the subtler intricacies of these in the middle of a playing hall can be embarrassing as well as painful and ignorance is no defence to the crimes of chess.

A draw may be agreed between the players at any stage in the game, including, tacitly, at its outset, where, for example, one player needs only half a point in the final round of a tournament in order to secure a prize, and the other is also happy with a draw. However, actually to agree a draw before the game begins is a breach not only of chess etiquette but also of the rules, and may in some cases be punished severely. This is obviously a difficult area, particularly as the question of what, exactly, constitutes an agreement is one that, even in the simple and harmonious world outside chess, has sustained a few thousand contract lawyers through dusty but lucrative careers. Chess players themselves find ways through the ethical labyrinth, learning to indicate, in unspoken demeanour as well as choice of moves, their readiness to consider an early half point. In any case, it is customary to play at least five moves, and generally twelve or more, before actually concluding the game and there is of course no obligation on either player not to change her mind and decide to play on.

In general quick draws should be avoided by young players, except in very occasional and exceptional circumstances, as they do not provide any real playing experience and create a bad impression among potential opponents, team mates and selectors. Where a draw is appropriate and acceptable to both players, this will generally become evident in the course of a normally-played game, with honour satisfied on both sides. It is important for Alice, especially towards the end of a tournament or championship, to know which games she needs to win and which she can afford to draw, but it is even more important for you to avoid anything remotely like horse-trading with other parents or coaches.

In normal circumstances, however, and once the game is properly underway, it is quite acceptable for Alice to offer a draw where she feels that her position, though tenable, is insufficient to win. The etiquette of professional chess requires that the draw be offered by the player with the advantage in the game, but at the lower levels, where the balance of power is constantly shifting with each mistake made, this convention is of lesser importance. What is essential is that the offer of a draw must be made by a player immediately after playing her own move and before pressing her clock. There are no set words for the offer; 'Would you like a draw?' or, more tersely, 'Draw?' are quite sufficient.

The other player may accept, ('yes' or 'okay' are generally unambiguous) and shake hands, upon which the game is concluded. To decline the offer, she can say no, or 'I'd like to play on' or simply make her own move, which acts as a refusal of the offer. If a player offers a draw before making her own move, the opponent can ask that the move be made before considering the offer. It is permissible to take time in assessing a draw offer, although obviously this time is on the clock of the player considering it.

It is considered bad manners in chess to offer draws repeatedly, especially when in a weaker position, and ambitious juniors in particular should guard against this temptation. If a draw has been offered and declined, the player who offered it should not ask again until and unless there has been a significant change in the position, normally not until several moves have elapsed. This does not, however, prevent the opponent, who has previously declined the draw, from reassessing the position and making her own offer very shortly afterwards. Certainly a game with more than three draw offers from one player will generally be frowned upon and, since a draw offer is normally represented in the margin of the scoresheet by an equals sign (=), the lapse in manners is published to the world (or whoever reads the scoresheet, which may not necessarily be quite the same thing). As well as being a breach of etiquette, a player who constantly offers draws will harm her own credibility and will find it less easy to get a draw when she really wants one (on the boy who cried wolf principle) as well as losing the opportunity to win games which might have been turned in her favour with a little more imagination and courage.

However the game is concluded, the players should ideally shake hands once more (though this is not quite as essential as at the beginning) and ensure that they are agreed as to the outcome. In most adult tournaments the result is recorded on the scoresheet, usually by the appropriate number: 0, ½ or 1 being circled on the top. In order to avoid any mistake, each player then signs the other's scoresheet and the top copy of each is handed in to the section controller. The carbon copy of the scoresheet can then be kept by the player. Sometimes, as in the British Championships, the scoresheet will comprise three copies, the first for the controllers, the second for the bulletin compilers and the third for the player herself.

Some, especially junior tournaments, do not require that the scoresheets be handed in but instead have a results slip to be completed with the game's outcome and handed it by one or both players. Finally, a few, less formal junior or rapidplay tournaments, simply ask that the winning player (or both, in the event of a draw) report the outcome to the organizers. It is obviously important that the results of games should be reported as quickly as possible in order that the draw for the next round should not be delayed. Inevitably there are always a few who forget, and it is one of many unenviable tasks of section controllers to spend their own lunch hour in plaintive pursuit of these absent-minded entrants. Try to make sure that Alice is not among them.

After the game, if there is another round to come, and the equipment is provided by the organisers, the players should set the pieces back in their opening positions. It is then usual for them to spend some time analysing it; i.e. going through the moves, explaining to one another what they were anticipating and planning and exploring what would have happened if different moves had been played. This analysis may sometimes be carried out immediately in the playing hall, at the board upon which the game took place, especially if it was one of the last games to finish and there is a reasonable break before the next round is due to begin. Generally, however, even if the players do their best to speak in whispers, it is distracting for others to have analysis going on in the playing hall and a separate room is therefore designated for this purpose.

In many ways the analysis room is the hub and heart of a tournament. Here players meet to analyse their games and stay to watch others analyse, joining in with their own observations and suggestions; here they play blitz, exchange bizarre new opening theories, eat huge quantities of crisps, and make legions of new friends. If Alice is really a chessplayer, then the analysis room will always be the first place to look for her.

It is not, of course, obligatory to analyse every game and there are sometimes excellent reasons for not doing so. If the game has been long, and there is another round due to begin shortly, then it may be more sensible for Alice to snatch a little rest, perhaps something to eat, than to plunge herself again into the morass of variations, counter-variations, tactical traps and interminable endgames. Similarly, if a round, particularly the Friday evening first round of a weekend tournament, finishes very late, then a long analysis may not be appropriate. Do bear in mind, however, that for many players the post-game analysis plays a similar role to the psychological debriefing of a released hostage and that if Alice is deprived of the chance to exorcise her moves here, they may hang around in her dreams for the rest of the night.

There are less objective reasons, also, why one player or the other may prefer not to look at the game again, particularly if an early blunder has made her loss inevitable. Some adults find losing to children so galling that they refuse to analyse the game afterwards while other players may simply be anxious to have lunch or a game of football. Where possible, however, Alice should try to look at the game with her opponent, particularly if she has lost. These sessions can in fact teach her more than the game itself and, if she has had the opportunity to play a really strong opponent, can provide an invaluable opportunity for a bit of free coaching. She should not, therefore, be afraid to suggest it to her opponent, however exalted. A simple request, 'Would you like to look through the game?' as they set up the pieces, will suffice, and even if refused, will demonstrate her professional attitude and commitment to the game.

Chapter Seven

Kibitzing[52]: Spectators and Support

'I wonder, now, what the Rules of Battle are,' she said to herself, as she watched the fight, timidly peeping out from her hiding-place...

...'It was a glorious victory, wasn't it?' said the White Knight, as he came up panting.

'I don't know,' Alice said doubtfully.

It is the first round of a tournament. Charlie is sitting dutifully at his board, armed with ball point pens, bottles of water, paper tissues and a comprehensive knowledge of the Scandinavian Defence. Now, as you hover about the margins of the playing hall, with the rest of the parents, wives, girlfriends and other human miscellany, the words echo dolefully around your head: Should I stay or should I go?

There are four main reasons why you might want to stay and watch the game (against a moderate list of four hundred why you wouldn't): to offer moral support, to give practical help, to see how Charlie could improve his play and, lastly, out of pure (or moderately pure) curiosity.

Moral support, in this context, consists basically of the idea that your mere presence in the playing hall, perhaps just visible out of the corner of Charlie's eye, will be a calming and inspiring influence, causing him to play each move with care and confidence, illuminated by the transcendent power of your parental love. How likely is this?

Or, to put it another way, you suspect that Charlie's opponent's father, who is six foot five (and that's just his circumference) intends to spend the entire game stationed behind his daughter's chair, glowering at Charlie, and you want to be there to do a bit of counter-glowering yourself.

---

[52] Watching a chess game while dispensing copious and unsought advice. Needless to say, kibitzing has no place outside the analysis room and even there is probably the activity least likely to win friends and influence people.

In fact, however, unless his attention is deliberately drawn to the facts, Charlie is likely to be equally oblivious of both his opponent's father's presence and of your own. It is also, unless you make a big issue of it, probably a matter of virtually complete indifference to him whether you are in the playing hall or not. You could, of course, emphasize to him the ominous and looming nature of his opponent's supporters, the possibility that they might succeed in disconcerting him and the consequent advisability of your constant presence. You could tell him that he need never worry, that you will always be there for him, a faithful shadow in the gloom, that whenever he feels anxious or perplexed he need only look up to see your smiling face. That should be enough to turn him into a miserable neurotic and to ensure that you have a nice substantial bundle of guilt and obligation to carry with you for the term of your natural life. Your smiling face might want, in the first flush of enthusiasm, always to be there for him, just as you promised when the midwife first presented him, all red and wrinkled and wrapped in a hospital towel. But he isn't red and wrinkled now, or only after a hard game of rugby, and your smiling face, not to mention the less than smiling other bits of you, may have other things to do during the next fifty years or so. Even if your martyr-complex is sufficiently well developed for you cheerfully to sacrifice your entire life to Charlie's putative chess career, there will be times when you simply cannot be there; when, as in some junior championships, parents are banned from the playing hall, when you cannot afford to follow him around the world, when, at a critical moment in the endgame, you can't postpone any longer that overdue dash to the Ladies.... In short, the whole thing is a self-fulfilling prophesy; if you tell Charlie that he needs you there, he will need you there. If, on the other hand, you suspect that you might like a life of your own one day, you can let Charlie get on with his games in peace, reminding him, if necessary, that annoying spectators can be summarily ejected by a sympathetic arbiter. As you walk out of the door, trying not to let it bang behind you, your heart may swell with a rush of unwonted parental affection, but try not to let this worry you. In an emergency you can always dive into the nearest newsagent and soak it up with a Beanie Baby.

Of course, while avoiding the situation where you have to be present at every game, you won't want to create a precedent in the other direction either, so that you are never there. Sometimes there may be games when your presence would be a psychological boost, to cheer Charlie up, perhaps, after a bad last round, or to remind him, during a particularly tortuous and bloody endgame, that life will still go on when the clocks have finally stopped. I am thinking particularly of occasions when his game has been very long, perhaps the last to finish, with the playing hall deserted except for the two players, the arbiter and a couple of hovering cleaning ladies. At the other extreme, he may be on the top board in the final round of a tournament, fighting for first place, with a scrum of spectators around him. He may not notice that you are there, but the spectators will, and your presence may encourage them to keep their distance.

Here, in your exciting role as crowd control executive, we are passing into the second reason for your presence in the playing hall; as purveyor and provider of practical assistance. But what kind of practical assistance can you actually offer (other than acting as an unpaid bouncer)? What you certainly can't do, first of all, is pop to the bookstall or to his laptop computer, and look up the position to see what he ought to play next. In fact, tournament rules forbid him from discussing the game with anyone at all, while it is progressing, and this is a prohibition that should be taken very seriously. Zealous officials, and officious zealots have even been known to rebuke parents for asking their offspring, mid-game, 'Are you all right? 'or 'Is everything okay?' It may seem ridiculous that anyone could accuse you, if your playing skills, like mine, are those of a slightly demented guinea-pig, of advising Charlie about his game, but there is no point in attracting controversy. In the same way, Charlie should remember not to talk about the games in progress with his friends, however innocent their enquiries.

If even responding to the vague queries of ignorant parents is suspect, then, obviously, looking anything up during the game is outright cheating and will be punished as such. Charlie should, therefore, take care to avoid even the appearance of scandal by waiting until the end of a round to visit the bookstall and keeping well away from any humming computers. (His own laptop, if he has one, should ideally be under lock and key or within your own remorseless vigilance. Unless Charlie constitutes an aberrant and unique genetic mutation in teenage or pre-teenage chess players, he will think nothing [literally nothing] or leaving two thousand pounds worth of silicon under his chair for four hours while he goes off to discuss the Caro-Kann and search for hot dogs.)

So, talking of hot dogs, we are left with the traditional forms of parental support: food, drink, clothing and cash. Unless Charlie really is very young indeed, you generally don't need to be on the spot to provide any of these (except the cash at the outset, of course, and a reminder about socks is usually timely). Some refreshments, drinks and snacks, are usually available at the venue and more substantial hot and cold meals may also be provided. Indeed, where refreshments are sold on the premises, there may be a prohibition against bringing them in from outside. It is only when Charlie is very young or in the extremes of calorie-starved time trouble, that you may need to perform a quick mercy dash to the bar, cafeteria or corner shop. And if he cannot put his sweatshirt on or take it off without assistance then one or other, either the sweatshirt or the child, is probably too small to be there.

The third reason for watching Charlie's game, to help him to improve it, sounds simple, even laudable. Behind it, however, as behind so many simple, laudable ideas, lurks a nest of misunderstanding, tension and blood-curdling death threats. We have all done it, at some time or other, maybe after a run of bad results, hovering about the margins of the playing hall, shifting from one foot to the other, dizzy and cross-eyed from the fervency of our concentration on the board. But what, exactly, are we looking at?

Well the moves, obviously. But why? During a normal long-play or junior tournament game, where the moves are recorded, even professional coaches do not normally stand watching their pupils' games live in the playing hall. It is so much easier and more productive to look through them later with the aid of the scoresheet, the player himself there to explain and half a pint of the local brew to lubricate the analysis. And generally speaking, if the game is not serious enough to be recorded, it is not serious enough to need any detailed investigation.

Then, if you really can't resist the urge to watch every single one of Charlie's moves as it is played, are you sure that you really understand them? It may be, of course, that you yourself are a gifted and natural chess player who has devoted many years of study to the game and are well qualified to act as coach to your own child. If this is the case, then you may indeed derive some benefit from watching the game (though the benefits of joining the other coaches in the bar might be even more substantial).

But most of us are by no means gifted players or natural coaches. Maybe we played a little chess long ago as children, maybe we have just plunged ourselves into a quick crash course, trying to stay a page ahead as we taught Charlie the rules and basic strategies. Now, however, as he moves into the world of clubs and tournaments, we have probably already been left behind. We may know the theories, the rather threadbare maxims; 'A knight on the rim is always dim', 'Don't move a piece twice in the opening', we may even be able to recite lists of opening moves, but we do not see the board as Charlie does, and we cannot trace the thoughts that pass through his head.

This is actually quite an odd experience, especially if Charlie is particularly young or similar in character to you yourself. You are accustomed to knowing, more or less, what he is thinking, to follow the patterns of his musing about the world, to anticipating, even if you cannot answer, his questions. Now, for the first time, he has gone forward without you. Of course, if Charlie is much older, perhaps already a teenager, you will be well used to the impenetrability of his thought processes. It may well be, however, that you are still accustomed to knowing more than he does about most subjects (with the possible exception of football and Nintendo) or at least to having the resources to find out. Chess, however, isn't quite like that: you can study every book in the chess publishers' catalogues and, without the extra spark, will still be beaten by a talented five year old. You may, if you try really hard, be able to tell whether Charlie is following the recommended opening lines, the theoretical principles, the correct endgame manoeuvres, but these in themselves will not tell you whether or not he is playing a good game.

The most common means for non- or novice chess players to judge a game is by the pieces captured, counting them as they line up beside their captor's elbow. 'Material' chess players call it, and, indeed, all other things being equal, the player with the material advantage is likely to win. All other things in chess, however, are very rarely equal, and an immense chunk, perhaps most, of opening theory would collapse if it were not for the undoubted advantages of an early pawn sacrifice. Later in the game the sacrifices can become more substantial, involving major pieces, even the queen herself, and appear to the pale and trembling bystander as ghastly, glaring blunders. (Often, of course, they are ghastly glaring blunders, though they may still be described by their maker as brilliant sacrificial tactics.)

As far as many players and parents are concerned, the proof of the pudding is in the eating, so that a truly inspired sacrificial sequence may be dismissed as a rash mistake if, despite its brilliance, its author goes on to lose the game, while a crass and thoughtless oversight by the victor will be hailed as a wise and cunning manoeuvre. As a spectator, who cannot discuss the game with Charlie until its conclusion, you eventually have the benefit of hindsight, but this hindsight can itself skew your vision. If you are lucky enough to have a gifted coach for Charlie then you will notice this; upon analysing his game you may hear the coach praising or criticizing moves which appear to bear no relation to the eventual outcome of the game. 'But he won!' we want to wail or, impatiently, 'Yes, but if he played so brilliantly, why didn't he win?'

We don't know, and unless we are struck by a shaft of divine illumination, we will probably never really know, however many barrels of midnight oil we waste ploughing through his books. We might save ourselves a lot of hassle and heartache by leaving the analysis to those who do: to Charlie's coach, if he has one, to the more experienced members of his club, to his opponents in their post-game analysis, and most of all to Charlie himself.

So, if you are not watching the individual moves, what else could you be watching for? Charlie's attitude, his behaviour at the board? If, by that, you mean whether he obeys the tournament rules, resists the temptation to chatter to his opponent, refrains from throwing pieces about when he loses and from sliding up and down the parquet floor, then something is probably wrong. If Charlie is at all likely to do any of these things then he should not be at a chess tournament at all, and you would be better taking him to an adventure playground instead for the next year or two. If, however, like most chess playing juniors, he would never dream of misbehaving, and would be mortified at the very thought, then you ought, at the very least, to be grateful and to demonstrate your trust in him by leaving him in peace for an hour or two.

You probably, however, don't quite mean his behaviour in that sense at all; but how hard he appears to be working at his game. It is a perennial criticism of juniors that they never seem to be concentrating on the board in front of them, but instead to be gazing about the room, their eyes fixed anywhere but on the pieces, their thoughts apparently miles from the conflict acted out before them. There are a very few young chess players who do not do this, who sit, almost motionless, staring at the board in what appears to be rapt attention. For the rest, however, the playing hall seems to be filled with invisible butterflies, flitting from corner to corner and demanding the attention of anyone beneath the age of twenty-one. If Charlie falls into the second category then he will be criticized for it, by opponents, officials and spectators, criticized both to his face and, more often, via you. If you hadn't noticed it before you will begin to, standing near his board in agonies, longing, as Bill Adams describes, to take his face and physically turn it towards the pieces.

But how much does it actually matter? The analogy in our adult minds, I suppose, is with school work, particularly anything that involves reading. If you are not looking at the book then you are not reading; if you are not reading then you are not working; therefore if you are not looking at the book then you are wasting time. It is a convenient deduction from the point of view of a mere invigilator who knows, simply from scanning the heads of his charges, who is deserving of rebuke. But, as any real teacher or student knows, there is more to learning than simply inputting text to the brain; ideas must be considered, mulled over, tested and refined. These activities need space and time, a background away from the remorseless progression of words across the page. Some of the pupils staring out of the window will indeed be daydreaming, but not all of those daydreams will be worlds away from what they are supposed to be learning.

And if this is true of school work, based on text and books, then how much more true it must be of chess. One of the principal signs of a naturally gifted player is said to be his ability to visualize the board without sight of it, and the breathtaking achievements of simultaneous blindfold play demonstrate the extent of this skill. When Charlie tells you that, when he gazes around the room, he is thinking about his moves, he is not necessarily making excuses for himself. What he says may well be the simple truth, that the future progressions and sequences of the pieces are better visualized against the background of a plain painted wall than superimposed on the board itself.

The other thing that juniors do, that infuriates and enrages their elders, is to wander about the playing hall looking at the other games in progress. No sooner have they made their first moves than they are up and about, threading their way down the narrow aisles to survey the openings employed by what seems like the entire tournament, although it may only be the top boards and thirty or forty of their closest friends. Even when they are sitting down at their own boards, they cannot resist the lure of their neighbours' games and it is a rare junior who cannot, at the conclusion of the round, give a pretty detailed summary of what has happened on at least the two adjacent boards.

If you are in the playing hall watching, or if you receive constant reports from well-wishing busybodies of Charlie's wanderings, then you too may be infuriated and enraged. He is here to play chess – his own game, not fifty-seven others. If he had wanted a walk then we could have gone to the park. At the very least, if all he wanted to do was watch other people's chess games then he could have come as a spectator and saved the entry fee and 5 a.m. alarm call. Et cetera, et cetera. And you may well be justified, especially if he loses his own game through carelessness or a lack of available time. (The trouble is, as we saw earlier, you can never actually know whether that is why he lost.)

But before you nail him to his seat in desperation, take a moment to think of the alternative. What kind of young player would want only to look at his own game and not those of his neighbours, friends, the most talented, titled players in the tournament? Only one, surely, for whom the result was all that mattered, who had no curiosity about the game, no desire to learn, to be inspired, to admire, no loyalty to his friends, delight in their achievements and sympathy with their predicaments. Is that the kind of chess player, the kind of person that you want Charlie to be? Obviously there are times, during the most critical games in the tournament, during the most critical points of every game, when he must concentrate upon his own play to the exclusion of all else. But Charlie himself knows this; he wants to win, probably even more than you want him to, he can find his own balance. A game in a long-play tournament like the British can last for up to seven hours and it would be sad and cruel to expect him to remain chained to his own game for the whole of that time.

There can, moreover, be positive advantages in looking at other games during the course of play. While it is statistically most unlikely that any other game will have the same position after the fifth or sixth move, it is not impossible that some tactic or sequence on another board will inspire Charlie to see his own game in a new light. It can also be of benefit to him to see how other players are doing; both psychologically, as he takes inspiration from the triumphs of his friends and the struggles of his enemies (yes, yes, I know that Charlie is much too pleasant to have enemies) and tactically, especially in the last round of a tournament when the outcome of other nearby games may affect whether or not he himself needs to press for a win or whether a draw will suffice to achieve the title or prize that he is aiming for[53].

The third misdemeanour in the triumvirate of junior chess crimes is another upon which every bystander is a self-appointed expert, and of which Charlie, unless he is extremely unusual, will be constantly accused: the sin of moving too quickly. Often the criticism is justified, for young players in particular, having formulated a plan or seen a clever tactic, are keen to play it as quickly as possible, to hasten their glorious victory. Longer consideration would, as their coaches wearily reiterate, reveal the flaw in the plan, the poison behind the offered pawn, the cunning behind the gift of the Greeks. Learning to move more slowly, to look before you leap, is a lesson that all of us, and not only chess players, learn to a greater or lesser extent on the rocky path to growing up. For the chess player, however, the results of thoughtless actions are swift and ruthless; their chickens come home to roost with unforgiving speed. But the child who plays far too quickly at seven years old will have slowed considerably by eight, more so by ten, and by the age of thirteen or fourteen will be in danger of running out of time altogether. It may seem cold comfort now, when Charlie trudges disconsolately out of the playing hall, having lost in five minutes flat, but he himself will be his own severest critic, even if he would never dream of admitting it to you. The lessons will be learned, though they may take some time, and neither your nagging nor anyone else's will drum them in further than the simple zero on the scoresheet.

Meanwhile, to say that juniors, in general, play too quickly is not at all the same thing as saying that Charlie ought to make a deliberate and conscious effort to take more time over all his moves. Dividing the time allowed in a certain time control by the moves available, e.g. two hours divided by 40 moves = three minutes per move, gives you only the absolute maximum average time per move and absolutely, definitively and certainly not a guide to how long each move should be considered. Some moves, such as those in a prepared opening, can be played almost instantaneously while others, at a crucial turning-point in the game, may require half an hour's thought before they can safely be made. Any attempt to impose an artificial fetter on Charlie's speed of play not only reveals your lack of trust in his own judgement but may well propel him into the opposite abyss, the lair of the hideous monster Time Trouble.

---

[53] It is always important to know, going into the final round in a strong position, what the effect of different results will be and in particular what the difference would be between a win and a draw. This is something that Charlie himself may not have calculated and that you may be able to help him with, provided, of course, that your own reasoning is sound.

Time trouble, briefly, is simply the situation where a player has too little time on his clock to be able properly to consider and make his moves. It may occur either at the very end of a game, whether long or rapidplay (blitz games being, by their nature, institutionalised mutual time trouble) or, commonly, before an earlier, e.g. forty move, time control. The severity of the problem ranges from the extreme, where there is insufficient time even physically to make the moves, never mind to think about them, to the mild, where the player has enough time to consider each move but feels under pressure to curtail his thinking at a critical point in the game. As important as the actual time available is the player's reaction to it. As in all such situations, some people function best under pressure, thinking clearly under the influence of the ticking clock, as the adrenalin flows and surges. For others the very suggestion that they may be in time difficulties acts as a fetter on their thought processes, causing them to panic as sequences of moves repeat themselves like a playground taunt. It is important, therefore, for Charlie not only to learn the skills of time management within his game but also to know how much time pressure he can cope with, how much urgency could even be beneficial.

As in the opposite problem, that of moving too quickly, there are no simple or artificial short-cuts to this kind of understanding, which will probably never be consciously formalized, but will come gradually, over the years, with Charlie's deepening experience and maturity. There is therefore little, unfortunately, that you can do to help, other than ensuring that Charlie knows the time control before the game (particularly if it is an unusual one) and refraining from criticizing him in the early days for playing too quickly. Pointing out, at the end of a lost game, that he appeared to be in time trouble is neither necessary, kind nor helpful.

What all these phenomena, wandering feet or eyes, moves made too quickly or under the nerve-wracking grip of time trouble, have in common, so far as you are concerned, is their potential capacity to induce Charlie to lose concentration and make a serious mistake, the type of mistake that chess players call a 'blunder'.

It is an evocative word, conjuring up visions of a young elephant trampling across the board, pieces and pawns rolling drunkenly in its wake. Some blunders, indeed, are rather like that; moments of blind panic upon which a game hinges, after which the remaining moves roll out with a ghastly speed and inevitability. During Charlie's early months and years of tournament play, he will almost certainly commit every one of the commonest type of blunder. There are the public ones; the well-worn opening traps that leave him humiliatingly checkmated before the rest of the room has finished shaking hands, the king moving the wrong way in a vital endgame, with a crowd of spectators, all of whom could do the manoeuvre in their sleep. There are the instant ones, when Charlie sees, as soon as he has touched the piece, exactly what he had overlooked before, and his opponent sees it too, and holds his hand, hovering, over the board even before Charlie has lifted the piece. There are the slow-fuse ones, the seemingly innocuous move that ticks away for half the game along with the clocks, its malice hidden until, imperceptibly but irreversibly, Charlie's position begins to crumble. Worst of all, there are the ones that come in the moment of victory, after a long and close-fought fight, when he has at last grasped the unambiguous advantage and relaxes for a moment and thinks of glory.

There are few things sadder for the parent of a chess player than to watch your child making the long slow journey out of the playing hall, down the corridor and across to where you are waiting. 'I blundered.' he says simply, with no excuses or justifications, so that you either want to provide them for him, smothering him with spurious reasons and reassurances, or you want to throw something, either him or at him, it doesn't really matter. And then you look forward, if you can, and daydream of the time, in two or three years, when he will stop making this kind of elementary mistake, and the dread and horrid word need never be heard again (except, obviously, in relation to baby elephants).

Unfortunately it doesn't work quite like that. Oh yes, he will stop making the elementary blunders, falling into the four-move opening traps, forgetting his basic endgame techniques, sacrificing pieces and material for an obviously dodgy swindle. The trouble is that his own expectations, his own standards will rise with his experience, so that after the subtlest miscalculation, one which, it turns out after hours of analysis, just tipped the scales imperceptibly in his opponent's favour, he will still return to you (or, more likely send a text message from his mobile phone) saying, as simply as ever, 'I blundered.' And the worst of it is, you still won't know what to say.

So, if it is counter-productive to watch Charlie's games to give him moral support, pointless to hang about for practical reasons and delusory to think you can teach him anything, then when can we safely be there?

When we want to be.

The wanting can take all sorts of forms: curiosity as to what on earth can make Charlie sit (moderately) still for four hours at a stretch, pride and the touch of a little reflected glory when he reaches the top board, the autograph hunter's quickened pulse as Kasparov strides into the playing hall, maternal (or paternal) anguish at having been separated from the little darling for forty minutes or simply an excuse to leave the ironing and mooch up and down the aisles with our own thoughts and the soothing patterns of black and white. The significant thing is that it is what we want, and for our own undisguised benefit, without any of the self-sacrificial gestures that invariably make everyone so unhappy.

Chess is unlikely ever to become one of the great spectator sports, up there with the Premier League and Formula One, but it can be surprisingly interesting to watch, whatever your level of understanding. Blitz, obviously, is the most exciting, with the pieces moving too quickly for you to be able to follow more than the crudest of the players' calculations, only the remorseless assault and final despatch. Thirty minute rapidplay games, while still swift enough to be interesting, give you long enough to look properly at the position, to begin to see the lines of attack and defence and to occupy yourself in trying to predict the moves that will be played. To watch a single long-play game borders upon masochism, but you may have your reasons; either Charlie has reached a world championship final or you have come across a grandmaster good-looking enough to be worth ogling for six or seven hours. (Of the two, the former is probably the more likely.)

Of course, there is no need to restrict yourself to watching only Charlie's games, and in a tournament of several hundred players you should find plenty to look at, whether chess analysis or people-watching is your real interest. Generally speaking, spectators are welcome to walk around the playing hall, provided that they can do so quietly (avoid clacking heels, small children and rustling carrier bags) and without crowding or distracting the players, although sometimes they may be restricted to a roped area or raised seating around the edge of the hall. The first few boards in the top section may be raised on a platform, sometimes with vertical demonstration boards on the wall behind them so that watchers can see the position without having to crane over the actual board. At the British Championships a separate commentary room exists where chess pundits discuss these games with the active participation of a lively audience. This room generally acts as an alternative to the analysis room for juniors when their games have finished and if you can't find Charlie in one, it is well worth checking the other.

Meanwhile, if you have decided that one chess tournament looks very like another and that, deep as your devotion undoubtedly is to Charlie, you can probably get through the next few hours without fixing your undivided gaze on to the back of his neck, or if the decision has been made for you by the edict of the controllers or the existence of Charlie's small but noisy siblings, what else can you do?

Bizarre as it may seem, one possibility is that you could play chess. Not, admittedly, with the small but noisy siblings still adhering (with peanut butter, chocolate spread or blood) to your person, but if you are a free agent, and the kitchen floor can wait another week, it may be worth a try. Chess is hereditary in the same way as insanity, in the old T-shirt joke: you get it from your children, albeit rarely in so virulent a form. Many parents of chess players do enter tournaments, and a few become moderately good players, though most merely dip a toe in the shallow end of the Minor section and retreat rapidly. The principal advantages of playing are that you have something to take your mind off Charlie's games, and that you begin to understand a little of what he is going through. The disadvantages are that you have no hope of getting anything else done during the weekend and that, since you almost invariably lose, you only share the downside of Charlie's experience, never the exhilarating bits. A further humiliation is the fact that, if you 'play' (the word is used loosely) enough games in a season, you will find yourself with a grade or rating, affording Charlie endless opportunities for gentle irony. But it is worth trying at least once, if you can, being just across the line from incest and Morris dancing. Then, if nothing else, you can put it on your CV with a clear conscience, and reminisce tediously for the rest of your life about the untapped potential of your chess-playing days.

If you are not intending to set up camp in the playing hall, either as a spectator or an entrant, but want to hang around, you will probably be consigned, depending on the venue, to a lobby, classroom or lounge. As we saw in Chapters 4 and 5, the facilities provided do vary enormously, and it is as well to be prepared for the worst, especially at a weekend tournament. Pack your bags on the assumption that you are going to be stranded for a fortnight; with books, newspapers, that report for work that has been overdue for the past three years, Charlie's Gameboy (this is your chance finally to have a proper go at Tetris) drinks and snacks (if the venue permit you to bring your own), and, if you have young children, spare nappies, a rug to sit on and the entire contents of the nearest Early Learning Centre.

Loaded with all this suburban paraphernalia (the pemmican and ice-pick can normally be omitted, at least south of Grimsby) you and your faithful sherpas should carry out an early reconnaissance and strike camp as soon as possible. Once established, you will be able to make short sorties from your base camp to the loo, coffee machine or in desperate search of a newsagent open on Sunday morning and selling anything but the News of the World.

You will also normally be able to carry out brief fact-finding missions to the playing-hall, checking up on the state of Charlie's game, clock, psyche and stomach. Some juniors find it off-putting to have their parents in the playing hall, but if Charlie can get used to your popping in and out from time to time it can be very useful, if only for him to place his Mars Bar order and for you to try to work out, from the pieces remaining, whether you have time for the Sea-Life Centre or only Sainsbury's. Equally, however, it is best not to encourage him to expect you at definite times or intervals if your not turning up on time is liable to make him worried or irritated. A chess player mid-game should be treated something like a hungry tiger; warily and from as great a distance as is compatible with a reasonable chance of predicting its movements.

Beware, however, of trying to do too much prediction from your sight of the board. For a start it may be difficult physically to see the position properly, especially if Charlie is playing in the middle of a crowded hall with narrow aisles between the tables and you are anxious not to distract him or any other players. Even if you can get close enough to count the pieces on the board, it is easy to miss one or two, a rook hidden in the shadow of an elbow or a pawn lurking behind the king, which may make all the difference to the balance of power. And if you can see all the pieces, possibly by standing behind Charlie or his opponent, you may not be able to see the clocks clearly and so be unable to judge what extra benefits or hindrances he may reap from a potential time scramble.

Secondly, even if you can see both the board and clocks clearly, you face the further hurdle of trying to interpret them. Sometimes the position may seem simple, with such an overwhelming material advantage to one player that his victory is inevitable. Beware, however, of rushing too quickly to raise the bunting or of slinking into the bar to drown your sorrows[54]. There may still be something you have misunderstood or overlooked: a recapture which turns an apparent advantage into a simple exchange, a perpetual check, neutralizing the position into a mere draw or even a forced mate by the disadvantaged player. And if this is the case with apparently straightforward positions, in the early years, it will become even more difficult to interpret his games as he grows older, when the advantage is generally limited to a pawn or two, and the pieces sit on solid, sensible squares, facing one another in what looks like an interminable stand-off.

Our difficulties in reading the subtle nuances of a mid-game position are made even worse by the fact that, watching your own child, it is almost impossible to be

---

[54] Technically Charlie's sorrows, of course, but while he is under age you had better bear the burden.

genuinely objective. According to our own psychological foibles, we either inflate or deflate our assessments of their chances. Most parents prefer to be pessimistic, at least in public, on the grounds that this softens the blow of a loss and sharpens the sweetness of a win. Others hope for the best, arguing that if Charlie does lose, at least they will have enjoyed the waiting, and if he wins, they will not have wasted the entire afternoon wallowing in unnecessary misery.

The sensible thing to do, of course, would be not to try to predict the outcome at all, but to view the position with a Zen-like detachment, preparing to meet with Triumph or Disaster and to treat those two imposters just the same, as Kipling put it so helpfully, not having been himself, so far as I can tell, either a serious chess player or the parent of one. The best that most of us can do, of course, is to pretend that we feel like that, and try to act accordingly.

Trying to interpret Charlie's expression as a guide to how the game is going is even more likely to be doomed to failure. Or, at least, you hope that it is. Chess is not quite poker, but a player who lets his thoughts and emotions appear on his face is handing his opponent an enormous advantage. Even the flicker of an eyelid can be enough to indicate a second thought, a flaw in his last move that could, he now knows, have cost him the game. So, the more inscrutable Charlie's expression, the better for his chances, however frustrating it may be for you (especially when he uses the same poker-faced skills to assure you that he has no maths homework this weekend).

For all these reasons and more, if we should beware of trusting our own sight of the game, we need to be even more chary of others' reports. And they will come, believe me, thick and fast, from the well-meaning, the officious and the just plain garrulous. Some will have been watching the game avidly since its beginning, but most will have given it only a cursory glance, insufficient for even the most expert to cull a proper analysis. When Charlie is winning you can brush them away like bluebottles, but when he is losing, or reputed to be losing, they cling to your thoughts; his friends with their desperate optimism, his rivals with a bitter tinge of schadenfreude.

The second worst thing we can do is to believe these bulletins. The worst thing we can do is to believe them and, as soon as we receive a really horrendous one, to rush to Charlie's board, face flushed with parental concern. If he wasn't losing before, he will be now. As time goes on you will discover who can be trusted, who will give you a considered opinion on the game without being afraid to say if he can't predict the outcome. These paragons will also be wise enough to appreciate that sometimes we don't want a report; we would rather be left with what shreds still remain of what was once our peace of mind. As for the others, the wild Pollyannas and the doom-mongers, we can nod and smile politely before consigning their communiqués, unopened, to the vast Recycle Bin of the mind.

Until you have experienced it, it is virtually impossible to imagine how exhausting it can be, simply waiting for a child's chess game to finish. It sounds like an easy life to the parents of young swimmers, footballers or skiers who must watch their children's star performances through rain, snow or a muggy chlorinated haze. At least, at a chess tournament, you can usually sit down and read a book.

This is true, and writing it here, on a summer Sunday afternoon in Torquay[55], out on the terrace with the sun shimmering gold on the sea, I feel like a hypocrite to even think of words like 'stress' and 'pressure'. But in a moment, when the sun gets too hot, I shall go indoors and look at Gawain's game, which he should be winning fairly comfortably, given the grading gap between him and his opponent. But if he is not (and notwithstanding everything I have said, I will still be trying to work it out) then my heart will start to beat more rapidly (in fact I can feel it already) and I will scuttle outside again, avoiding the glances of the friends I pass and gaze out, distracted, at the sea until the game is over.[56] And this is just a friendly rapidplay tournament, with little but pride at stake, and I have plenty to occupy my mind, and have had eight years to get used to it.

It isn't only mothers who feel like this, or even only parents. Grandparents, coaches and managers all find the same thing. I suppose that it is partly the helplessness of the adult, the fact that we can't, like the parents of rugby or football players, jump up and down, cheering ourselves hoarse, trying simultaneously to encourage our offspring and to give ourselves the illusion of doing something to help. By contrast, the plucky little smile we offer across the playing hall seems feeble in the extreme.

Then there is the unpredictable nature of the game itself, the fact that nothing can be said with any kind of assurance until it is all over. Goals in football act as tangible achievements, solid gains that must be neutralized before the opposing team can begin to progress towards a win of their own. In chess, however, although a material advantage is usually significant, it can never act as an automatic barrier to a swift and unexpected checkmate. Similarly, although we know the theoretical maximum length of each game, we know very little more than that about precisely how long it will take. At any moment, therefore, from five minutes until eight hours, the door to the playing hall may creak open and a relieved or disconsolate face appear.[57]

Finally, there is the indivisible character of the player's responsibility, the fact that, in the ultimate analysis, there is no one for him to blame but himself, no goalkeeper to reproach, no prevailing wind or poor turf conditions. And, where a child is to blame, we all know where the true fault lies...

Chess is not really a test of mathematical aptitude, or military potential or logical intelligence or character or any of the other things that it is supposed to measure, but simply a test of how good someone is at a particular game. Unfortunately, knowing this doesn't keep us, during the long classroom vigil of the soul, from reflecting over again upon all the mistakes we made in bringing Char-

---

[55] British Championships, 2002

[56] He was winning comfortably, and I did fail to realise it, being unable to count up to two when it came to his knights, never mind the four or five pawns which were completely beyond my arithmetical abilities.

[57] The good news is that most of us do eventually develop a kind of sixth sense as to when the game is likely to finish, allowing us to pull up outside the chess club just as the phone rings. The bad news is that it takes a good eight or nine years to reach this stage, by which time Charlie can probably get home under his own steam anyway.

lie up, the times when we left him to cry himself to sleep, thus fuelling the sub-
merged Oedipus complex which will stop him from sacrificing his queen, even for
a mate in two, the times when we were too lazy to read him a bedtime story,
when we let him off cleaning his teeth, when we couldn't understand his maths
homework... there is nothing, absolutely nothing, that we can't blame ourselves
for, and, by extension, blame ourselves for Charlie's imminent and undeserved
defeat...

...We need to get out more. Now. We need to get out now, right out of this chess
tournament. Whatever we do and wherever we go, with the possible exception of
white-water rafting with the Salt Lake City toddler group, will be less stressful,
less exhausting and generally healthier than sitting quietly here with a book and
a flask of lukewarm coffee. In fact, the more physically demanding, expensive
and logistically impossible the alternative activity, the less room it will leave us
to think about chess and the more likely we will be to be able to greet Charlie as
a fellow human being when he finally emerges from the tournament hall.

For emerge he will, eventually, however long the organizers allow him to analyse
his game, peruse the wall charts and generally mooch about. They have homes to
go to, even if Charlie seems ready to abandon his in favour of a sleeping-bag on
the playing-room floor. And then you have to think of something to say to him.

The first bit, if you meet him directly out of the playing hall[58], is comparatively
easy. You don't need a diploma in therapeutic counselling to know that 'How did
you do?' is likely to be a safer bet than 'I suppose you lost again?', however authentic to our inner feelings the latter may be. It is with the answer that our
problems really start. A win is fairly easy to deal with: 'Well done!' with varying
degrees of emphasis upon the 'done' in accordance with the improbability of the
result. A draw needs more careful handling and sometimes a supplementary
question to find out how he himself feels about it. A draw against a highly rated
player is generally a cause for unfettered enthusiasm and against a weaker
player a signal for rueful sympathy. Against an opponent of equivalent strength
the correct response is dependent upon the circumstances, nature of the game,
phases of the moon and current fortunes of Charlie's favourite football team. If in
doubt, say little.

Years of meticulous research carried out in carefully controlled laboratory conditions (i.e. the car journey home and breakfast next day) have led to the tentative
but cogent conclusion that shouting at a child for losing a chess game achieves a
precise outcome of zero. ('Shouting' in this context encompasses any form of immediate and emotionally charged disciplinary action including *sotto voce* hissing,
silent disapproval, and throwing the latest volume of ECO[59] out of the window[60].)
Who, you might ask, but a crazed psychopathic control-freak would even think of

---

[58] and even, sometimes, when you already know the result but are too tactful or cow-
ardly to admit it.

[59] Encyclopaedia of Chess Openings. See Chaper Nine.

[60] The withdrawal of Playstation privileges will inevitably be perceived by Charlie as
a punishment, more cruel if not unusual than any of the above, however attractively
packaged as a rest cure for the cerebral cortex.

shouting at their child for losing a chess game? Well, most of us, for a start. And if you think it's that easy to resist then, on behalf of all crazed psychopathic control-freaks out there, I would like to shake your hand, kiss the hem of your flowing garments and grill a couple of bacon rashers under your halo. If the accumulated irritations of cold, boredom, expense and lack of sleep are not in themselves sufficient to loosen our grip on the parental pieties, then the shattering of our fond daydreams can easily be enough to push us over the edge into temporary apoplexy. And we do have daydreams of success, probably more vivid ones than the children themselves, knowing better than they what it could mean to be exceptionally good at something, even something as little regarded and poorly rewarded as competitive chess.

Sometimes, it is true, Charlie will be at fault; sometimes he will have played carelessly or lazily, more concerned to finish the game and get outside than to play properly. These occasions, however, will be rare if he is really a keen chess player. If not, if he really prefers football, then we might usefully ask ourselves what we are doing at a chess tournament with him in the first place? More often, of course, he will make silly mistakes, but only despite his best efforts otherwise and to his own intense chagrin and disappointment. It hardly seems fair to add to the punishment he is already heaping upon himself. What is more, it doesn't work. Different players have differing tendencies to blunder, just as certain of us (I use the first person advisedly) are more liable than others to knock glasses over, usually expensive ones that have only just been filled. It isn't something any of us intend to do; Charlie will no more go into a chess game saying to himself, 'I think I'll lose concentration after about forty minutes and blunder a couple of pieces' than I go out for dinner thinking, 'I'll just chuck the Chianti over the antipasti to get the evening off to a good start.' The differences are that Charlie's chess game matters to him a lot more than my social embarrassment, however much he may try to conceal it, and that within a few years he will have grown out of the worst of his lapses. Unfortunately, there is no evidence to suggest that this process will be accelerated by reproaches, emotional blackmail, nagging or the detonation of short-range ballistic missiles under his bedroom window.

This is not to suggest that the whole arena of chess preparation, tournaments etc. should be a punishment-free zone. Misbehaviour at tournaments is exactly the same as misbehaviour anywhere else, and there is no need to make allowances for an artistic temperament. The same applies before the tournament and if Charlie gains exemption from the washing-up on the grounds that he is working on his chess, only to be discovered on the seventh level of the latest Playstation punch-em-up, then you are probably entitled to a United Nations sanction for any reasonable retaliatory action. Similarly, a loss at chess, however long drawn out and bloody, is no excuse for snapping at junior siblings, themselves probably shattered after a seven hour vigil under the crosstables.

Right at the beginning, when Charlie has first started to play chess, he may react in the same way to any loss. Very soon, however, he will develop sufficient appreciation of the game and of his own play to distinguish between different types of defeat, and to react differently to these. A loss to a player whom he would never have expected to beat is, understandably, the easiest to cope with, and if he feels that he has acquitted himself creditably, he may come out of such a game looking positively cheerful. Next comes a game against a slightly better or roughly equal opponent where Charlie has played well, especially as Black, and the game could have gone either way. These games, too, he will eventually begin to take philosophically, managing a rueful smile and promise of revenge at their next encounter. It is the games which Charlie judges that he should have won, but did not, whether owing to his own blunder, or to an unforeseen complication or coincidence, that really hurt. This is when he needs you and, sadly, when there is really very little that you can say. 'It's only a game' is idiotic and insensitive; quite clearly, to Charlie, and even to you, having gone to all the trouble and expense to get him there, it is already more than a game. I tried 'Never mind' once, in the hearing of the then Chairman of the British Chess Federation, who informed me immediately that he should mind, that all real chess players mind, and that without minding there was no point to the game at all. All of this is no doubt true, if not very helpful to a tongue-tied parent. Maybe it is best not to say very much at all, just to listen and make appropriate noises. You may not understand much of what Charlie is telling you, but that doesn't matter. He doesn't want expert analysis from you, he certainly doesn't want, or expect you to tell him where he went wrong, he just needs someone to talk to. Or not; if he doesn't want to talk about it then don't try to force him. If he is really little then you might hazard a hug, if not then one of those awkward English pats on the back will have to do. Apart from that, if it is the end of the day then get him home and rested, if he has another round then feed and water him and get him back into the playing hall ready to thrash his next opponent. And there always is another opponent, however disastrous the last game seemed to be, always another opportunity to prove what he can do. Any player can have a bad game, a bad tournament, even a bad season. What matters is not these but his best results, the flashes of brilliance which show what he can really achieve.

Chapter Eight

Starflights and Distant Opposition[61]:
Coaching, Selection and Beyond

'It's a great game of chess that's being played – all over the world – if this is the world at all, you know. Oh, what fun it is! How I wish I was one of them! I wouldn't mind being a Pawn, if only I might join – though of course I should like to be a Queen, best.'

The word 'coach' is a strange one. First used as a noun in the sixteenth century, it apparently derives from Kocs, a village in Hungary renowned for its large horse-drawn carriages. The verb followed shortly afterwards and in the mid-nineteenth century became university slang for 'to prepare for an examination'. The idea was, presumably, that with the benefit of sufficient fact stuffed in his head by a private tutor (later 'coach') the fortunate undergraduate would be transported to success without any effort of his own, would, as we now say, 'sail through' the exam. Later the concept was extended to include athletic training and thence to today's celebrated or maligned soccer and baseball coaches.

Whether from its commercial origins, or its connections with the less cerebral sports, there is still a slightly suspect odour hovering around the word, a suggestion of disreputable crammers, of the mindless reiteration of rote-learned exercises. Nothing could be further from real chess coaching.

'Have you got a coach?' Alice may be asked, by fellow players, parents, even professional chess teachers on the lookout for new pupils. But the fact is, whatever her answer, she will almost certainly have had some kind of coaching ever since she first crept into a club or joined the throng in a tournament analysis room. Chess education goes on all the time, for every level of player, whether the source is Dad, Fritz[62] in training mode, the junior team captain, an up-and-coming IM or

---

[61] Starflights, at least until intergalactic tournaments really take off, are the four squares diagonally adjacent to a king, while distant opposition is the position of two kings (usually on the same file) with three or five squares between them.

[62] A chess program (see Chapter Nine), not the dachshund next door or last summer's German exchange student who ate all the sausages.

a World Championship second[63]. If you are really fortunate, as we were, you may find, at your local club, players willing to make extraordinarily generous sacrifices of time and energy to support enthusiastic beginners. Gawain's first club was run by a retired teacher, who gave up many hours, for the first couple of Gawain's chess-playing years, teaching him the basics of opening theory and endgame technique, how to record and analyse games, how to think strategically and tactically, and generally setting his chess on a strong and permanent foundation. We will always be grateful to him, not least for compiling a perfect record of Gawain's early games, when his scoresheets, though conscientiously completed, defied even expert palaeographic analysis. If you are lucky enough to have this kind of support from your local, junior or school club then there is probably no need, at least for the first year or two, to look further afield.

In these early stages the coach's own chess ability (provided that he is at least a moderately good club player) is far less important than that he (or occasionally she) should be sympathetic and sensible, a good teacher and most importantly someone with whom Alice feels relaxed and comfortable. At this level Alice will not be memorizing reams of opening theory or solving complex problems but being introduced to some basic and flexible opening ideas, to simple endgame techniques and imaginative ways to think and plan during the middlegame. She may, of course, not need a regular coach at all, teaching herself from books and videos, supported by the occasional training session at a local club or school. There are no absolute rules; everything depends upon what Alice herself feels happy with, subject, of course, to your own budget and the availability of coaching in your local area[64].

As Alice grows older and her chess develops, her coaching requirements will similarly change. It may be that, as she reaches a certain stage, she will need a regular coach for the first time or may find that her ability and needs have progressed past the level that her original teacher is able to meet. If your coach has Alice's best interests at heart then he will be able to anticipate and appreciate this move and to advise you as to who might best help her in the future.

Even if Alice becomes a very strong player, it is not essential for her to have a rigid weekly schedule of coaching. To have a personal coach who knows her well, her character as well as her playing style, can be an enormous benefit, but this does not, especially with the availability of email, need to be limited by geography or the conflicting commitments of busy players. A sympathetic coach, one who is a friend as well as a teacher, can be an incalculable help to you as well as to Alice, taking from you the burdens of understanding the chess side of her life and leaving you free to be her parents. He will be able to advise, not only what openings would suit her, what areas of the game she needs to study but also about which tournaments she might enter, which teams she might hope to be

---

[63] Yes, grandmasters have seconds in major international events, much as gentlemen once did for duels, only now they have to research openings and fetch bacon sandwiches instead of holding the spare pistols and carrying the body home.

[64] If you have difficulty in finding a coach, then the BCF or other national federation will normally be able to supply you with a list.

selected for, when and how to begin thinking about FIDE ratings and, for the strongest players, even international titles.

An interesting test of the coach-student relationship comes when they have to play one another for the first time in a serious tournament, after many hours of mutual analysis, friendly and blitz games. For Gawain this experience came at the age of nine, in his first ever weekend Open, when he found himself paired in the first round against his then coach, one of the strongest players in the region. Perhaps fortunately, he has not yet been thrown into the ring with IM Angus Dunnington, who took over as his coach in 1999. Watch this space...

□ S.Marsh ■ Gawain Jones

Hartlepool Open 1996

King's Indian Attack

1 g3

Avoiding the lines which we had studied together, Sean chose this irregular opening where White plays calmly, simply developing his pieces.

1...Nf6 2 Bg2 d5 3 d3 e5 4 Nf3

This opening is the King's Indian Attack (or KIA for short).

4...Nc6 5 0-0 Be7 6 Nbd2 0-0

So far White has simply developed his pieces, allowing Black to control the centre. However, with his next move White begins the central fight in earnest.

7 e4 Bg4 8 h3 Bh5 9 Re1 d4.

An alternative approach to the position is to take on e4.

10 a4!? Qd7 11 Nc4

Hitting the e-pawn. 11 g4!? is another possibility, when Black's light-squared bishop would be out of the game.

11...Bxf3 12 Qxf3 Rfe8

Simply developing the rook and also trying to defend the e-pawn after the bishop moves.

13 Bd2 Bb4

Black is trying to swap off more pieces as White is slowly improving his position while Black has yet to form a plan.

14 c3 Bf8 15 Qe2 Rad8!

Eyeing the weak d-pawn.

16 Bf1

White could have also played 16 Rb1!?, the point being to attack the b-pawn after 16...dxc3 17 bxc3 Qxd3 18 Rxb7.

16...h6 (diagram 39)

Preventing White from playing Bg5.

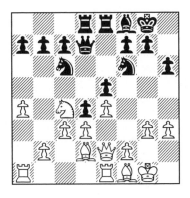

Diagram 39

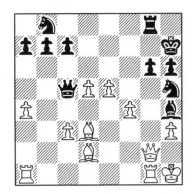

Diagram 40

17 f4!?

White starts an attack. If White does not play this then Black should be fine.

17...Bc5

17...exf4! would perhaps be better as Black seems to have a slight advantage after 18 Bxf4 Nd5!.

18 Kh1 dxc3

Again 18...exf4 19 Bxf4 Nd5! would keep Black slightly better.

19 bxc3 exf4 20 gxf4

Here White has the centre but a weak king and Black's pieces are actively placed.

20...g6

Trying to stop f4-f5.

21 Qg2!

Threatening f4-f5 and d3-d4.

21...Kh7

Preventing the white plan of 22 f5 g5 and now 23 h4!.

22 d4!

Taking over the centre and leaving Black passive.

22...Be7?

Instead 22...Bf8 was the only move, although it still leaves White is better. Now, however, White has a fabulous position.

23 d5! Nb8?

The natural try but in fact 23...Nxd5! was the only move, sacrificing the knight for two pawns and stopping White's attack. After this White would still be better but Black would at least have some activity.

24 Ne5! Qd6 25 Nxf7 Qc5 26 Nxd8 Bxd8.

Here White is an exchange[65] and a pawn up as well as having the centre and more active pieces. Now it should be simple for White. But...

27 Bd3 Nh5!?

Trying to get something going ...

28 e5! Rg8 29 Rg1

This position looks very good for White. Not only is he material up but he also has a good attack. After 29...Qb6 30 e6! Black is no longer able to defend g6.

29...Bh4! (diagram 40)

Sacrificing a pawn to try and get some play.

30 Qg4?

A very odd move. White is trying to prevent ...Ng3 but the alternative of Qf3 would be better.

30...Qxd5+ 31 Rg2

The only move, as 31 Qg2 Qxd3 wins a piece and if 31 Kh2 Qxd3 then 32 Qxh4 Qxd2 also wins.

31...Ng3+ 32 Kh2 Qxd3 33 Qxh4 Nf1+?!

After 33...Nf5 White would still be better but Black would have some play, despite being the exchange down.

34 Kh1?!

34 Rxf1! looks good for White as after 34...Qxf1 35 f5! his attack is too substantial.

34...Nxd2 35 Rd1

Winning back the piece.

35...Qxc3 36 Rdxd2 Qc4

Inaccurate. Instead 36...Rg7 seems okay as, while White still has the advantage, Black would at least have a pawn for the exchange.

37 Qf6 Qb3!

Hitting both the h- and a-pawns.

38 Kh2 Qxa4 39 Rd8

Played too late. Instead 39 e6! looked better.

39...Nd7!

Developing with gain of a tempo.

40 Qh4

---

[65] i.e. has captured a rook in exhange for a minor piece (knight or bishop).

The only move to carry on playing for the win as after 40 Qf7+ Rg7 41 Qe8 Qxf4+! Black has perpetual check.

40...g5?

Missing White's trick. Instead 40...Rg7! would give Black two pawns for the exchange, when he would not really be worse.

41 Rxg8!

The trick. Now Black cannot take the queen because of 42 R2g7 mate.

41...Kxg8 42 Qg4 Kh8! 43 Rd2! Nf8

The only move to stop White's attack.

44 f5!

Now White has two connected passed pawns which will decide the game for him.

44...Qa5

Exchanging queens is hopeless – White will promote the e-pawn.

45 Qd4! Kh7 46 Rf2

Defending the pawn, enabling e5-e6. However, the immediate 46 e6 was also strong.

46...c6 47 f6 Qc7 48 Kg2 Ng6?

This allows White an easy win but the position was already hopeless for Black.

49 e6! Nh4+

If 49...Nf4+ then 50 Rxf4! gxf4 51 Qe4+ Kh8 52 e7! f3+ and 53 Kh1! is winning for White.

50 Kf1 Qg3 51 Qd7+! 1-0

Selection, at its most basic, could simply mean being chosen for an inter-house tournament at school or a friendly rapidplay match at the junior club. At a slightly higher level it may involve Alice in playing for her school or club. Above this, the next rung on the ladder for most British juniors is selection for her county team.

County championships are organized on an Under-18 basis and also for Under-11s, under the auspices of the English Primary Schools Chess Association. Teams for these events are drawn from shire counties or from metropolitan areas and normally compete first in regional heats and from there to a final in a central location. The events are in a 'jamboree' format, which is not quite so exciting, though almost as chaotic as it sounds. Only one or two rounds are played but the various teams are jumbled up so that, for example, Board One for Devon may play Board One for Somerset, Board Two for Dorset may play Board Two for Kent, etc. Parents may attend these events, transport permitting (you may well find that you are the team transport if you show too much enthusiasm) but there is generally no particular need to do so, unless your county team is in need of accompanying adults. These are serious events, especially for the top performing teams, but they are also cheerful, noisy and, on the whole, unpressured. Alice will have a marvellous time playing blitz on the back seat of the coach, eating her squashed peanut butter sandwiches and discussing the finer points of the Benko Gambit and last night's *Neighbours*. Unless these are pleasures for which you have an unquenchable craving, you might as well stay at home with the herbaceous border or the gin bottle.

Gawain made his county Under-18 debut at the age of seven, when his chess was considerably more advanced than his knowledge of English geography.

'Which county are you from?' he politely enquired of his teenage opponent, as they sat down to play.

'Surrey.'

A little louder, then. 'Which county are you from?'

Eventually the penny dropped.

□ **M.Campbell** ■ **Gawain Jones**

Surrey v Cleveland Under-18 1995

Sicilian Defence

---

1 e4 c5 2 Nf3 d6 3 d4 cxd4 4 Nxd4 Nf6 5 Nc3 a6 6 Bg5 e6 7 f4 Be7 8 Qf3 Qc7 9 0-0-0 b5?!

This is a mistake. 9...Nbd7 is the normal move.

10 Bxf6 Bxf6?!

10...gxf6 would be better as it prevents the tactics which now follow.

11 Ndxb5!?

Sacrificing the knight for three pawns and opening up Black's king. 11 e5! is also a good move here, e.g. 11 e5! Bb7 12 Ndxb5! (12 exd6 also looks good) 12...axb5 13 Nxb5 Bxf3 (or 13...Qb6 14 Qxb7! Qxb7 15 Nxd6+) 14 Nxc7+ Kd8 15 Nxa8 Bxd1 16 exf6 Bh5 17 fxg7 which looks very good for White.

11...axb5 12 Nxb5 Qc5 13 Nxd6+ Kf8 14 Nxc8 (diagram 41)

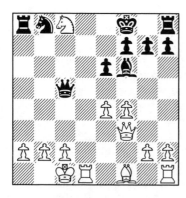

Diagram 41

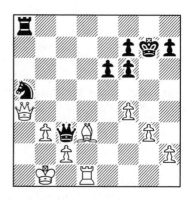

Diagram 42

14...Rxa2!

Avoiding a nasty trap. If 14...Qxc8 then 15 e5! attacks both the rook on a8 and the bishop on f6.

15 e5! Qb4!

15...Qxc8 would be too dangerous, allowing 16 Kb1! Ra5 and 17 exf6 which is good for White.

16 b3

This is White's only possible move to guard against the threat of ...Ra1 mate. 16 Kb1 is met by 16...Qxb2 mate and 16 Qc3 by 16...Ra1+ 17 Kd2 Qxf4 – not mate this time but nonetheless very good for Black.

16...Ra1+

16...Qa5! might be better, forcing a repetition, e.g. 16...Qa5! 17 exf6 Ra1+ 18 Kb2 Ra2+ 19 Kc1 Ra1+.

17 Kb2 Qa3+ 18 Kc3 Qc5+?!

This is probably a mistake as it allows White to develop and defend his king.

Instead 18...Qa5+! would give Black at least a draw after 19 Kb2 Qa3+. It would be very risky for White to try to play for more from this position, e.g. 19 Kc4? (19 Kd3?! Rxd1+ 20 Qxd1 Qd5+ 21 Ke2 Qe4+ 22 Kf2 Qxf4+ is good for Black) 19...Qa6+! 20 Kb4?! (20 Kd4?! allows 20...Rxd1+! and 21 Qxd1 Qxc8 when White cannot take on f6 due to ...Qd8+! which skewers[66] king and queen; 20 Kc3 Qxc8+ and Black stands well) 20...Nc6+! 21 Kc5 Ra5+! is winning for Black.

19 Bc4 Rxd1 20 Rxd1 Qxc8 21 exf6 gxf6

White has fought off the attack and now has a pleasant position.

22 Qd3 Nc6 23 Qd6+?!

This move allows Black to develop the rook on h8. It would be better to play the king back to b2 where it is more adequately defended.

23...Kg7 24 Qc5 Qb7 25 Qb5?!

White is trying to force the exchange of queens but again 25 Kb2 would be better, improving the safety of White's king. Alternatively, 25 g4!? going straight for the attack was possible.

25...Qc7!

Exchanging queens would give White has a very good ending with two connected passed pawns.

26 g3 Rc8 27 Kb2

At last White drops the king back to safety.

27...Na5! 28 Bd3?

---

[66] A 'skewer' is a situation in which a comparatively important piece is attacked and, moving out of the line of attack, allows a less valuable piece or pawn to be taken. A 'pin' is a similar tactic, in which the piece directly attacked is the less vaulable of the two, and so cannot move out of the line of attack.

White fails to appreciate how strong the black attack really is. The right move would be 28 Rd4 but after 28...Qa7 Black still seems to have a very comfortable position.

28...Qc3+ 29 Kb1 Ra8

Threatening 30...Nxb3 followed by 31...Ra1 mate to which White has no adequate defence.

30 Qa4 (diagram 42)

Forced to stop the mate threat.

30...Nc4!!

Now Black is getting every piece into the attack.

31 Bxc4

The only possible move to stop mate but White is now lost.

31...Rxa4 32 bxa4 Qxc4 33 Kb2 Qxa4 34 Rd3 e5!

Creating a passed pawn.

35 f5 Qe4 36 g4 Kh6

Bringing the king into the game. Note that Black has to avoid 36...Qxg4?? as after 37 Rg3 White has a chance to get back into the game.

37 h3 Kg5 38 Kc3 h5!

Breaking up White's pawns.

39 gxh5 Qxf5

The rest is simple for Black.

40 Kd2 Kxh5 41 c4 Qe6 42 Rc3 f5 43 c5 Qc6 44 Kd3 f4 45 Kd2 e4 46 Ke2 e3 47 Ke1 Kh4 48 Ke2 Kxh3 49 Ke1 Kg2 50 Rc2+ Kg3 51 Rc3 Kf3 52 Rc2 Ke4 53 Rc4+ Kd3 54 Rxf4 Qxc5 55 Kf1 e2+ 0-1

Strong British junior chessplayers, at the age of eleven or twelve, may be selected for the British Chess Federation's Junior Squad. The principal competitions for existing and potential members of the Squad are the Junior Squad Championships, with categories from Under-12 to Under-16 and the Mini Squads, for the Under-7 to Under-11 age groups. Entry to these, like the London Junior Championships, is by invitation only. You would need to accompany Alice to the Mini Squad events, but the Junior Squads are normally held in boarding schools and so can provide dormitories for unaccompanied older players. In addition, the Junior Squad organizes trips abroad, e.g. to France and the Czech Republic, combining a series of matches or a tournament with sightseeing and experience of communal life.

At this level, Alice may also be invited to play in the Smith & Williamson Young Masters, a week-long junior event held at the beginning of July. The top section, the Masters, is restricted to invited players with ratings of over 2200, including several titled players from around the world. There are also tournaments open to invited players of Junior Squad standard and a FIDE rated event to help improving players to obtain their first rating.

Another source of FIDE ratings, challenging games and late-night pizza for strong British juniors is the 4NCL: Four Nations Chess League – Britain's only semi-professional league, in which games are played on five weekends between September and May, usually in the Midlands. The top teams are principally made up of titled players, but there are many opportunities for strong juniors to play for regional or Junior Squad teams. The playing conditions are generally very good, the atmosphere is friendly and there is the opportunity to see top players in action and to play experienced opponents. There are particular opportunities for women and girls, as the 4NCL rules require that the teams in the top divisions include at least one female player in every round. In his first couple of seasons, Gawain, playing on the lower boards for his home, Yorkshire-based team, faced frequent female opposition, as in this game when he was eleven, against one of the Kasparov scholars at Oakham School.

□ Z.Lazhevskaya ■ Gawain Jones

White Rose v Wood Green, Four Nations Chess League 1999

Sicilian Defence

1 e4 c5 2 Nf3 d6 3 Nc3

This normally transposes to a Main Line Sicilian after a later d2-d4. The point is simply to block out any early deviations.

3...Nd7

3...Nf6 is more natural, developing the knight without hindering the progress of any other piece. Besides, in most lines the knight is better placed on c6 than d7. I was anxious to prevent White from playing e5 after ...Nf6 but in fact it is not in the least threatening for Black.

4 Bc4 Ngf6 5 d4 cxd4 6 Qxd4!

Taking advantage of the fact that Black has already played ...Nd7 and so can no longer kick the queen away with ...Nc6.

6...e5!?

Kicking the queen and speeding up development but creating a big weakness on d5. Black must pay careful attention here to the threats of Bxf7+ and Ng5-e6 or even Ng5 first.

7 Qd1 h6

Stopping Ng5 although Be7 is also playable.

8 0-0 Nc5

This is a good square for the knight, simultaneously hitting the central pawn and assisting in the development of the Black pieces.

9 b4!

Now 9...Ncxe4? doesn't work on account of 10 Nxe4 Nxe4 11 Qd5!, attacking the knight and also the pawn on f7.

9...Be6!

Developing the bishop and gaining a tempo[67].

10 Bxe6

10 bxc5 isn't possible due to 10...Bxc4 hitting the rook.

10...Nxe6 11 Re1 Be7 12 Nd5!

Playing the knight into the central outpost.

12...Nxd5

I was anxious to remove the knight, but in fact it looks better to leave the knight there for the moment and continue developing with either Rc8 or 0-0.

13 Qxd5 Qc7 14 Be3 g5!?

Going for the attack but Black's king is also weak. Instead 14...0-0 would leave White with a slight edge.

15 Nd2 Qd7!?

A weird-looking move! My plan was to bring the queen out to g4 after the e6 knight moves.

16 Rad1!

Bringing the last piece into the game and eyeing the backward d-pawn.

16...Rg8

This move doesn't seem to do much. Instead 16...Rc8 would be better with the idea of ...Qc6 after Nc4.

17 Nc4! Rd8

The only way to defend the d-pawn.

18 Bxa7?!

This gives Black good chances. Instead it would be better for White to keep up the slow improvement of her position, perhaps with 18 Na5! focusing on another of Black's weaknesses

18...Nf4

Playing for the attack but perhaps the immediate 18...b5! hitting bishop and knight would be better. After 18...b5! 19 Na5! (19 Bb6 would transpose to the game after 19...Nf4! 20 Qd2 as 19...Rb8 fails to 20 Nxe5!) 19...Qxa7 20 Nc6 Qd7! 21 Nxd8 Kxd8! (21...Qxd8 22 Qxb5 looks good for White) gives White a rook and a pawn for the bishop and knight with an approximately equal position.

19 Qd2

---

[67] A tempo in chess is a unit of time, equivalent to one move. To lose a tempo is to make unnecessary moves in completing a manoeuvre and to gain a tempo is to achieve an objective in fewer moves than would normally be required.

19 Qa5 leaving White a pawn up is better as Black doesn't have much of an attack after 19...Qg4 20 Ne3!.

19...b5! 20 Bb6

The only other move was 20 Na5 but after 20...Qxa7 21 Nc6 Qc7 and 22 Nxd8 Qxd8 Black looks better.

20...bxc4

20...Rb8 is bad on account of 21 Nxd6+.

21 Bxd8 Kxd8! (diagram 43)

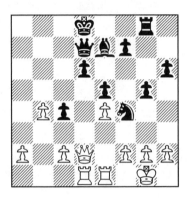
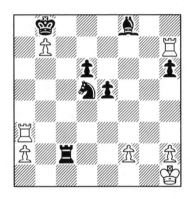

Diagram 43   **Diagram 44**

Keeping the queen on its best post on d7, defending against the a4-pawn break and also contemplating a kingside attack with ...Qg4.

22 b5!

An extremely good move: the only way to keep up an attack against my king. 22...Qxb5 is too dangerous after 23 Rb1 when I have no good defence against Rb8+.

22...c3!

Counter sacrificing!

23 Qxc3 Qg4! 24 Qf3

The only other ways to stop the mate were 24 g3 and 24 Qg3 but both are met with Ne2+ winning the exchange.

24...Qxf3 25 gxf3

Black has a knight and bishop for White's rook and two pawns. The black bishop is not much of a piece so Black tries to get some activity against White's king as compensation.

25...g4!

Hitting White's weak king and also helping to activate the bishop.

26 fxg4 Rxg4+ 27 Kh1 Nh3!

Hitting the weak f2-square.

28 Rf1?!

Instead 28 Rd2! (28 Re2 Rxe4! 29 Rxe4 Nxf2+ wins the rook back with interest) 28...Ng5! would leave the game wide open.

28...Rxe4 29 b6 Kc8 30 Rd3! Nf4 31 Rc3+ Kb8

Not 31...Kb7 as 32 Rc7+ wins the bishop.

32 Rb1 Nd5!?

Bringing the knight back to defend and dislodge the rook from its good c3-square. 32...d5! is also possible, defending a3. After 33 b7, 33...Rc4! looks good for Black.

33 Ra3 Rc4 34 Ra5 Nc3 35 Rb3 Bd8 36 Ra7

White brings her rook to the seventh rank hitting the weak points f7 and d7.

36...Nd5?!

Black misses a chance. Instead 36...Na4 would have left Black on top as the b-pawn drops.

37 Rd7!

Showing up the weakness of the Black's last move. If now 37...Bxb6 38 Rxd6 Rc5 (38...Rd4 loses to 39 Rd3! but these are the only moves to keep up the defence of both bishop and knight) 39 c4! and Black can't maintain the defence of both pieces.

37...Bh4

Now it is White who is better.

38 Rxf7?!

38 Rxd6 seems a lot more sensible.

38...Rxc2 39 b7 Be7

Missing 39...Rc1+! 40 Kg2 Nf4+! 41 Kf3 Ne6.

40 Rh7 Bf8 41 Ra3 (diagram 44) 41...Nc7?

Black should be content with a draw with 41...Be7 when White's best plan is to defend b7 with 42 Rb3 and Black's best reply is again 42...Bf8 etc...

42 Rf7!

Now I can't defend both against the mate and the bishop as 42...Ne6 allows 43 Ra8 mate.

42...Kxb7 43 Rxf8 Nd5 44 Kg2 Kc7 45 Rf7+ Kc6 46 Rh7 h5!

Keeping hold of the pawn as after 47 Rxh5 Nf4+ forks the rook and king.

47 Kf3 Nf4 48 Rh8 Kd5 49 Ra5+ Ke6 50 Ra3?!

Better was 50 Ra6!, stopping the d-pawn and also leaving room for White's a-pawn to start advancing.

50...d5 51 Kg3 d4 52 Raa8 Kf5! 53 Ra3?!

Here White overestimates the black attack. 53 Ra5! would still be okay for White.

53...h4+!

A neat move, decoying the White rook from the active post on h8. If 54 Kxh4 then 54...Ng6+ wins the rook.

54 Rxh4 Rc3+! 55 Rxc3 dxc3 56 Rh8 c2 57 Rc8 c1Q 58 Rxc1 Ne2+ 59 Kf3 Nxc1

We have now reached a position where Black has a knight and pawn against three pawns. However, with white pawns on opposite sides of the board it is impossible for the knight to stop both of them and so the game should be drawn.

60 a4 Nb3 61 h4 Nd4+ 62 Ke3 Nc6 63 h5!

Forcing the black king away from the centre.

63...Kg5 64 Ke4 Kxh5 ½-½

Obviously the time has come, as the Walrus said, to talk of many things, not least the mysterious and exotic world of the FIDE rating.

Although anyone who plays more than a couple of games in a tournament or league will receive a national grade or rating, however derisory, only around one in ten club players will ever achieve an international rating from FIDE, the Federation International des Echecs.

FIDE ratings are expressed in four digits, beginning at 1800 and extending, in the case of the most astronomical 'super-grandmasters' to around 2900. You may sometimes see figures of under 2000 appearing in the place of FIDE ratings on wall charts and crosstables but these are only conversions into ELO[68] format of BCF grades or other national ratings.

The traditional conversion of a BCF grade into an ELO figure multiplies the first by eight and then adds 600. Thus a BCF grade of 200 translates to around 2200. A similar rough conversion of USCF ratings may be obtained by subtracting 50, so that a US rating of 2100 is equivalent to an approximate FIDE rating of 2050. It is important to remember, however, that these conversions are not actual FIDE ratings and that they are only approximate, used for purposes of comparison.

In order to achieve a FIDE rating, Alice must play at least nine games in a FIDE rated tournament against rated opponents and achieve a rating performance of at least 2000. If she plays fewer than nine rated opponents in one event then she may still gain a partial FIDE rating. These partial ratings are then amalgamated to produce her first full rating.

Gaining a FIDE rating is an important step for a junior chess player, often marking the transition from junior and amateur events to participation as an equal in senior tournaments. As such, many juniors are anxious to obtain a rating at the earliest possible moment. Progress in chess often comes in sudden bursts, after a

---

[68] Not, as I first supposed, an acronym, but simply named after Professor Elo, who invented the system.

plateau when little achievement seems to have been made. It is therefore understandable that, having caught this moment of rapid improvement, Alice would want to take advantage of it by seeking a FIDE rating as soon as she can. There can, however, be some advantages in waiting for a few months, until her improvement has consolidated a little. Because of the way that changes in ratings are calculated, a player who obtains a first rating of only just over 2000 may find it difficult to increase it in line with her actual performance. It might therefore be better for her to delay her first rating for a short period so as to gain a higher initial rating and thereby start a few rungs further up the ladder. On the other hand, juniors who achieve an unrealistically high first rating, perhaps as a result of being entered for tournaments above their current level, often have the discouraging experience of seeing their rating decrease in the next FIDE list.

Maybe the best plan is not to have a plan at all. If Alice is a sufficiently strong player, participating in a reasonable variety of events, then the opportunity to gain a FIDE rating will arise naturally, either within a specific ratings tournament or another strong event such as the Major Open. Whatever her initial rating, whether accurate, slightly too high or too low, it will be adjusted over the next few months and years until it becomes a realistic barometer of her true ability.

The calculation of changes in FIDE ratings is a complex business, very different from the simple formulae which govern BCF grades. Very roughly, the system takes an average of Alice's rated opponents in a particular event and predicts, based upon her own rating, what score she would statistically be expected to achieve. If she does better than this, then the additional points or half point are multiplied by her 'K factor' to give the figure by which her rating will increase. If she scores fewer points than expected then the same calculation is carried out to give the extent to which her rating will be reduced. Her K factor will be twenty-five during her first thirty games, after which it will decrease to fifteen and, should her rating reach 2400, it will reduce again to ten. This means that the first few tournaments after her initial rating will serve as a quick means of adjustment if her initial rating was too high or low. After this period it will of course take longer for a rating to increase or decrease. Ratings are published regularly on the FIDE website and separate rapidplay ratings are now available.

If Alice proves to be a sufficiently strong player to obtain a FIDE rating while still a young junior, she may eventually progress even further, to be awarded an international title[69]. The best known of these are the International Master (IM) and International Grandmaster (GM) titles, but there are also Candidate and FIDE Master awards to players who reach ratings of 2200 and 2300 respectively, or who win certain international junior championships. In order to gain the International Master title, a player must achieve at least two or three 'norms', i.e. score sufficiently highly against a field of opponents including several International Masters or Grandmasters from different countries. It is rare, though occa-

---

[69] Titles at a lower, national level, Club, County and Regional are also awarded by the BCF to players achieving particular scores in weekend and other tournaments, while in the US the Master and Senior Master titles are given at USCF ratings of 2200 and 2400 respectively.

sionally possible, to attain the title before the player's late teens or early twenties, but, once obtained it cannot be removed, however low her rating should plunge in the future. The IM title is, to some extent, a rite of passage separating the amateur from the professional, opening doors to higher level closed tournaments, often with appearance fees and expenses paid[70], and holding open the possibility of a precarious living in the world of chess. There are also separate women's Fide, International, and Grandmaster titles. These are achievable with slightly lower ratings and lower-rated opponents than the main titles and so strong women players often achieve titles from both sets simultaneously, e.g. Women's Grandmaster (WGM) and International Master. After the IM comes of course the Grandmaster title, although only a small proportion of IMs achieve this, the highest title in chess. All the same, there are still several hundred grandmasters in the world and so the new unofficial word 'Super-grandmaster' has been coined to denote the very few players with ratings in the 2700+ category, those, like Kramnik, Anand, the Englishman Michael Adams, and Garry Kasparov himself, who dominate the heights of world chess.

Down on the lower slopes, however, things can still get pretty exciting, especially if Alice finds herself doing exceptionally well in comparison to her peers in the same age-group. In England a rough comparison can be made from the tables published each year at the front of the BCF grading list. However, since lists are based upon the players' BCF grades they do not necessarily tell the full story, especially for the older age-groups where FIDE ratings are more significant. Similar information is given on the USCF website for the highest rated American juniors in each age group. For a few of these players, usually those in the top four or five of the list, there may be the possibility of representing their country abroad, in events such as the World, Pan-American or European Championships[71] or, for older players, the Youth Championships, Olympiads and international team competitions. Most of these tournaments have sections comprising two year-groups, e.g. Under-10, Under-12 etc, using the calendar year to determine eligibility and with separate sections for boys and girls.

Selection procedures will, of course, vary between federations[72], but most major chess-playing countries try to send at least one player to each section and sometimes more than one, if there are several particularly strong players in an age-group, and resources allow. The federation may write, several months before the event, to potential players to advise them that they are being considered and to request details of their past year's results. This is very important, as the games upon which the player's current grade or rating are based may, by this stage, be

---

[70] Known to chess players as 'conditions'.

[71] Other parts of the world have their own regional championships. Selection procedures will of course vary between federations and change from time to time. If you are interested, therefore, I would recommend that you contact your federation for the latest information.

[72] In this respect the British Chess Federation is in fact a misnomer, as it deals only with English selection, while the Scottish and Welsh federations send separate teams. Details of the criteria used for selection in the United States are given on the USCF website.

relatively old and therefore be an inaccurate reflection of her present performance. If you have encouraged Alice[73] to keep a tidy file of her scoresheets, or, even
better, copy her games on to a reliable computer database, then this will be easy.
If not, then you will spend a happy weekend or two crawling under beds, excavat-
ing coat pockets and carrying out major archaeological research in your glove box
in a desperate search for any scrap of paper that may provide a clue as to where,
how and against whom Alice has played chess in the past twelve months.

This can be a difficult time; for the junior players, their parents, and perhaps
most of all the poor beleaguered panel of selectors, who must frequently choose
between several equally deserving players. Federations would often like to send
more entrants than they do, but are constrained by financial constraints as well
as by championship regulations. In Britain, for example, chess receives almost no
public funding of any kind and, not being officially recognized as a sport, remains
ineligible for help from the Lottery or similar bodies.

Finally the letter will come, after Alice has hijacked the postman every morning
for a fortnight, and she will at last know one way or another. If she hasn't been
selected then please try to keep her (or you, your spouse, mother-in-law, hair-
dresser or spider plant) from getting too despondent. Although it may loom
enormous at the moment, no one will remember in the future who competed and
who did not, unlike, say national age-group champions whose names are usually
recorded for posterity. In certain exceptional circumstances it may be possible for
a player, not selected by their federation, to compete independently, if you can
bear the financial and administrative burden of travel, accommodation, chaper-
oning and coaching. Even so, her entry would still have to be through official
channels, and so you would normally have to approach your national federation
to discuss the issue.

If, on the other hand, the letter offers her a place, you will have different decisions to make. There will be several issues to consider: firstly, the dates of the
championship and whether she will need to be absent from school. Most schools
are happy to allow time off for such important events, but some may create difficulties, so it is as well to check this as soon as possible. Secondly it may be necessary for parents to contribute towards the costs of travel, accommodation and
coaching. If this is likely to be a problem for you then it is important that you
speak to an appropriate person at your federation in confidence as soon as possible. Thirdly, you will have to decide whether you, or any other members of your
family, wish to accompany Alice. Again, this may be principally a matter of time
and money, and you should not feel at all guilty if you are not able to go with her,
even on the first occasion. Most national teams include several parents, coaches
and a designated team manager *in loco parentis*. It may, even be an advantage
for her not to have to cope with your anxiety and expectations in addition to her
own. You may, on the other hand, be able and wish to accompany her, especially
on the first occasion or if she is very young. These international tournaments are
generally held in holiday resorts and so it may be an opportunity for an off-peak
holiday with the family. Remember, however, that Alice will need to work very

---

[73] 'Encouraged', being a euphemism for begged, cajoled, pleaded, bribed, threatened,
and finally done it yourself.

hard: generally spending most of the morning preparing for her game, and playing through the afternoon and early evening, so that there will be little opportunity for her to join in with the rest of the family. Everything that I have said in previous chapters, about the stress of tournaments, must be multiplied in the case of an international event, and you should be prepared for tears and tantrums. (Alice might get a bit upset as well.)

Gawain celebrated his tenth birthday at his first World Championships and since then has been fortunate enough to represent England on several occasions. In this game he was paired against the current European Champion, and decided on the secret weapon strategy. The only difficulty was that he didn't have a secret weapon. No problem, said Angus[74], and taught him a new opening from scratch in the hour or three before they started playing. His opponent had a potentially even more devastating tactic; presenting a signed photograph of himself before the game, but somehow Gawain managed to overcome even that psychological body-blow.

□ **Gawain Jones** ■ **B.Predojevic**
World Under-12 Championship 1999
Sicilian Defence

1 e4 c5 2 Nc3 d6 3 f4

The Grand Prix Attack, so named after it was played to good effect in the Seventies and Eighties in weekend tournaments.

3...Nc6 4 Bb5 g6 5 Bxc6+ bxc6 6 Nf3 Bg7

White has a pleasant game due to Black's doubled c-pawns.

7 d3 Nf6 8 0-0 0-0 9 Qe1!

This move may look odd but White wants to play the queen to h4 where it will have good attacking options.

9...Ne8

Black moves his knight, preparing to transfer it to his queenside. Afterwards if I play Qh4 then Black can play ...e6 or ...e5 and try to swap queens.

10 f5!?

Theoretically a pawn sacrifice but if Black takes then White can launch a major attack on Black's king with a move such as Qh4.

10...e6 11 fxg6 hxg6 (diagram 45) 12 e5!

Sacrificing a pawn to break up Black's pawn structure and help bring the c3 knight to the kingside.

12...dxe5

Instead 12...d5 would allow 13 Na4! when Black cannot defend the pawn as after 13...Qe7 14 Be3! looks very good.

---

[74] Dunnington – International Master, coach and fellow Yorkshireman.

13 Kh1 f6

Black defends the pawn on e5 as well as giving the king an escape square on f7 and stopping White's knight from going to g5.

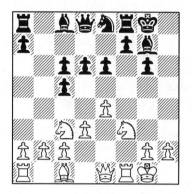

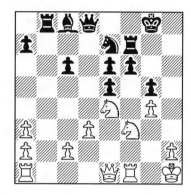

Diagram 45   Diagram 46

14 Ne4 Nd6

14...c4!? was interesting.

15 Nxc5

Having regained the pawn White is now clearly better.

15...Nf5 16 Bd2 Rb8 17 Bb4 Rf7 18 Ba3 Bf8 19 Ne4!?

White allows Black to double the a-pawns, judging that the attack on the kingside is more relevant.

19...Bxa3 20 bxa3 g5 21 g4!? Ne7? (diagram 46)

This blocks the black queen from the defence of the pawns on g5 and f6. Instead, any other square would have left Black only slightly worse.

22 h4!?

Missing 22 Nxf6+!! Rxf6 23 Qxe5! hitting both rooks and winning.

22...gxh4 23 g5!?

Again, 23 Nxf6+!! looked good.

23...Nd5?

Here Black misses 23...fxg5, after which the position would be approximately equal.

24 gxf6 Nxf6 25 Nxe5 1-0

After 25...Rf8 26 Rg1+ is mating for White – 26...Kh8 27 Qxh4+ Nh7 28 Qxd8 Rxd8 29 Nf7 mate.

Three years later, when he was fourteen, Gawain travelled with an English team to compete in his first World Under-16 Olympiad in Kuala Lumpur.

☐ **Gawain Jones** ■ **Wee Zhen Yang**

World Under-16 Olympiad 2002

Caro-Kann Defence

---

1 e4 c6 2 c4

More usual is 2 d4 but the text is also fine.

2...d5 3 cxd5 cxd5 4 exd5 Qxd5 5 Nc3 Qd6 6 Nf3 Nf6 7 Bc4 e6 8 0-0 Be7 9 d4 0-0

We have reached a typical position where White has more space and better developed pieces but the d-pawn could become a weakness and Black has a solid position.

10 Bg5

Instead 10 Qe2! would be normal.

10...Nc6 11 Qd2 Rd8 12 Rfd1 Bd7 13 a3!?

Allowing the bishop to retreat to a2 if attacked and also preparing to expand on the queenside with b4.

13...Be8 14 b4 Nd5 15 Nxd5 Bxg5 16 Qxg5

Probably better than 16 Nxg5 as the queen is more active here and the knight may want to go to e5.

16...exd5 17 Bd3 f6

Black is trying to get his bishop back into the game.

18 Qh4 Bg6 19 Bxg6 hxg6 20 Qg4 g5?! (diagram 47)

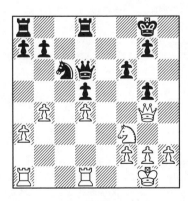

Diagram 47

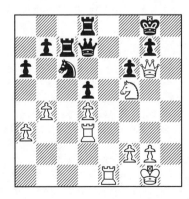

Diagram 48

This creates big holes on g6 and f5. Instead 20...Kf7 or 20...Ne7 would be better.

21 h4!

Preparing the way for the knight to jump into the position.

21...gxh4 22 Nxh4 Qd7?!

Black needed to play 22...Ne7 to stop the knight getting in.

23 Nf5! Rac8

Black would like to swap off pieces but unfortunately for him 23...Ne7 fails to Qxg7 mate and he cannot take the open e-file with 23...Re8 as 24 Nh6+ follows, winning the queen.

24 Rd3

Bringing the rook in.

24...Rc7

Desperately trying to defend the pawn on g7 but the white attack is too great.

25 Re1 a6 26 Qg6! (diagram 48) 1-0

It is still equal on material but White's threats are overwhelming.

If Alice reaches this international level, and even possibly before, you may consider looking for commercial sponsorship in order to help with the expenses of travel, accommodation, computer equipment etc. Your success in this will probably have very little to do with Alice's chess, but much more with your own contacts among family and friends. There are obviously financial advantages in obtaining some form of sponsorship, but there may also be a price to pay, in that your choice of tournaments, coaches etc may be constrained by the wishes of the sponsor. If no commercial funding is sought or found, there are sometimes other modest awards available to promising junior players, usually under the auspices of the national federation.

Finally a word about the media. In general there is very little serious coverage of chess in the English-speaking media, with the notable exception of India, news and comment generally being confined to regular columns in the quality daily and Sunday papers. However, the stereotype of the infant chess prodigy is an enduring one and good for a picture or two, especially if the child is small and photogenic, sitting at the board with legs dangling a foot or so from the ground. You may find, therefore, that any media interest in Alice comes at the beginning of her chess 'career', when she least needs or deserves it. Young children beating adults, which is bound to happen from time to time, is a particularly hoary old theme and Alice may suddenly, as a result of what seemed to her like a perfectly normal, run of the mill game, find herself in the spotlight of press attention. Be careful if this happens: enjoy it if you can, but don't feel obliged to do anything with which either you or Alice are uncomfortable. Whatever you say will, almost inevitably, be distorted by the national media, and both you and Alice could finish with a nasty taste in your mouth. Try to make sure, so far as you can (and it may be virtually impossible) that the emphasis is placed upon the chess, rather than upon Alice's cuteness or those horrible words 'genius' and 'prodigy'. The local media is a little different, being usually calmer and more interested in reporting the actual facts and events, especially if there is a local tournament to publicize. It can be very exciting for a young child to have her photograph in the local paper and even more so if she is invited to be interviewed on a local radio station. Even these, though, should be entirely her own choice. In the long run, her ability and application will determine how high she rises on the chess ladder, not the number of her appearances on *Blue Peter* or T-shirts from snazzy dot.com sponsors. Many of the best and strongest chess players have had no sponsorship or media attention, other than the quiet reporting of their achievements in the civilized obscurity of the chess columns.

Gawain enjoyed (on the whole) a brief flurry of notoriety not long after his ninth birthday when he entered a local rapidplay; generous sponsorship of which had attracted a fair contingent of international and grandmasters. These included the chess correspondent of the *Daily Telegraph,* IM Malcolm Pein. Gawain had a particularly good tournament, was paired in a late round with Malcolm and managed to beat him on time, albeit in a lost position. We congratulated Gawain lightheartedly on his good fortune and went home thinking little more about it. However, as the chess correspondent of the rival *Guardian* quickly realised, Gawain had in fact broken a world record, being the youngest player ever to defeat an IM in a tournament game. His photograph appeared in a few national newspapers, the *Telegraph* giving up two pages to Malcolm's own humorous account of the débâcle, but the fuss was largely forgotten within a fortnight, with the arrival of an alternative excitement in the form of a new baby brother. All the same, there is an agreeable nostalgia in looking back at the cuttings, especially at the incongruity of a little boy's game being solemnly analysed in the august pages of the *Spectator*.

□ **M.Pein** ■ **Gawain Jones**
ICI Quickplay 1997
Sicilian Defence

During this game I didn't know my opponent was an IM, I just sat down to play!

1 e4 c5 2 Nf3 d6 3 d4 cxd4 4 Nxd4 Nf6 5 Nc3 g6

By now I had switched from the Najdorf to the Dragon Variation of the Sicilian Defence, which seemed to suit my style better.

6 f4

The Levenfish Attack in which White launches an early offensive.

6...Bg7

6...Nc6 might be better, preventing the e4-e5 push.

7 Bb5+

Instead 7 e5!? would have made it harder for me, as the natural 7...dxe5 is followed by 8 fxe5 Ng4? 9 Bb5+! where I cannot block with 9...Bd7 owing to 10 Qxg4!. The best line for Black after 7 e5!? is probably 7...dxe5 8 fxe5 Nd7 but this would still be slightly unpleasant after 9 e6!.

7...Bd7 8 Qe2

Here 8 e5! still looks good for White.

8...0-0 9 Bxd7 Qxd7

It is normally considered better to take with the queen in such positions to allow the knight to get to c6.

10 Be3 Qg4

Trying to exchange queens but the simple developing 10...Nc6 looks better.

11 Nf3

White declines the exchange but instead 11 0-0-0 would have left White with a development advantage.

11...Nc6 12 0-0-0 Nh5

Going after the f-pawn.

13 Qd2?!

Not the best move. Instead, 13 Nd5! looks good, e.g. 13...e6 (13...Rac8!? is also interesting) 14 h3! Qg3 15 Bf2! Qxg2 (the alternative 15...Nxf4 would be followed by 16 Qe3! – not 16 Bxg3? when 16...Nxe2+ is winning for Black – 16...Nxd5 17 exd5 after which Black cannot save both the queen and the c6-knight) 16 Rh2! and the queen is trapped. White must avoid 16 Rdg1 as Black then has the brilliant 16...Ng3! staying in the game, e.g. 17 Qe3 (17 Rxg2 Nxe2+ 18 Kd1 exd5 leaves Black much better) 17...Qxh1! 18 Rxh1 Nxh1 and Black is better.

13...Rac8?!

Missing 13...Bxc3! when 14 Qxc3 Nxf4 leaves Black a pawn up and 14 bxc3 could be followed by 14...Na5! giving a good attack against White's king.

14 h3 Qd7 15 e5! Ng3 16 Rhe1 Nb4

Launching an attack on the queenside though it is not as powerful now with the 'Dragon Bishop' on g7 cut out.

17 a3 (diagram 49)

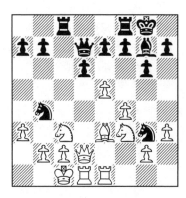

Diagram 49

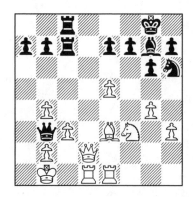

Diagram 50

17...Rxc3!

A typical sacrifice in the Dragon, trying to blow open White's queenside.

18 axb4

White was short of time so this is probably a good decision. 18 bxc3 would leave Black with a good attack for the exchange.

18...Rc7 19 Bf2 Qa4 20 Kb1

White can't take the knight on g3 because of the mate threat on a1.

20...Rfc8 21 c3

Instead 21 Bxg3 Rxc2 would leave Black with a sizeable attack for the piece and if 21 b3 then 21...Qa3 22 Bxg3 Rxc2! 23 Qxc2 Rxc2! 24 Kxc2 Qa2+! 25 Kc3 Qxg2! wining the piece back.

21...dxe5?

A mistake. It was better to retreat the knight straight away, e.g. 21...Nf5 22 g4 Nh6 when the black position seems to hold. Alternatively 21...Nh5!? 22 g4 Nxf4! 23 Qxf4 Rxc3! allows Black to maintain a good attack as if White takes then Black wins with 24 bxc3 Qb3+ 25 Ka1 Qxc3+ 26 Kb1 (26 Ka2 Qc2+ 27 Ka1 Qa4+ 28 Kb1 Qb3+ 29 Ka1 Rc2 transposes to 26 Kb1) 26...Qb3+ 27 Ka1 Rc2 and White cannot stop mate!

22 fxe5 Nf5 23 g4

Now White commences his attack in earnest and the knight runs out of squares.

23...Nh6 24 Be3!

The knight is trapped.

24...Qb3 (diagram 50) 25 Nd4!

Cutting out any play by Black.

25...Qa4 26 Bxh6 Bxh6 27 Qxh6 e6 28 Nf3?!

Eyeing the weak h7-pawn and also contemplating the manoeuvre Nf3-g5-e4-f6.

28...a5?

Missing 28...Rxc3! after which Black is in the game again.

29 Rd3

Trying to defend against the ...Rxc3 threat.

29...axb4

Again, 29...Rxc3! was possible as after 30 Rxc3 Rxc3 31 bxc3, Black has perpetual check with ...Qb3+.

30 Red1! Re8 31 Ng5 0-1

White lost on time.

White took too long over this move and his flag fell. He is winning easily as after 31...bxc3 32 Qxh7+ Kf8 he has 33 Nxe6+!! Ke7 (33...Rxe6 34 Qh8+ Ke7 35 Qd8 mate and 33...fxe6 34 Rf3+ mates), 34 Qh4+! is mating.

Chapter Nine

Greek Gifts[75]: Resources and the Internet

There was a book lying near Alice on the table, and...she turned over the leaves, to find some part that she could read, '-for it's all in some language I don't know,' she said to herself... 'Somehow it seems to fill my head with ideas – only I don't exactly know what they are!'

The first thing you need to play chess is a chess set. Or, to be more precise, a board and some pieces. As mentioned in Chapter One, it is usually best to be rather boring and conservative about this, sticking to the traditional Staunton design and resisting the allure of Star Wars, dinosaurs and even Lord of the Rings. As for the sets which comprise thirty-two variously-sized spirit glasses, designed to be filled with whisky for Black and gin for White; you really don't need so elaborate an excuse to drink, and it just isn't the same with Ribena and orange squash.

You will probably find, in fact, that you need at least two or three sets. An attractive set, perhaps wooden, in the living room allows Charlie to re-enact his victories in comfort, as well as adding a certain touch of class to the Lego-strewn decor. This type of set can be bought from good toyshops or stationers or alternatively from specialist chess suppliers from around £20, although you can, if you feel so inclined, fork out up to £500 for a luxury version. Then, for Charlie himself, a magnetic travel set will be invaluable for journeys and impromptu analysis. Remember that several pawns will disappear within the first ten minutes so don't spend too much more than the minimum of around £10. Be careful, however, with the very small plastic sets, in which it may be difficult to distinguish one piece from another. He may possibly want a further medium-sized set for his bedroom (although if he does most of his preparation on a computer, this may be less important). Many serious players now seldom touch an actual chess piece, except during games. Dominic Lawson, in his excellent book about the 1993

---

[75] Chess players, like Trojans, need to beware of these. They generally take the form of a sacrificed bishop, rather than a gargantuan wooden horse, but can signal an equally devastating assault.

Short-Kasparov World Championship match, *The Inner Game*[76], notes that, while playing Kasparov in the World Championship final, Nigel Short in fact had no chessboard or pieces either at home or in his rooms at the venue. Nonetheless, in the early stages it will probably be helpful for Charlie to see the pieces three-dimensionally on the board as well as on the screen before him.

Note that players in US tournaments, unlike British and European ones, are obliged to bring their own boards, pieces and clocks. Standard, base level plastic sets with roll-up boards are generally used, often transported in a special bag. This type of set is available from all specialist chess suppliers for around £10, although for home use you may wish to replace the roll-up board with something more rigid and less liable to roll itself up again mid-game. Digital clocks are gradually replacing the old clockwork type at high-level tournaments, although you should, if possible, check the requirements for each individual tournament beforehand. For general home and friendly use a digital clock (from around £35) will probably be more exciting and flexible although both types need careful handling to preserve their delicate mechanisms.

Stand alone chess computers have been around for some time and you may even have had one yourself as a child, a small bleeping forest of plastic in which you and the processor never seemed able to agree about where your knights were sitting. The major breakthrough since then has been hand-held computers, something like a Gameboy, with an LCD screen showing the game in progress. These generally cost between £25 and £70, depending on the strength of the computer opponent, which at the maximum is only equivalent to a BCF grade of around 115. They are unlikely, therefore, to represent a serious opponent to Charlie for very long, if he is improving quickly, although they may be helpful in the early stages, particularly if you travel a lot, or do not have a PC available for Charlie to use.

Traditional portable desktop chess computers, incorporating a board and pieces, are available from around £50 and in various strengths ranging from the beginner to a BCF equivalent of around 210. At the top end, however, the cost, around £750, approaches that of a basic PC, which would be able to run much stronger and more useful chess software as well as word-processing, Internet access and the rest of the caboodle.

The personal computer has in fact revolutionized chess and nothing, short of a tame grandmaster in a the broom cupboard, is likely to help Charlie's development more than access to a machine and basic modern software. There are various packages available, most of which, in addition to acting as a ubiquitous opponent, incorporate training modes, beginners' courses and opening databases. Probably the best known is Fritz, which is also available for the Pocket PC, and which, in its multi-processor Deep Fritz incarnation, has proved itself a worthy adversary even to the super-grandmasters. Other programs, notably Junior and its big brother Deep Junior, provide similar features and the pleasant young men who staff chess shops will be happy to expound these in meticulous detail for many happy hours.

---

[76] Macmillan 1993.

Later on, when Charlie begins to study openings in more depth, and to prepare for specific, experienced opponents, he will want to progress to a more comprehensive database. ChessBase, as mentioned in previous chapters, is the major product in this field. A starter pack generally costs around £100, but it may be possible to obtain an earlier version for a reduced price. It will include hundreds of thousands (in the latest versions millions) of games, which can be sorted and searched by reference to openings, variations, tactical themes or players. An additional benefit is the player's encyclopaedia with potted chess biographies, opening repertoires, playing statistics and even photographs, so that Charlie can (perhaps) recognize his next opponent across a crowded room. If these are not enough, the games can be supplemented by upgrades, additional databases and the bimonthly ChessBase magazine. The product also has links to make it easy to send a game by email, submit it to Fritz for analysis or play on from a given position.

Other computer products are of course available, including stand-alone beginners' courses and training CD-ROMs covering particular openings, strategies, endgames and even biographies. As such, they cover similar ground to the wide range of chess videos which deal with opening, strategic, tactical and endgame themes as well as the games of great masters and important modern matches, such as world championship finals. Videos can be particularly helpful to Charlie if his chess develops early, before he is able to read quickly and fluently enough to make great use of books upon these subjects. Audio tapes are also available, although, without any visual content, they are obviously disadvantaged in the immediacy of their presentation. It may, however, be worth trying them, especially if Charlie can listen with a board and pieces in front of him.

Despite all these other media, books are still essential to most chess players, and even the most reluctant readers somehow manage to overcome their distrust of the written word for long enough to romp through the latest bodice-ripping saga of the Queen's Gambit Declined[77]. There are enough chess books in existence to stock a medium-sized Eastern European state, and your difficulty will not be in trying to persuade Charlie to read them, but in restraining him from purchasing the entire bookstall at every weekend tournament. New books come out every month, adding to the hundreds already available and so it would be foolish to attempt a complete analysis of the material available. Instead, I will give a summary of the major types of chess book, with one or two examples of each. The books mentioned here are listed in the bibliography at the back of the book and are, on the whole, texts which either Gawain or I have read or referred to, although several may have been updated or superseded since.

Initially, you may be looking for something from the beginners' range, in which titles vary from the anthropomorphic *Checkmate at Chess City* to the straightforward *Starting Out in Chess,* written for adults and teenagers and recommended for your own late-night homework when you've forgotten the intricacies of queenside castling. After this, however, there is probably not much point in bothering with too many beginners' books, especially as Charlie may well be in-

---

[77] No, sorry, not a swashbuckling tale of nymphomania in high society, though books with 'pawn' in the title can raise grandmotherly eyebrows unless spelled out carefully.

undated with them next Christmas, when the family grapevine whispers tidings of his new interest.

The next stage is usually openings, and here the steady flow of chess books across Charlie's bedroom floor threatens to become a major tidal wave, threatening life, limb and that last pair of almost clean socks. Initially, he will need a general overview of the openings and defences available to him, from repertoire books such as *Attacking with 1 d4* or *Attacking with 1 e4*. Having decided, perhaps with the assistance of a coach or teacher, which openings he wishes to study, Charlie will then be looking for specialist books about each. These include the Everyman *Starting Out* series, specifically designed for the junior player, as well as heavier tomes, often translated from the Russian. As his opening study becomes more comprehensive, he may venture into the terrifying (to us, not him) depth of an opening encyclopaedia, hundreds of pages of dense notation, leavened only by the occasional name or tournament reference. These are available in a one-volume format (only just: you would probably need planning permission to leave it in the garden) as the '*NCO*' or *Nunn's Chess Openings*[78] or in the multi-volume and magisterial *ECO* or *Encyclopaedia of Chess Openings*.

Similarly, a wide range of books deal with general chess strategy and tactics, from the startling *Steve Davis Plays Chess*[79], to classics such as Nimzowitsch's *My System*, first published in 1929 and still an inspiration to a new generation. Here, especially, it is important for Charlie to be able to browse, look at books on subjects which interest him and by authors whose style and analysis he finds helpful. Some chess players read a lot of these books, some hardly any, without any appreciable difference in strength between the two groups. Other books deal with the games of a particular player or with an important match, including the recent contests between the top grandmasters and the latest computer programs. Again, if Charlie enjoys these then he will almost certainly derive benefit from them, but if not then there is no point in pressurizing him to read them.

One type of book which juniors often find particularly helpful is the chess quiz book. These range from simple puzzles like those which often appear in newspaper columns, to complex analytical assessments in *Test Your Positional Play* or *Rate Your Endgame*. The more fantastically-minded may enjoy Raymond Smullyan's *Chess Mysteries* in which characters from Sherlock Holmes and the Arabian Knights illustrate puzzles in which the solution is found by working backwards from a given position.

Finally, what about you? Apart from this book, of course, is there anything that you can read to help Charlie, to understand him better or just to get through the next four hours until his round finishes and you can get back home? A reliable reference for tournament rules is always useful and can be found in *The Chess*

---

[78] Nothing to do with cloisters or bad bishops, John Nunn is a British grandmaster and leading chess writer.

[79] Not actually as strange as it sounds; Steve Davis (yes, that one) was the President of the British Chess Federation for several years in the 1980s.

Organiser's Handbook[80] or, for American events, the *US Chess Federation's Official Rules of Chess*. Less essential, but invaluable for surprising Charlie with your chess erudition is the *Oxford Companion to Chess* or, on a lighter note, *The Even More Complete Chess Addict*. Chess humour is not a vast bibliographic category but is well represented in William Hartston's books, which should get you ejected for the odd giggle if you are foolish enough to read them in the tournament hall. Chess history is an important subject in its own right, led by the scholarly works of Harold Murray, and a little corner of it is attractively illuminated by the children's book *The Lewis Chessmen and what happened to them*.

As far as the game itself, its psychology and politics are concerned, I can recommend Dominic Lawson's *The Inner Game* which deals with the 1993 Short-Kasparov World Championship match. At a slightly less exalted level, *Searching for Bobby Fischer* (later made into a film) describes the evolution of a junior American player while Bill and Michael Adams' *Development of a Grandmaster* does the same, in a nicely modest and understated English way, for the only Briton in the current world top ten.

Chess in literature has a long pedigree from the Arabian Nights, through the medieval tale of Gawain (no relation) and the flying chessboard, to Lewis Carroll, Tolstoy and Nabokov. Recent novels with a chess theme which I have enjoyed include *The Luneburg Variation* and *The Flanders Panel* while my own comic thriller *Trotter's bottom* investigates the mysterious death, in Yorkshire, of a Russian grandmaster's wife.

Chess magazines cover a spectrum of interest, from the serious analysis of *Informator* (published by Sahovski Informator, who produce the ECO) to the mildly subversive *Kingpin* (traceable via a link from chess.co.uk). The principal publications in Britain are *ChessMoves,* published by the BCF and distributed free to direct members, *Chess Monthly* and the *British Chess Magazine*. The US Chess Federation publishes *Chess Life* while *New In Chess* is published in Holland but entirely in the English language.

In general, high street bookshops do not stock a wide selection of chess books and chess magazines are virtually unknown to conventional newsagents. Chess books can of course be ordered from bookshops or internet sites but, especially in the early days, it will be more important for Charlie to be able to browse amongst the books to find out what appeals to him. The best place to do this is generally at a tournament (not during a game, remember!), where chess suppliers usually run a stall selling books, magazines and equipment. Alternatively, if you can travel easily to central London, both *Chess Monthly* (as the London Chess Centre) and the *British Chess Magazine* have shops with comprehensive stocks of chess and bridge supplies.

If chess had not already existed for a few thousand years, it might have been invented now specifically to demonstrate the glories of the Internet. As an international game, but a minority interest, chess would always be an ideal subject for the kind of detailed, contemporaneous information which the Web can provide so

---

[80] Not just for organisers: it includes the FIDE laws of chess and lots of useful appendices for calculating ratings.

much more efficiently than any other channel of communication. When you consider that chess is already so dominated by the computer; in analysis, databases and even as opposition, and that a chess game itself can be enacted in diagrammatic form in a way that would be ridiculous in most other sports, you can see why the Net is so central to the contemporary game.

First of all, there is the simple function of information and contacts. All chess federations, many individual leagues and clubs and most chess societies have their own websites, with links to many others. Among the most useful are:

fide.com	
fideonline.com	FIDE
bcf.org.uk	British Chess Federation
	(with links to Welsh, Irish federations)
scottishchess.com	Scottish Chess Federation
uschess.org	US Chess Federation
auschess.org.au	Australian Chess Federation
nzchess.co.nz	New Zealand Chess Federation
braillechess.org.uk	Braille Chess Association
englishdeafchess.org.uk	English Deaf Chess Association
bcmchess.co.uk	British Chess Magazine
chess.co.uk	Chess Monthly magazine & London Chess Centre
chesscenter.com	Chess Monthly magazine & London Chess Centre
newinchess.com	New In Chess magazine

In addition, many large tournaments and championships now have their own websites which include pairing lists and results, news, photographs and tournament games which can be viewed live or downloaded in ChessBase format. These sites are especially helpful to parents, grandparents, friends and computer-literate gerbils who can check up on Charlie's progress (and possibly even catch a glimpse of him on a wandering webcam) when he is on the other side of the world and his text messages, sent faithfully after every round, have disappeared somewhere in the telecommunications ether. Individuals may also have their own personal websites, (Gawain's is gawainjones.com) which can be fun to design as well as a good source of information for family, friends and other chess players.

Finally, and most importantly from Charlie's own point of view, he can actually play chess on the Internet. There are various sites which provide this service, the best known of which is probably the Internet Chess Club (chessclub.com). Based in New York, the club has over twenty-five thousand members of whom, according to the club, over two thousand are often on-line at a time. It is suitable for players of any standard, from beginner to grandmaster, and it is generally possible to find an appropriate opponent within seconds of logging on. Most games are blitz, usually with a three minute time limit, but variations can also be played. Online tournaments are organized, from friendly one-minute contests to official World Blitz Association matches, and members are invited to 'watch' the encounters of the great. Players have their own handles or nicknames, and internet ratings, usually comfortably above their FIDE or national rating. During or between the games they can 'chat', by typing onto the screen, with their opponent or any other member online and it is not uncommon for friends in the same town to exchange news of tournaments, homework and general gossip via the New York server. It is also, of course, a relatively cheap way for Charlie to keep in touch with other chess players from around the world whom he has met at tournaments. English is generally but not exclusively used and so it can even provide the opportunity to practice other languages (or to get the evening's French exercise translated by a native!). A one year membership for juniors or students currently costs $24.50 and a one-week free trial is offered.

Obviously there are potential drawbacks, principally, as usual, involving time and money. Players are often online for a long time, which can be expensive, especially if you do not have a package with a fixed fee and unlimited internet access. Additionally, of course, the time spent on the ICC may be that designated for other activities; little things like homework and sleep. Unless Charlie is exceptionally self-disciplined, there may be one or two battles to come. However if, as a normal teenager, Charlie would be likely to spend long hours in any case either playing computer games or in an Internet chat room, this is probably a better alternative to either. Online blitz games give him the opportunity to test openings, strategies and tactics against similar or stronger players, most of whom he will never meet in a formal match. The use of handles, with further information only available if the player chooses to reveal it, and the chess-dominated nature of the 'chat' makes the environment relatively safe, although you will obviously wish to monitor the online conversations of a young or vulnerable child and discourage any from revealing personal details online.

Chapter Ten

The Eighth Rank: Where do we go from Here?

'Now you talk like a reasonable child,' said Humpty Dumpty, looking very much pleased. 'I meant by 'impenetrability' that we've had enough of that subject, and it would be just as well if you'd mention what you mean to do next, as I suppose you don't intend to stop here all the rest of your life.'

As soon as you get the hang of this chess parent business, of knowing the right kind of enthusiastic squeak to greet an unexpected win and sympathetic grunt to mourn a loss, when you've mastered the sleight of hand necessary to smuggle half a pound of grapes in with the week's supply of chocolate bars, when you've worked out how to set up the board and to recognize a family fork[81], you gradually find that you don't need it any more. Or, to be more accurate, that Alice doesn't need you.

It doesn't happen overnight, of course. From the first time that you sneaked out to the supermarket during the second round of the Under-8's, you have been gradually giving her more independence, freedom and control. As she moves into her mid-teens, Alice's actual playing is far beyond your comprehension and her knowledge of the chess world will also probably be greater than your own. She will be beginning to decide for herself, with the assistance of coaches and others, which events she wants to enter, although you will still be called upon for financial and travel assistance and retain your ultimate veto. She will still need you, though, if not to test her openings and pack her suitcase, at least to watch as she demonstrates her triumphs and to commiserate with her on the occasional disaster. (At least, we work on the assumption that she does, none of us liking to be that dispensable.)

Most junior chessplayers, though by no means all, go on to university after school, sometimes taking a gap year in between to travel and play chess. Admissions officers seem generally to look favourably upon the game, either for its effi-

---

[81] Not the bent one left in the dishwasher, but a sneaky version of the common or garden fork we first saw in Chapter Four. A family fork simultaneously gives check and attacks the queen, sometimes adding one or two minor pieces to its bloodthirsty assault.

cacy in instilling habits of discipline and hard work or in the belief (occasionally mistaken) that chess playing students are less likely than others to consume large quantities of vodka-spiked cider and smash up the union bar. Some universities have thriving chess clubs and strong teams, others virtually nothing at all, but, unless she has chosen a particularly isolated institution, this is unlikely to matter very much to Alice, who will be able to travel, during weekends and vacations, to play in appropriate events. In the United States, chess scholarships are offered by many universities, often restricted to residents of a particular state but sometimes open to all.

That is, of course, if she still wants to. Odd as it may seem to those of us whose houses remain shrines to the sacred Caissa[82], chess players, even the most ardent, do occasionally give up playing chess, sometimes completely. For most of the youngest, the testing time comes at eleven, or at whatever other age they transfer from primary or elementary to secondary or high school. If the interest manages to survive this upheaval, and the turbulence of early adolescence, then it generally continues into the student years, albeit perhaps fading in the glare of new activities and friends. The real crunch comes after university, when the great wide world beckons and bright young graduates are lured into the clutches of the professions and the multinationals. Here, too, chess players are often at an advantage, should they care to take it, as their esoteric skills are rated highly, especially by technological and financial institutions. Chess players who work for these companies often continue to play chess, at least for a few years, but in general the pressures of work and the derisory rewards of competitive chess gradually reduce their active involvement. A few, to their great credit and the immense gratitude of the chess-playing community, then offer financial support to the game, either by corporate sponsorship or personal donations. Without this type of generous help, chess, particularly in Britain, would be very much the poorer.

At the other end of the pecuniary spectrum, a few brave souls each year decide not to look for a job at all, but to play chess professionally and full-time. A living, albeit a precarious and frugal one, can be made from chess for the exceptionally talented, although only a handful in the world are likely to achieve this by competitive play alone. Most professional chess players are also coaches, peripatetic teachers, journalists, proprietors of bookshops, writers of chess books, organizers or providers of multifarious other services tangentially linked to the game itself. Others steer a middle course, taking a relatively modest paid job which will keep them in food, books of opening analysis and the occasional pair of shoes while giving them sufficient time off to play in tournaments and leagues. Alice need not, of course, make her mind up immediately, and might choose to take a year or two after university to play professional chess before settling down to something more conventional. New relationships will have their influence, of course, though

---

[82] The muse of chess, otherwise known as Schacchis (*scacchi* is the Italian for chess) for whom the game was invented, at the instigation of Mars who had fallen in love with her. As a seduction technique it is, admittedly, subtler than most employed by the ancient gods. However, as legions of lonely chess bachelors down the ages can attest, it is not invariably successful. Dinner is still a better route to most girls' hearts than 1 c4.

not necessarily in the way that you might expect, owing to the distinct tendency of professional chess players to live with, marry, and produce offspring with one another rather than with dangerous intruders from outside the tribe[83]. The genetic effect of having two chess-playing parents is no doubt fascinating to biologists, but, as yet, most of the said offspring are too young to demonstrate marked tendencies one way or the other.

When our children grow up, as our own mothers and fathers know to their cost (literally, in most cases), we will not cease to be their parents. The same is true, in a rather straightforward sense, of the peculiar hybrid creature the chess-parent. More than once, at a professional tournament, you may see a middle-aged couple or two strolling along the corridors, scanning the wall charts with a practised eye, their brows faintly furrowed and yet serene. These are the veterans, the parents of current Grand or International Masters, those who have served their time in the vandalized classrooms and earned the honour and respect of all us novices. For the chess world is, once you have penetrated it, a fascinating and welcoming one, and the friendships and interests which you find there can stay with you for as long as you wish. Whatever Alice chooses to do in the future, with or without chess, she will have learned invaluable lessons during these years, made lasting friends, discovered the resources of her own mind and shared with hundreds of others her own gifts of intelligence, imagination and tolerance. And we, as the memories of those chilly tournament vigils fade, will look back with pleasure and affection, grateful for the developments we have witnessed of our children's minds and characters, and for the rare opportunity to glimpse the world through the eyes of that most mysterious and enigmatic character, the true chess-player.

---

[83] This is, of course, a wild generalisation, with copious examples to the contrary, but the phenomenon is, nonetheless, striking to the outsider. There is also a linked tendency of chess players, with their international outlook, to choose partners from another country, which is generally a cheering occurence and conducive to world peace, livelier parties, better cheese sandwiches etc.

List of Complete Games